Food
Not
Lawns

Food
Not
Lawns

How to Turn Your Yard
into a Garden
and Your Neighborhood
into a Community

H. C. Flores

Foreword by Toby Hemenway

Illustrations by Jackie Holmstrom

Chelsea Green Publishing Company · White River Junction, Vermont

Illustrations by Jackie Holmstrom

Editor: Ben Watson
Managing Editor: Marcy Brant
Copy Editor: Laura Jorstad
Proofreader: Nancy Ringer
Indexer: Beth Nauman-Montana, Salmon Bay Indexing
Designer: Peter Holm, Sterling Hill Productions
Design Assistants: Daria Hoak and Abrah Griggs, Sterling Hill Productions

Printed in the United States of America
First printing, September 2006
13 12 11 10   4 5 6 7 8 9 10

Our Commitment to Green Publishing

Chelsea Green sees publishing as a tool for cultural change and ecological stewardship. We strive to align our book manufacturing practices with our editorial mission, and to reduce the impact of our business enterprise on the environment. We print our books and catalogs on chlorine-free recycled paper, using vegetable-based inks, whenever possible. This book might cost slightly more because we use recycled paper, and we hope you'll agree that it's worth it. Chelsea Green is a member of the Green Press Initiative (www.greenpressinitiative.org), a nonprofit coalition of publishers, manufacturers, and authors working to protect the world's endangered forests and conserve natural resources.

  Food Not Lawns was printed on Natures Natural, a 30-percent postconsumer recycled paper supplied by Thomson-Shore.

Library of Congress Cataloging-in-Publication Data
Flores, H. C., 1971–
Food not lawns : how to turn your yard into a garden and your neighborhood
into a community / H.C. Flores ; foreword by Toby Hemenway ; illustrations
by Jackie Holmstrom.
    p. cm.
Includes bibliographical references and index.
ISBN-13: 978-1-933392-07-3 (pbk.)
ISBN-10: 1-933392-07-X (pbk.)
1. Permaculture. 2. Edible forest gardens. I. Title.
S494.5.P47F56 2006
631.5'8--dc22

                                    2006014226

Chelsea Green Publishing Company
Post Office Box 428
White River Junction, VT 05001
(800) 295-6300
www.chelseagreen.com

Dedicated to Mushroom and Linda Kapuler,
whose enduring wisdom, steadfast creativity,
and humble brilliance have illuminated
the most delicious path to peace.

Contents

Foreword

As I write this, one of America's busiest highways, the Dan Ryan Expressway in Chicago, is being torn up and enlarged. Long traffic delays have led thousands of commuters to leave their cars at home and ride buses or the city's famous El to work. And they hate it. Mass transit takes longer, but that is not the real issue. For too many people, the car commute is the only time they are alone, away from the pressures and demands of family, boss, and coworkers. The fuel-saving and pollution-reducing bus or train, rather than being a relaxing and meditative time to read, listen to music, or simply stare out the window, is felt as a theft of the few moments they have to themselves. Car commuters may complain about the time wasted in traffic jams and the soaring cost of gas, but faced with the prospect of riding among strangers for an hour each day, most would much rather simmer alone indefinitely on a highway-turned-parking-lot.

This dilemma points to some colossal design flaws in our culture. Who would create a system in which so many forces conspire against the ecological act of leaving your car at home and taking public transportation? Why do we need so badly to escape our families, friends, jobs, and those with whom we anonymously share our communities? How do we begin to disconnect from the pressures and ugliness forced into our lives, and to reconnect, by choice, with the people, places, and things that give us joy?

The title of this book may have led you to believe it is simply about trading turf for vegetables. It is far more: It is a road map for a personal and cultural transformation that begins on our own lawns and carries us into our neighborhoods, communities, and society. If we follow this path, it will leave us healthier, wiser, and more joyful.

Food Not Lawns is a radical book. I write that with some irony, because the simple suggestions and techniques that Heather Flores offers—grow a garden, talk to neighbors, and try to notice the consequences of our actions—would have been plain common sense to our forebears of just two or three generations ago. But today, when saving a seed can result in a lawsuit, catching water from your roof risks fines from the health department, and a gardening workshop in Sacramento ends in arrests for terrorism, small acts of self-reliance require not merely courage but unusual vision and persistence in the face of a deeply apathetic culture.

Although Heather's stance is anti-corporate and anti-polluter, this book is not about stopping anything. It is about starting to create the world we want to see, a remarkably positive vision of a more fulfilling life gained in small, easy steps. Her writing unites science and magic, mechanics and mystery. She offers practical tools for reducing our manufactured dependencies and building our interdependence and helps us reconnect with ourselves, our land, and our communities.

This is a book about grassroots practice, even though grass is antithetical to what Heather stands for. She helps us see our sterile swards as the embodiments of waste, overconsumption, and emptiness that they are, and she shows us ways to rebuild them into sources of physical and spiritual nourishment. Moving from our yards to the global terrain, she outlines the work that we face. But she wisely stays focused on the local and shows us what we can do right here without feeling overwhelmed. She can wade with grace and balance into taboo topics such as using human waste for fertilizer, and I can attest that she writes from not just a theoretical acquaintance with this and many other topics. She has done nearly everything she describes in this book, and done it well.

Read this book. But don't stop there. Help create the paradise gardens and communities that Heather herself is bringing into being. I'll see you there.

Toby Hemenway
June 2006

Food
Not
Lawns

1. Free Your Lawn

Humans still live in prehistory; indeed, all things still stand before the creation of the world. . . . The real Genesis is not in the beginning, but at the end, when society and human existence become radical. When we engage our roots—the history of human as worker, creator, molder—and have grounded our possessions in a genuine democracy without alienation, then there will appear in the world something glimpsed in childhood, a place where nobody has yet been: Home.

—**Ernst Bloch, *The Principle of Hope***[1]

I teach self-reliance, the world's most subversive practice. I teach people how to grow their own food, which is shockingly subversive. Yes, it's seditious. But it's peaceful sedition.

—**Bill Mollison**[2]

This is not just another gardening book. Several parts of it are about gardening, but in the context of a garden that's deeply rooted in a complex community ecosystem. This book is about how to be healthier and more self-reliant, and thus improve the ecological integrity of the community you live in, through growing diverse organic gardens and sharing the surplus.

The natural world is in deep decline due to the grossly unsustainable habits of humankind. This is no secret. You can find evidence everywhere, from global warming to rain forest destruction to mass extinctions, all of it done in the name of free enterprise and short-term profit. Fortunately more and more people are waking up to these facts and working to find solutions on all scales. Let's just hope it is not too late.

I do not know a magic word that will make a wasteful society into an ecologically healthy one, or even just turn a lawn into a garden—these things take time, practice, and dedication. But I do know some powerful strategies that, in my experience, make these goals more attainable, and I have done my best to bring them together here in this book.

The average urban lawn could produce several hundred pounds of food a year.

Whether you live in an apartment, in the suburbs, on a farm, or anywhere in between, growing food is the first step toward a healthier, more self-reliant, and ultimately more ecologically sane life. Gardening may seem like just a hobby to many people, but in fact growing food is one of the most radical things you can do: Those who control our food control our lives, and when we take that control back into our own hands, we empower ourselves toward autonomy, self-reliance, and true freedom.

I know . . . social and environmental justice are the pipe dreams of every generation, and they seem especially obscure and remote in this age of corporate control, perpetual violence, and widespread environmental devastation. But before you dismiss me as another bleeding-heart tree hugger, remember that *radical* comes from a Greek word meaning "root," and let me share a short autobiographical tale.

How It Seems to Me

The eldest of four in an addicted, abusive, and estranged family, I had little access to alternative education or informed choices. Though born in Oregon, I grew up in the slums of suburban Los Angeles in the 1980s, where I didn't learn much about self-reliance, natural living, or ecological harmony. Not that growing up in suburban Cleveland, rural

Arizona, or New York City would have been much different. There are few places in America, or the world for that matter, that provide working examples of environmental responsibility in action.

For the first twenty years of my life I never thought about where my food came from; nor did I question the deeper workings of the food system or society as a whole. Though marginalized by my half-Mexican blood and low-income status, in many ways I was just like any other kid in the suburbs: I struggled to fit in, I fought with my parents, and I ate sugar and industrial meat almost every day.

Public school taught me to obey authority, and that words are more important than actions. Television taught me to buy my way to happiness, and that I should starve myself and keep my opinions to myself so I could find a husband and make babies. My family taught me to tolerate abuse in the name of love, and the mainstream workforce taught me that my time isn't worth a living wage.

Ironically, none of these lessons seemed to benefit me in any real way—on the contrary, these lies I had been indoctrinated with seemed to lead only to a doomed and heartless culture. I realized this but didn't know how to do anything about it, and at twenty-one I was clinically depressed over my lack of place or purpose.

I was lucky enough to have a few friends who encouraged me to question the mainstream values I felt so oppressed by, and to reach out for more information. I spent my last fifty bucks on a bus ticket from LA to San Francisco and quickly found work there, canvassing for Greenpeace. I had no experience with fund-raising or environmental activism, but the other canvassers welcomed me, and I discovered the world outside the working-class consumer box I'd grown up in.

I soon found that I could unlearn the bad habits of my upbringing and renew myself as an ecological being, and I began to try to live in concert with the other species around me. I became a vegetarian; I started recycling and riding bikes. I lost interest in shopping and watching television and started reading poetry, playing guitar, and paying attention to local, national, and international environmental issues. I learned that the planet is a mess because of human impact, and I resolved to do something about it.

Still, fund-raising for a bureaucratic organization in a big city wasn't exactly the Earth-mother connection I was looking for. I quit

Greenpeace and went to northern California to help defend the last of the ancient redwoods. For the next three years I worked with a wide variety of groups, doing actions and demonstrations in support of forest conservation, social justice, and food security.

Food Not Bombs

In 1998 I settled in Eugene, Oregon, and opened a communal household that would soon become the hub of a large activist community. The people I worked with were well educated and extremely well informed, and now I began to develop a deeper analysis of how best to channel my energy. As a full-time activist, I was inspired to make changes in the world and in my own life. I dove into the work, passionate about my newfound power and eager to learn as much as I could about building community and living more ecologically.

Still, much of the work was about *stopping* something—logging, mining, violence, et cetera—and not much seemed to focus on *starting* real alternatives. One exception was a group called Food Not Bombs. Most activists are cash-poor, having devoted their lives to volunteer work, and Food Not Bombs helps meet the need for good vegetarian meals.

Not that you have to be an activist to eat with Food Not Bombs. In hundreds of cities worldwide, local FNB chapters cook and serve free

Food Not Bombs offers free vegetarian meals in over a hundred cities around the world.

vegetarian meals to the public, using donated ingredients that would have otherwise gone into the trash. Through cooking with Food Not Bombs and interacting with the people we fed, I learned that it is not just activists who are concerned about the issues. Everyone is. Everyone wants to live peacefully, take care of the earth, and be good to one another. Sadly, people feel disempowered by the system and are struggling just to survive. They don't feel they have the time or the ability to change their own lives, let alone the whole culture.

Yet the more we ate together and shared ideas, the stronger we became. I was relieved to find something to do that created alternatives instead of focusing on problems. I was actively seeking and implementing positive, meaningful solutions, and by turning waste into food I was simultaneously reducing pollution, increasing my own quality of life, and building community.

Going Organic

As I learned more about agriculture and food in relation to health, the environment, and social justice, I quickly developed a deep commitment to eating an all-organic diet. And while it seemed expensive and difficult at first, the rewards were obvious: Within a few months I noticed a huge difference in how I felt—my energy levels were more stable, I wasn't getting sick as often, and my complexion looked better than it had since before puberty. Within a year the manic depression that had plagued me for a decade was gone, and I was physically and mentally healthier than ever.

It is a proven fact that organic food is fresher and more nutritious than conventional food, and better nutrition translates into better health for humans and the environment. Many people prefer organic food because they say it tastes better, and a number of studies have attested to its superior nutritional quality. On average organic food contains higher levels of vitamin C and essential minerals such as calcium, magnesium, iron, and chromium, as well as cancer-fighting antioxidants.[3] In addition, it doesn't contain food additives, which can cause health problems such as heart disease, osteoporosis, migraines, and hyperactivity.[4]

Genetically Modified Foods

The last few years have seen an overwhelming flood of genetically modified foods into stores and kitchens around the world. In fact, since 1999 genetically modified organisms (GMOs) have constituted more than 70 percent of the corn and soy crops grown annually in the United States.

GMOs can cause insects and plants to mutate, rendering them either exceedingly weak or super-resistant to even the most toxic controls. Either way spells disaster for long-term agricultural viability. Long-term effects on humans and animals are still largely unknown but could, and most likely will, include similar results in the form of cancer, plague, gross overpopulation, or worse.

The top fifteen companies that make, patent, and serve up genetically modified foods are listed below. In general, chances are that if you're eating nonorganic corn, corn syrup, potatoes, soy, or dairy, you are ingesting GMOs on a daily basis.

In a recent talk about the threats behind GMOs, consumer advocate Ralph Nader said,

> Genetic engineering of food and other products has far outrun the science that must be its first governing discipline. Therein lies the peril, the risk, and the foolhardiness . . . without commensurate advances in ecology, nutrition-disease dynamics, and molecular genetics, the wanton release of genetically engineered products is tantamount to flying blind.
>
> The infant science of ecology is underequipped to predict the complex interactions between engineered organisms and extant ones. As for any nutritional effects, our knowledge is also deeply inadequate. Finally, our crude ability to alter the molecular genetics of organisms far outstrips our capacity to predict the consequences of these alterations.[5]

The companies that make, patent, and sell these life-forms reject any responsibility for the irrevocable changes they cause to the natural environment. In fact, Monsanto's director of communications has said, "Monsanto should not have to vouchsafe the safety of biotech food. Our interest is in selling as much of it as possible. Assuring its safety is the FDA's job."[6]

This is like saying that a car company doesn't have to make sure its cars are safe, but the Department of Transportation should take responsibility for any accidents that occur because of equipment failure or bad design. The solution is obvious: If the suppliers of our food cannot be responsible for the safety of that food, then we need to take that responsibility into our own hands.

By refusing to consume GMOs, and by supporting organics instead, we send the message that we want food that is grown responsibly and with the best interests of all species in mind. Read the list below and stop eating the foods these companies produce. Call or fax them and tell them you don't want GMOs in your food. Support local, national, and international movements to ban genetically engineered foods.

THE FRANKENFOODS 15

Company Name	Phone	Fax
Campbell Soup	800-257-8443	856-342-3878
Coca-Cola	800-438-2653	770-989-3640
Frito-Lay	800-352-4477	972-334-5071
General Mills	800-328-1144	612-764-8330
Heinz	888-472-8437	412-456-6128
Hershey's	800-468-1714	888-431-7429
Kellogg's	800-962-1413	616-961-2871
Kraft/Nabisco	800-543-5335	847-646-2922
McDonald's	630-623-6198	630-623-6942
Nestlé	800-225-2270	818-549-6952
Procter & Gamble	800-331-3774	
Quaker Oats	800-367-6287	
Safeway	877-723-3929	925-467-2005
Shaw's	888-431-7429	508-313-3111
Starbucks	800-235-2883	206-447-3432

(This list comes from a flyer by the Organic Consumers Association.[7] See the resources section for contact information and a list of other excellent resources on this issue.)

Organic farming prohibits the use of polluting, carcinogenic chemicals, replacing them with tried-and-true methods such as composting, mulching, cover-cropping, traditional plant breeding, and the use of carefully planned designs and crop rotations to build healthy soil and balance essential nutrients. Organic farmers reject genetically modified organisms (GMOs), and their livestock is free of drugs and hormones. Organic practices can also support wildlife health and habitat, and they produce less waste and pollution, including carcinogens and global-warming gases.

However, the term *organic* has lately been co-opted by the federal government and corporate profit-mongers, and I feel it is important to note that even "certified organic" farms often engage in harmful practices such as covering the ground with black plastic or using excessive fossil fuels, whereas many small, ecologically sound farms choose not to certify themselves organic for a number of reasons.

I encourage you to look at where your food comes from with a critical eye and choose according to your own ethical beliefs. Certification, after all, may be merely a piece of paper acquired by paying fees and jumping through bureaucratic hoops. Real ecological integrity in agriculture comes only through personal accountability, and what better way to learn about gardening than to go to where food is grown and ask questions? Support the local farmers and gardeners you trust, and build that trust by getting to know them. I guarantee that your body, your gardens, and your bioregion will mutually benefit from the extra effort.

From this point on I will assume that you agree that eating organic food and supporting ecological agriculture is better for your health and that of the planet than chemical agriculture and the industrial food system. My purpose in this book is not to convince anyone of these facts, but to make it easier for those of us who choose an organic lifestyle to apply these ethics to our diets, our gardens, our homes, and our communities.

If you need more convincing about the toxicity of industrial agriculture, see the sidebar on pages 8–9 or refer to the resources section at the back of this book. Now on with the story . . .

Toxic Agriculture

In *The Soul of Soil* activist educator and agronomist Grace Gershuny points out that all land-dwelling animals, including humans, are members of the soil community. She writes, "Humans disregard this fact at their own peril. Soil fertility has historically been squandered for the immediate enrichment of a few at the expense of future generations. Cultural values—ethics, aesthetics, and spiritual beliefs—have a profound influence on how soil is treated. [Because of this] political and social activism are essential components of soil stewardship."[8]

Unfortunately this is not the mainstream attitude toward growing food (or anything else having to do with the soil). Irresponsible agriculture has been responsible for the collapse of civilizations since time immemorial, and much of what are now the world's vast deserts were once agricultural lands where the soil was not carefully cared for, such as in Peru, most of the Middle East, and large parts of Africa. In the last century the Dust Bowl of the Midwest was caused by unsustainable agriculture. Unless we put a stop to the excessive tillage, chemical inputs, and general disregard for the life in the soil, we are headed for a similar situation with what's left of the prime agricultural lands in California and Oregon and beyond.

In the late 1800s chemical companies and government agencies started promoting chemical fertilizers, miracle pesticides, and laboratory-developed seeds. This trend led to a rapid decline in soil and human health, which was promptly met by a continued increase in dependency on more chemicals. As is their basic nature, insects, diseases, and weeds have adapted to each new, stronger dose of poison with increasing vigor, developing resistances that force chemical companies to develop even more lethal toxins each year. This chemical dependence is a self-perpetuating cycle, and it is passed on to consumers, who routinely suffer from malnutrition or straight-up poisoning as a result of a lifetime of eating toxic food. This is evident in the increased dependency of humans on pharmaceutical drugs and vitamin supplements to provide the essential life-giving nutrients that stripped, dying soils cannot.

Commercial agriculture is one of the most polluting, destructive industries in the world. Some

Food Not Lawns

As my personal health and eating habits improved I became convinced that food—the source of our energy and, often, the root of consumerism—was also at the core of personal and community empowerment. It is extremely difficult to build an organic life on an empty stomach. When we are well nourished with good local food, we can work hard, get along, and build beautiful, ecological communities.

Healthy food is a basic right for everyone, but geographic, social, and economic boundaries often limit or deny access, both to food itself and to the land needed to grow it. Most people I talk to want to eat healthy, organic food and live in harmony with the earth and one another, yet they don't know how turn these ecological ethics into a real, daily lifestyle.

Often the primary problem is not supply but distribution. Through cooking with Food Not Bombs, I learned that in every city in North America, truckloads of nutritious food go to waste every day. Much of

two and a half billion pounds of chemical fertilizers, pesticides, and herbicides are used every year in the United States alone to mass-produce fast food for a consumer population that insists upon convenience at every corner. These chemicals poison drinking water worldwide and devastate soil communities.

Modern industrial agriculture is so toxic that 68 percent of farmworker pregnancies end in miscarriage, and cancer is the leading cause of death among farmers and farm laborers. Hundreds of different chemicals are routinely used in conventional farming, and residues are often present in nonorganic food, including high levels in baby food, spinach, dried fruit, bread, apples, celery, and potato chips. Many agricultural chemicals are made with known cancer-causing agents such as organochlorines, heavy metals, and chemical industrial wastes. The very same companies that profit from these poisons also control the advertising, research, and marketing sectors of the industry. Do you really want to continue to eat food from the same companies that make cleaning supplies, rat poison, and weapons?

It seems obvious, but chemicals such as pesticides and herbicides, manufactured for killing, do not stop with the bugs and weeds shown on the box. They kill everything, from butterfly eggs to beneficial nitrogen-fixing bacteria. Please never use these horrible substances in your garden. At best a cruel hoax, they are more likely a devastating curse upon humanity.

When we blanket the garden with deadly poisons and artificial fertilizers that destroy insect communities and shock the plants into unnatural growth spurts, we not only upset the balance of the natural community but also rob ourselves of the opportunity to learn what nature has to teach. This is an example of our dysfunctional relationship with nature. We see the evidence of this dysfunction everywhere, in widespread famine, war, and environmental devastation.

We can look back at history and see where societies structured much like our own have failed due to inadequate and unsustainable stewardship of agricultural lands.[9] We can avoid repeating history by going organic, not just with our food, but throughout every aspect of our lives.

this food is organic, and diverting the flow into the mouths of community-minded people is like sending water into a dry garden: It makes everything grow and bloom.

Further, food is only one of the deep diversity of resources found in the waste stream—and recycling the waste stream is the key to long-term urban sustainability. Beyond food, shelter, clothing, building materials, plants, seeds, tools, and of course many acres of fertile soil sit idle in every town in America.

As I began to realize this, I continued to cook and serve free meals in the park but changed my focus from providing resources to teaching others how to find them on their own. The old adage still rings true: Give a person a fish and feed her for a day; teach her to fish and feed her for a lifetime.

It was with this in mind that a few of us founded Food Not Lawns, a grassroots gardening project geared toward using waste resources to grow organic gardens and encouraging others to share their space, surplus, and ideas toward the betterment of the whole community. Why *Food Not Lawns?* Most obviously, the name was a natural evolution from *Food Not Bombs*.[10] But more importantly, we called ourselves Food Not Lawns because the more we learned about food, agriculture, and land use, the more the lawns around suburban Eugene began to reek of gross waste and mindless affluence.

While looking for a garden site, we asked our landlord to let us grow a garden in the grassy front yard of our rented house. He refused, saying he wanted to keep the lawn intact, and while I tried to see his point, to me it was absurd. In a world where so many lack access to basic needs such as food and shelter, and where a lawn of a thousand square feet could grow more than a hundred edible and beneficial plant species, becoming a lush perennial "food forest" within three years, mowed grass seems an arrogant and negligent indulgence (see the sidebar on pages 12–13).

We did eventually find a nice spot in an abandoned section of a local park, where we grew a diverse organic garden. We ate some of what we grew and gave the rest away. We grew starts and seeds and gave them away, and we hosted workshops in the garden space. The produce nourished us, the starts and seeds inspired gardens around the neighborhood, and the workshops helped spread the knowledge gained from our experience.

The garden flourished, and other activists in the neighborhood became intrigued. All summer long people dropped by with plants, seeds, or tools to donate, or to volunteer for an hour or three, chatting and sharing ideas within our peaceful oasis. It was so easy and so much fun, and the positive effects were exponentially obvious as the neighborhood got greener and the people got more educated about organic food and urban sustainability. Our neighbors and their gardens bloomed with an abundance of food, goodwill, and inspiration.

Food Not Lawns started several more gardens and circulated seeds, plants, and information. We planted food all over town—vegetables and fruit trees in public parks, berries along the bike path, squash down by the river—anywhere that looked like it would get water and sunshine. Over the next several years we organized dozens of events, including seed swaps, farm tours, resource exchanges, and workshops on a wide range of topics, such as natural building, composting, organic orchard care, self-education, and community organizing.

In the spring of 2000 I helped put on a weeklong community gardening festival during which a small affinity group planted a vegetable garden in a vacant lot around the corner from our house. Several months later, just before the juicy tomatoes and giant zucchini were ready to harvest, the landowner sold the lot to a developer who wanted to build an apartment complex.

The locals protested, saying there was ample vacant housing in Eugene (true). One neighbor locked himself to the bulldozer, with a sign saying SQUASH THE STATE! to prevent the garden from being destroyed, but he was arrested and the apartments were built. We lost that garden, but the event spurred a new flow of local and national interest, and ten more gardens popped up in other places around town.

Local and national media caught on, and we gave several interviews about sharing land and resources to promote peace and sustainability. Soon e-mails and letters flowed in encouraging our work, asking for more information, and telling of new chapters of Food Not Lawns in Washington, California, Pennsylvania, and Montreal. We soon connected with a global community of like-minded people—activists, some, but mostly a diversity of working-class people: healers, midwives, single moms, artists, musicians, lawyers, teachers, librarians, and plenty of organic farmers and gardeners. Apparently organic gardening with the larger goal of community sustainability appeals to people across many cultural and economic boundaries and unites activists, apathists, and many in between.

My own political views changed profoundly as the gardens taught me their lessons. I had lived and worked in a radical, anarchist/activist community for years and was inspired by finding a beautiful, positive way to manifest these philosophies. Notions of violent revolution dimmed next to visions of multicolored paradise and peaceful abundance. Dreams of industrial collapse became prayers for communities feeding and healing themselves.

Paradise Gardening

While reading up on similar projects in other towns I came across a book titled *Avant Gardening*, an anthology of stories and insights about

Wasted on Grass

French aristocrats popularized the idea of the green, grassy lawn in the eighteenth century when they planted the agricultural fields around their estates to grass to send the message that they had more land than they needed and could therefore afford to waste some. Meanwhile French peasants starved for lack of available farmland, and the resulting frustration might well have had something to do with the French Revolution in 1789.[11]

Today fifty-eight million Americans spend approximately thirty billion dollars every year to maintain more than twenty-three million acres of lawn. That's an average of over a third of an acre and $517 each. The same-sized plot of land could still have a small lawn for recreation *and* produce all the vegetables needed to feed a family of six. The lawns in the United States consume around 270 billion gallons of water a week—enough to water eighty-one million acres of organic vegetables, all summer long.

Lawns use ten times as many chemicals per acre as industrial farmland. These pesticides, fertilizers, and herbicides run off into our groundwater and evaporate into our air, causing widespread pollution and global warming, and greatly increasing our risk of cancer, heart disease, and birth defects. In addition, the pollution emitted from a power mower in just one hour is equal to the amount from a car being driven 350 miles.

In fact, lawns use more equipment, labor, fuel, and agricultural toxins than industrial farming, making lawns the largest agricultural sector in the United States. But it's not just the residential lawns that are wasted on grass. There are around seven hundred thousand athletic grounds and 14,500 golf courses in the United States, many of which used to be fertile, productive farmland that was lost to developers when the local markets bottomed out.[12]

Turf is big business, to the tune of around forty-five billion dollars a year. The University of Georgia has seven turf researchers studying genetics, soil science, plant pathology, nutrient uptake, and insect management. They issue undergraduate degrees in turf. The turf industry is responsible for a large sector of the biotech (GMO) industry, and much of the genetic modification that is happening in laboratories across the nation is in the name of an eternally green, slow-growing, moss-free lawn.

These huge numbers are somewhat overwhelming, if not completely incomprehensible, but they make the point that lawns not only are a highly

community gardening, organic living, and urban sustainability. An article by Joe Hollis was of particular interest. In this he wrote:

> Our world is being destroyed, in the final analysis, by an extremely misguided notion of what constitutes a successful human life. Materialism is running rampant and will consume everything, because its hunger will never be sated by its consumption. Human life has become a cancer on the planet, gobbling up all the flows of matter and energy, poisoning with our waste. What can stop this monster? Nothing. Just this: walk away from it. It is time, indeed time is running out, to abandon the entire edifice of civilization/the State/the Economy and walk (don't run!) to a better place: home, to Paradise.[13]

inefficient use of space, water, and money but also are seriously contributing to the rapid degradation of our natural environment.

I have traveled in the United States, Canada, Europe, Mexico, and South America, and most of the people I've met will agree that eating organic food is a good idea, as are recycling, conserving wilderness areas, and otherwise taking care of the earth. Nevertheless, as a society we continue to degrade our lands and cultures with pollution, mining, logging, a toxic and devastating agriculture, and a string of other abuses. We display our rejection of ecological responsibility through an irreverent consumer culture rife with waste and injustice, and we demonstrate our affluent denial by growing miles upon miles of homogeneous green lawns.

If we truly feel committed to treating the earth and one another with equality and respect, the first place to show it is by how we treat the land we live on. It is time to grow food, not lawns! The reasons include reducing pollution, improving the quality of your diet, increasing local food security, and beautifying your surroundings, as well as building community and improving your mental and physical health. You will save money and enhance your connection with the earth and with your family.

Whatever happens, you may still choose to keep a small lawn for playing croquet and sunning with the chickens. Good for you! The term *Food Not Lawns* is meant as a challenge to the notion of a homogeneous culture; it is not a call for the eradication of all green grassy places.

A small lawn, incorporated into a whole-system design, helps provide unity and invites participation in the landscape. Lawns offer a luxurious and comfortable place to read, stretch, or exercise. If you are the kind of person who uses a space like this, you should have one somewhere near your house.

And why not enhance the lawn with edible flowers, fruits, vegetables, or other useful plants? Or what about turning your whole yard into an organic food garden and using a local park, school, or natural area for recreation? If we can change our land-use philosophy from one of ownership and control to one of sharing and cooperation, we can renew our connection with the earth and one another and thus benefit through increased physical and mental health, an improved natural environment, and stronger local communities.

What have you got to lose besides a few blades of grass?

I found these words to be so real, so poignant, that I went with a friend to visit Joe at his place in the hills outside Asheville, North Carolina. It was spectacular. Everything still glistened with morning dew, though we arrived well after noon. The humid Appalachian forest steamed with the aromas of moss and worms, humus and biodiversity. Flowering vines spiraled up the banister as we climbed to the house.

We met Joe and chatted for a while, and he encouraged us to explore the garden. He motioned the way we had come, and I realized that the dense forest we had walked through on the way to his door was actually a diverse, multilayered garden, packed full of fruit trees, annual and perennial edibles, medicinal herbs, and more.

Joe calls his approach "Paradise Gardening" and recommends that, instead of continuing to occupy niches in society, we return to our ecological niche: intentionally, as stewards of the earth. This attitude

The consumer waste stream is overflowing with valuable resources.

makes so much sense to me, as a gardener and as a human being, that I decided to use the word *paradise* to describe the type of gardening I write about. I will explain how to create such a garden, and I'll use the term throughout to refer to the holistic attitude and natural gardening approach described in this book.

Ecology and Community

Growing paradise gardens and giving away the surplus makes communities better in the most fundamental ways: First, we regain control of the quality and availability of our food supply, which results in healthier, more confident people. Next, when we share the harvest, our neighbors become more like family. This reduces waste from all directions.

Finally, and perhaps most importantly, organic gardening reconnects us to the earth and allows us to place ourselves within the context of the larger ecological whole. This realization inspires us to live as if the earth mattered and encourages us to take responsibility for ourselves and our families.

Becoming a paradise gardener means cultivating an attitude of equality with all species and embracing a role as willing participant, rather than master and commander, of the garden and surrounding ecology. This egalitarian attitude shapes our actions and approaches and defines the types of strategies we use to develop our homes, gardens, and communities.

Ecological living is not so much about understanding nature as it is about understanding ourselves. We must learn how to provide for our own needs without degrading our natural surroundings. This is primarily a social transformation, because humans are doing most of the damage. Humans are a part of the larger ecological community, and it is our blatant disregard of this fact that has gotten us into so much trouble.

Living ecologically means changing our whole way of being with the rest of nature, and gardening provides the setting for this transformation. If each of us grows even a small organic garden and shares the surplus, we will see a distinct cultural shift toward healthier people and stronger communities, not just through a direct increase in available food and information but also, and more importantly, through the way these actions change how people think.

In the garden, by stepping outside economic and social constructs for a moment to envision ourselves in the cradle of nature, we can get to know the ecological self. Through this eco-self we can place ourselves in the context of the ecological community in which we live, learn how to cooperate with natural systems, and eliminate or decrease the disharmony caused by our current unbalanced state.

The more we can understand ourselves in relation to the natural world we depend upon, the closer we will come to integrating into a healthy, ecological whole. More simply, by rejecting the consumer culture and instead embracing an outdoor life that is rich in organic foods, personal interactions, and intentional learning, we can live in a lusher, more natural alternative: paradise.

In cities around the world Food Not Lawns collectives work to set the stage for these transformations. We share a vision of freeing ourselves from a toxic, artificial culture and reuniting with our natural ecology through community interaction and paradise gardening.

But it is not flowers and strawberries the whole time. While we build gardens and educate ourselves, our governments wage war around the globe, and the corporations wage war on the environment. Even in our little neighborhood people can't seem to get along well enough to take care of a local park, let alone save the world. For every seed that we save, every garden we start, whole ecosystems go down.

So while paradise gardens provide food, sanctuary, and many lessons about the earth, these lessons won't endure unless we also apply them to the rest of the community—and to every other aspect of our lives.

Beyond the Garden

Paradise gardens are at the heart of a healthy urban ecology, and the next few chapters will provide many practical examples of healthy ways to make your garden grow. However, your own garden becomes a hundred times more bountiful when placed in the context of the larger community, and the rest of the book is about how to bring what you learn from the garden into your daily life, and how to build community through sharing food, resources, and ideas.

Many people today are talking and learning about ecological, economic, and social sustainability, each of which has varying definitions, depending upon whom you talk to. Unfortunately most models of one type of sustainability tend to inhibit the sustainability of another, such as when a logging project creates jobs but destroys the forest.

Overall, the whole of modern culture is not sustainable on any of these fronts. The current world population will double in just a few years, and again a few years later. Nothing can sustain such exponential growth in a finite area, and unless we begin to redesign the whole, starting with local communities and spiraling outward, we are, frankly, doomed. We must learn how to balance economic need with ecological priority—and, perhaps most important, how to get along with one another while we're at it.

The extent to which the global situation is ecologically and economically unsustainable is well documented elsewhere, so I will spare you the grim details. In short, the last threads in the web of life are fraying rapidly in the shadow of global development and scientific progress, and our survival as a species will be utterly dependent on our ability to change. It is time to think beyond our own gardens and put our ecological ethics into action throughout the rest of our lives as well.

Environmentalism and *ecological living* are often terms associated with activists, but you don't have to be an activist to want to live as if nature mattered, or to want to change your community. As I said

The average urban lawn could produce several hundred pounds of food a year.

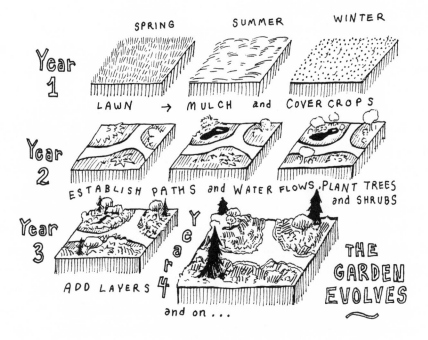

before, most of the people I meet do want these things but don't know how to manifest them.

The first step is to start making choices that balance autonomous thought with integrated ecology. To create a sustainable future we must focus on exponential learning rather than exponential growth, and on accumulated wisdom rather than accumulated wealth.

By insisting that human communities not only provide for their own needs but actually contribute to and improve the natural environment, we can work toward a *thriving* human ecology that might have a chance at perpetuity. In short, when we work with nature, rather than against it, everything gets easier, more delicious, and potentially more sustainable.

This attitude, while sadly foreign to our fast-paced consumer culture, works quite well in the garden, and it can work in the rest of the community too. The garden is an excellent place to start, but we must go beyond it to find the path to whole-system ecological health.

Permaculture and Ecological Design

Around the globe, as people wake up to nature, ecological living, and ethical land stewardship, they are devoting themselves to building communities that are environmentally, economically, and socially balanced. In the past thirty years the ecological design movement has proven itself as an excellent resource for strategies and techniques that help communities realize this vision.

In 1979 Bill Mollison coined the term *permaculture* to describe his methodology for the "conscious design and maintenance of agriculturally productive ecosystems which have the diversity, stability, and resilience of natural ecosystems."[14] Since then many more great minds have contributed their own insights and experiences to the global movement of ecological gardeners and designers who call themselves the permaculture community. Today there are thousands of working demonstrations around the globe, all organized by people who have jobs, families, busy lives, and often minimal funding.

Permaculture designers use a succinct set of principles and techniques to establish homesteads and communities that provide for their own needs, require minimal care, and produce and distribute surplus food and goods. These principles and techniques merge well with the paradise gardening approach, and a paradise garden fits perfectly into the heart of any permaculture design. Like paradise gardening, permaculture emphasizes relaxation, sharing, and working with nature rather than against it. Meeting our own needs without exploiting others is the primary goal.

Further, the principles that make permaculture so successful in the garden also apply to other endeavors, such as home design, community events, and interpersonal relationships. These include activities like food preserving, natural building, environmental repair, ecological education, resource recycling, and using renewable energies including solar and wind power.

Permaculture stems from a triad of ecological ethics: First, care for the earth, because the earth sustains our lives. Second, care for the people, because we are people, and because people are the primary cause of damage to the earth. Third, recycle all resources toward the first two ethics, because surplus means pollution and renewal means

The classic permaculture triad of ecological ethics

survival. By allowing these three primary ethics to provide a foundation for our garden, design, and community work, we can move toward our goals of a peaceful culture and a healthy human ecology.

This transformation has exponential effects on the land and the people and has the potential to spark a global culture of peaceful, responsible communities. Maddy Harland, editor of *Permaculture Magazine*, says it well: "Contact with the soil reminds us that we are an integral part of nature, rather than feeling shut out and excluded. The simple acts of growing and eating our own food, recreating habitats in which nature's diversity thrives, and taking steps to live more simply are practical ways of living which connect us to an awareness of Nature's seamless whole. Permaculture is a spiritual reconnection as well as an ecological strategy."[15]

Permaculture is not just about the elements of a system; it is also about the flows and connections among those elements. You can have solar power, an organic garden, an electric car, and a straw-bale house and still not live in a permaculture. A project becomes a permaculture only when special attention is paid to the relationships between each element, among the functions of those elements, and among the people who work within the system.

Through a design process like permaculture, we can organize these relationships for optimum success. Our creativity is our most powerful tool for overcoming the ills of our culture, and design helps us harness that creativity and put it to work.

Yet, while the word *permaculture* does refer to a few specific techniques, most of what permaculture teaches is not new information. It stems from the wisdom of the ancients, blended with science and critical thought, and distilled into design formulas for modern use.

I sometimes hear people say, "Permaculture is just common sense!" Yes, many of the techniques seem like common sense, but they are not common practice—yet. Why not? Perhaps it is because people do not know where to begin. The goal of this book is to help you create that starting point and, further, to develop a long-term implementation plan that will help you manifest your thriving gardens and communities.

I will always adhere to the ecological ethics I learned through permaculture and devote my work to caring for the earth, caring for the people, and recycling resources toward those ends. I believe that these ethics will lead us down the path to an abundant human ecology, with plenty of yummy things to eat along the way. However, while I would never abandon the permaculture movement as a whole, I caution against allowing this or any other catchphrase to replace a working human ecology.

Don't get me wrong: I love permaculture. I love to geek out on design theory and play with the principles and to study the techniques and try to apply them to my life, my home, and my garden. I love Bill Mollison for his silly jokes, his codgerish reputation, and his brilliant writing. I have studied permaculture and have met many amazing, inspired, and capable people who self-identified as "permaculturists."

I have also, however, studied several other topics, such as biodynamics, kinship gardening, direct action, dance, music, and visual arts. All of these play as strong a role in this book as permaculture, and to call this a "permaculture book" would be to diminish both my own hard work and that of my dedicated mentors in these other areas. In truth, I am uncomfortable with the word "permaculture" and with the assumption that we as a species are entitled to permanence on this earth. My purpose here is not to alienate anyone, but to integrate a broader and, in my opinion, more inclusive perspective into the eco-organic-permaculture-sustainability mindshed.

This is obviously a conversation that needs to continue far beyond these pages, but for now I will summarize by saying that when I take action toward caring for the earth, and toward designing my life in concert with my ecological community, it feels right. Some call it permaculture, some call it common sense, some might even call it enlightenment. Personally, I do not seek enlightenment or exaltation, only the occasional bellyful of homegrown peaches and a chance to interact with the growing global community of like-minded people. I always welcome comments, critiques, constructive criticism, and, of course, sweet little envelopes full of organic seed! So let us engage as a community of individuals who think our own thoughts, do our own work, and yet trust and rely upon each other as we move toward a common and fruitful future.

Radical As a Radish

Is this just the latest grasp at Utopia, another random idea from the radical fringe? At first glance it may seem so, but Utopia is a rigidly controlled world with no problems, no conflict, and no fear. We must rather embrace the reality that, as humans, we will grapple with these and many other difficult issues.

The scope and quality of our survival is largely dependent upon how we deal with the inevitable and sometimes horrible facets of humanity. Therefore, while Utopia prescribes an authoritarian and impersonal recipe for perfection, this book insists that small, localized communities develop and support their own unique systems. In this type of flexible, individualized approach lies our true power.

My own work stems from a deep dedication to an autonomous, egalitarian attitude that some might associate with traditional anarchism, and many might label "radical." I see this attitude as radical only in that it comes from, and returns to, the root of the problem: namely, how to live on the earth in peace and perpetuity. Each of us has only herself to be, to blame, and to rely upon, and our own behavior is at the root of any social or environmental change. If we want peace, we have to be peaceful. If we want to live in paradise, we have to grow it, now. I see this work as evolution, not revolution, and as the ultimate adventure: a fantastic way to simultaneously enjoy life on this earth and improve it for future generations.

Flowers are not the only thing that bloom in the garden—people do. When people participate in an ecological community, they tune in to the subtle voices of nature and tend to become more attentive to their bodies, more mindful of their impact on the environment, better at listening and communicating, and more able to overcome fears and obstacles.

By putting our hands in the soil, we gain access to the wisdom of the earth, and by putting our heads together we learn how to use that knowledge for the benefit of all. When the members of a community start living more ecologically, they improve the soil, purify the water, plant trees, encourage wildlife, and reduce pollution and waste. By giving back more than it takes, every ecological project increases the overall health of our planet—and thus our capacity for peace and sustainability.

People balk at this vision, call it unrealistic, even fear it. Indeed, it is hard to imagine such a community in these grim and violent times, but with a devoted effort I think we can achieve peace and sustainability through paradise gardening, ecological design, and grassroots community interaction. These varied strategies and techniques help renew our connections to our instincts and enable us to ask the questions that will lead to real, long-term solutions. And once we learn to ask questions—relevant, useful questions—then nothing can stop us from learning what we need to know.

How to Use This Book

The primary goal of this book is to give tangible shape to these ideals, and to show how easy it can be for you and other people who care about the earth to grow gardens and build communities accordingly. We'll start with gardening, then move on to communities.

The first half of this book focuses on how to establish and maintain ecological paradise gardens, using the resources we have available here and now. We will tap into the wasted resources around us and look at the varied elements of the garden, including the water, soil, plants, and seeds. Then we will use my own ecological design formulas to bring these elements together into a multifunctional, low-maintenance paradise garden.

The next several chapters go beyond the garden to show how the ecological skills learned there can help improve our communities. Here you will find examples and suggestions for meeting people, forming collectives, and organizing projects such as seed swaps, community gardens, educational performances, or workshops on any range of topics. I finish with a special chapter on integrating children into our gardens and community projects. I also include a resources section to help you find more information on the topics in this book and connect with like-minded people in your community.

Unfortunately this book alone will not solve all your problems; nor will it teach you everything you need to know about organic gardening, sustainable living, or community organizing. What it will do is ask the question *How can human beings thrive together, in peace and perpetuity, without destroying the ecology that we depend upon?* and identify some potentially viable answers, starting with growing and sharing food where you are now.

I am not trying to prescribe a template for a perfect, "sustainable" culture. You must design your own life, your own community, around the ecology you live in. Nor am I telling you to don a loincloth and live on grub worms and roadkill. You must find your own niche in your community, make the best use of the resources at hand, and work with steadfast intention toward a long and natural life.

Ultimately the best way to learn these skills is to do them. Just reading this book won't get you much farther than the armchair—you have to get out there and try this stuff in your own yard, in your own community. To these ends, I offer you some theories and examples, and a thorough list of references for further study. What you do next is up to you.

By putting our hands in the soil, we gain access to the wisdom of the earth.

2. Gaining Ground

Our goal is to naturalize ourselves in the environment. This will involve changing ourselves and changing the environment: convergence toward "fit." Perfect fit means the free and easy flowing of matter and energy between ourselves and our environment; life lived as a complete gift—from the garden to us, from us to the garden.

—Joe Hollis[1]

The sad reality is that we are in danger of perishing from our own stupidity and lack of personal responsibility to life. If we become extinct because of factors beyond our control, then we can at least die with pride in ourselves, but to create a mess in which we perish by our own inaction makes nonsense of our claim to consciousness and morality.

—Bill Mollison[2]

Urban Ecology

Many people see ecological living as something they will do later, when they can finally afford a big place in the country, but I say, "Start now!" Even, or perhaps especially, if you live in a tiny apartment surrounded by a concrete jungle, you can usually find simple ways to repair the earth, educate others, and prevent further destruction of the natural world.

Growing ecological gardens, wherever you can, is never a waste of time. Nothing lasts forever, and if you can get a few baskets of food without damaging the environment, and perhaps leave behind some long-living fruit trees, then the larger ecological community will surely benefit from your labors. If you can do these things while also educating others, then your work will succeed many times over.

Further, not everyone wants to live in the country, and if everyone moves there it will all become the city. Many people plan to spend their lives in the city, happily, and have no plans to go rural. This is good, because if we want to support the growing human population for more than another few centuries, we are going to have to grow up, not out. We also must ensure that urban communities can provide for their own needs, using resources from the local area. These needs include food, building materials, water, medicine, and much more, and currently there are no cities to provide a working model, though some cities, like Portand, Oregon, are starting to gain ground.

We can create local models by simultaneously caring for the earth, caring for the people, and recycling resources. In these models rural food surpluses will supplement urban subsistence gardens, and the ecological integrity of each bioregion will depend upon how well the city dwellers can provide for themselves.

Improving the ecological health of cities is crucial to achieving a healthy bioregional community, and if the ideas in this book inspire you, then begin doing these things now regardless of where you live or whether you rent or own your garden site. Do it for the land and to experience the personal transformation; consider the harvest a bonus, rather than the goal. The sooner and more fully we embrace an ecological ethic in our daily lives, the better our ability to place ourselves within the deep ecological context of our communities, and the clearer that context, the more possible our goal of sustainability.

Urban ecology is not so much a matter of "saving the earth" as it is a chance to improve the ecological viability of our own human lives and, thus, our chances of survival as a species on earth. The earth probably does not care whether we save her. She will most likely continue to turn and breed life long after humans have gone extinct. If we continue our current trend of wanton consumption and shameless waste, this will occur much sooner than later.

I know I sound like Chicken Little saying, "The sky is falling!" However, this deep impermanence, while it may seem like so much doom and gloom, is actually a blessing: Our own fragility gives us the impetus to act now to create healthy lives that harmonize with nature, and to know the comfort, joy, and inspiration brought on by an organic life. Why waste years and decades locked into jobs and consumer boxes that kill and oppress us when paradise is the alternative?

In my experience most people want to eat healthy food, care for the earth, and do other things that help create a better future for humans and other species, but they feel powerless against economic and social constraints. This has a lot to do with the fact that millions of people don't have a place to grow food, and the people who do have access to land, such as in rural and suburban areas, rarely steward it to the extent we need.

In addition to land, we also need tools, seeds, plants, and other materials, and most people can't afford to just go out and buy it all. It is a common misconception that you need a lot of money to transform your home, garden, and community into paradise. But you can't buy your way to a healthy ecology—you have to innovate it.

Integral to growing paradise gardens is recycling resources to do so. Every city in the world is rife with useful waste, and recycling it is an essential component of a healthy urban ecology. By understanding the flow of resources in the community around our gardens, we can better place those gardens within their deeper ecological and social context. Yes, growing organic food is always worth doing, but what of the truckloads of good organic produce that farmers and distributors throw away? This waste could be food on your table and compost in your garden.

Focus on making best use of what is near you.

Get acquainted with locally available, free resources—land, food, and otherwise. This is the first step in turning your yard into a garden and your neighborhood into a community, and recycling those resources is the next step. Focus on making best use of what is near you now, and buy new stuff only as the very last resort. The more we recycle the waste stream toward meeting our basic needs, the closer we come to closing the ecological loop.

Urban ecology is a big issue, and one that will take many years and many ideas to understand, but if we start with growing food where we can, we will be moving in the right direction. We can find space and resources that don't cost money; we can build gardens and communities that make social and ecological sense.

This chapter will focus on making these resources more accessible. We will look at how to find a garden space if you don't have one, and how to make the most out of the spaces you find. Then we will see how to tap into the flow of useful surplus that goes to waste every day, in every city in America, and how to divert that flow toward your garden and community.

Look Before You Leap

Before we can build ecological gardens and communities, we must first take the time to look deeply into our surroundings and try to see how best to integrate ourselves with the natural ecology. Humans are notorious for their inability and/or unwillingness to look at the natural signs around them, and this tendency is probably how we got in such deep water with the natural environment.

Sure, you might be all fired up to bust out some fabulous project, and I don't want to discourage spontaneous creative action, but it is essential that we learn to look. Only through careful observation can we avoid making the same mistakes twice and determine what to do next.

During this observant, assessing phase, you should start a journal to keep track of what you find and to document the ideas and designs you come up with later on. Include garden maps and design ideas, seed harvests, lists of where you find good resources, contact information for fellow gardeners, drawings of your projects, and whatever else comes to mind. Such journals will become treasured community heirlooms, so choose a well-bound book with acid-free paper, and try not to leave it out in the rain!

Observation means more than just looking around with your eyes at what you see right now. There are many ways and many levels on which to see things, and I will describe a few important ones here. Before you read any more, take this book and go sit outside, where you have a decent panoramic view of your neighborhood. Now, as you read, look at your surroundings and try to see them in the ways I describe. Do this every morning for a few days.

This exercise might feel a bit contrived, but you really must do it, because it will help train your subconscious mind, and you will be surprised at how quickly your perception changes. Just as a dance step or a piano riff may seem difficult or impossible to do at first but can become easy, even automatic, over time, so can we train our minds to see and respond to nature. Ready?

Look Deep

This is a proverb familiar to hunters, who must learn to look deep into the woods for deer and other prey. Use your eyes and try to see as far into a landscape as possible. Look past the first layer of foliage, through the gap between trees, and past the tops of small plants.

One of the first times I went to the garden of my friends and mentors Alan, or "Mushroom," and Linda Kapuler, we spent the afternoon wading through a dozen or so varieties of giant marigold plants in bloom. There must have been millions of flowers, and I had never seen marigolds that were different from the little pom-poms sold out in front of supermarkets.

Mushroom said, "Look at these flowers! Aren't they beautiful?" I replied, "Oh, yes, so many different reds and oranges." Then he said, "No, *look*." And pointed at a single flower just inches from our faces.

I followed the line of his long finger into the center of the flower and saw, to my utter amazement, that it was one of a kind. All of the flowers were marigolds, and the ones in this patch had come from the seeds of a single flower, but each flower had a unique shape and color. By looking deep into the garden, then into the patch of marigolds, then into each flower, I was able to begin to understand what it means to be diverse.

Looking deep also means using all our senses. You should look with your eyes, but also listen, taste, touch, and smell your surroundings. Practice looking deep into a garden, into the woods, into a handful of soil, and at your community. Look in every direction: up, down, under, behind, around, through, and at different times of the day. Write down what you see. Deeper, use your spiritual sense—your intuition—and make note of what your instinct sees.

When developing ecological gardens and other community projects, we need to make observations on different levels. The two main ones are the macrocosm and the microcosm. Each includes important sublevels of observation, which I will elaborate on below. Look deep at each level to create a fractal-like sense of what you see. Look past the obvious, check your assumptions, and use all your senses.

Macrocosm

From seeing your garden in the context of your neighborhood to seeing yourself in the context of the universe, the macrocosm is the big picture. This includes the embedded energy in every tool and resource, such as how much pollution was caused by manufacturing and trans-

Developing a balanced understanding of microcosms and macrocosms helps us find a harmonious place in ecological communities.

porting the greenhouse plastic, or how much forest was destroyed for the lumber to build raised garden beds. When you use recycled materials you minimize embedded energies and help prevent pollution by intercepting waste, rather than creating waste through consumer demand.

Looking at the macrocosm means searching for patterns in space and time. Look at all the big things and see how they fit together to make the whole. Look for large-scale patterns and relationships. Try to determine where they go and where they come from by following the connections from one observation to the next. In most cases these patterns will repeat themselves on each smaller scale, and through them we can find ways to make our small work resonate with the big picture.

Microcosm

Now tune in to the subtler details of what you see. Look deep into the macrocosm and pick out the microcosm that is your life, your garden. In the garden look deeper into each detail, from an individual tree to the smallest soil organism. Again, look for patterns and notice opportunities.

Within each microcosm there will also be many microclimates—special niches that yield special circumstances, which you can change or take advantage of. I'll get into microclimates in a minute. For now focus on training your senses to see the details.

Volunteer at a Local Farm or Help Friends with Their Gardens

Most organic farms offer free produce to volunteers, and some will lease you a small plot of your own. This gives you an opportunity to learn from the farmer and access to the farm infrastructure, which includes important resources such as irrigation, seeds, surplus starts, et cetera. Some farms also hire seasonal workers, which can be a great opportunity to spend your summer learning, exercising, and eating fresh produce.

If you can't find a local farm to work with, volunteer to help your neighbors with their small garden. More options usually reveal themselves as new relationships mature, so build community through voluntary interaction and you won't be without a garden for long.

Garden in Pots and Containers

Most annual vegetables are well suited for container gardening. Even a small patio can hold a few planters—get pots out of a garden center dumpster or use other recycled containers such as sinks, bathtubs, wine barrels, and plastic buckets with holes drilled in the bottom. Try strawberries, carrots, beets, tomatoes, cucumbers, zucchini, herbs, and salad greens.

Try a self-contained potato garden: Take some chicken wire and make a round cage. Put a layer of thick straw in the bottom and toss some potatoes in. Cover with straw, leaves, or soil, water often, and keep adding more mulch on top as the shoots emerge. Soon you will have a basket full of fresh potatoes.

Use the Roof

If you lack patio or yard space but have a flat, accessible roof, consider building raised beds or planter boxes on the roof. There are fabulous rooftop gardens in big cities all over the world, with everything from small containers of herbs and salad greens to large planter boxes filled with trees and perennials. Get creative with the space you have now and better options will unfold later.

De-pave Your Sidewalk or Driveway

Rent a concrete cutter or just get together some friends with crowbars and rip out the pavement around your house. It doesn't take that much work to convert a driveway or parking area into a garden. I have seen several wonderful examples, and the residents didn't regret the lost pavement for a second.

The broken-up pieces—aptly called "urbanite"—work great as stepping-stones or patio pavers or for building raised beds and terraces. Park on the street and enjoy the extra exercise while walking home through your new garden.

You may even want to tear down a whole building, such as a garage full of junk; recycle the junk and building materials, and grow plants instead. I would much rather have a living, edible garden next to my house than a dirty old box full of consumer crap. Think about it—you probably wouldn't pave over an orchard to build a driveway, so why choose the pavement over the trees just because it's there now?

Grow Food in the Existing Landscape

You don't have to turn over a big area or even disrupt existing plantings to integrate some food plants. We once rode bikes around town with a big bag of zucchini seeds, planting them wherever we saw a gap in the landscaping. Later we saw big plants in some of the spots and harvested some delicious zucchini! I have also planted fruit trees into existing beds in front of local businesses or at the edge of a park.

This strategy works well, because the city or property owner maintains the landscape, and your plants get watered—sometimes even weeded and fertilized—right along with the plants that were already there! The downfall is that whoever is in charge of the site may notice your plant and pull it out or may spray it with toxins. Still, this is a good option for generating more food around town, and it can be great fun.

Also look for good spots in alleyways, along back fences. Often there is a garden on the other side of the fence, and you can plant small beds along the outside that benefit from the surplus water and fertility.

Start a Garden in a Vacant Lot

You can do this with or without permission. Sometimes property owners will let you plant vegetables and fruit trees in a sunny, under-used corner. Others may say no if you ask but won't notice for a long while if you just do it without telling them.

When the Food Not Lawns collective started our first garden, in an overgrown section of the park, the city didn't know we were there for almost a year. We got the combination to the gate from a neighbor, cleared out all the trash and debris, and started gardening. By the time folks from the city came along to ask questions, we had a beautiful garden established, and they let us continue to use the space. They even sent park workers to drop off chip mulch once in a while!

There are countless examples like this, where people took over an area, grew food, and maintained access for many years. Some of these squatted gardens eventually gained ownership of the land. Sadly, there are just as many examples of gardens that were eventually bulldozed and paved over. In my opinion it is usually worth a try, and you will probably get at least a season's reward for your audacity. This and the previous option are often called guerrilla gardening—see chapter 9 for more tips along these lines.

As you look for places to grow, ask yourself some important, practical questions: Will you actually go there to garden? Will you be inspired by the surrounding space? Will the plants have an opportunity to reach maturity? Will you want to eat the produce? Grow what you love, what you eat, and what you want to look at, in a space that makes you feel healthy and empowered.

Making the Most of a Space

Don't let the idea of the perfect garden spot keep you from planting things right where you are now. Making the most of every space is one of the primary purposes of paradise gardening and ecological design. Here are some important pointers for maximizing the space you have available now.

Grow Up

Using vertical space wherever possible will double or even triple your yield, because for a tiny amount of ground space, you get lots of produce. Grow plants that climb, such as cherry tomatoes, cucumbers, gourds, and beans. Hang a salad garden near the kitchen door. Or grow plants up a trellis, rooted in large pots or small beds.

Try growing upside-down tomatoes by planting a handful of seeds in a hanging bucket with a hole cut in the bottom. Water often and watch

An ugly urban lot can be transformed into a lush organic garden in just a few months.

tomato vines grow out from all directions. Thin to the strongest few vines and harvest often.

Grow in the Shade

Many gardeners value only the sunny spots, but thousands of edible and beneficial plants thrive in partial to full shade. True summer veggies usually prefer full sun, but try spinach, kale, collards, raspberries, mints, beets, and most salad greens in an area you thought might be too shady. You may be pleasantly surprised.

Think Outside the Raised Bed

Filling big square areas with annual vegetables is but one of the many varied and wonderful ways to grow good organic food. Even a small corner can become a fruit-bearing oasis filled with cherries, currants, grapes, or any number of perennial shrubs and trees. Carve out odd-shaped sections where a large bed won't fit. Convert curvy strips around your lawn into garden beds, leaving wide grass paths in between. Or just plant little islands around the yard.

Also try mixing annual vegetables with existing landscape perennials. Plant long-living fruits such as blueberries, plums, grapes, apples, and pears, and enjoy the bounty of your ingenuity for generations to

Using vertical space, containers, and rooftops to grow gardens can help make the most of small, urban spaces.

come. Most garden fruits will bear within the first three years, depending on the variety and age of the tree when planted.

Make Use of Available Water and Fertility

In areas that are naturally soggy, such as near a dripping hose or by the roof drain, plant a garden filled with plants that will thrive on the moist soil. Along the same lines, if an area is naturally dry or the soil seems barren, find plants that prefer the dry soil or can improve it, rather than trying to force plants to grow in a soil to which they are not suited.

This principle also applies to soil fertility—if you have a rich area, use it to grow your most important plants, even if it doesn't seem to be the most aesthetically or socially appropriate area. By this I mean do it in the front yard, y'all! Don't underestimate the beauty of your food garden. If well designed and tended with love, it will far surpass the beauty of any ornamental landscape, and your neighbors will prefer it to the static lawn that was there before.

Make Microclimates Work for You

Take plenty of time to carefully observe the site—sun, water, soil, traffic, and natural and industrial influences—and make a note of the apparent microclimates around your garden area. The term *microclimate* refers to the specific conditions of a particular site within a larger ecosystem. This could be your individual garden versus the local growing area, or a specific spot within that garden versus the whole site. Around even a small home or garden site there may be a dozen or more types of microclimates, each with a distinct set of conditions: hot and dry; cool and wet; sunny and moist; shady, dry, and acidic; and so forth.

There are a number of factors to consider when looking for and designing microclimates, including soil, wind, frost, heat, water, and of course function. First, look at the soil. Where is it dry, wet, warm, cool? Is it thriving with life or is there not a bug to be found? Next, notice how the wind moves through the garden; it can be very easy to filter and direct (more or less) wind through a site.

Cold wind often has a devastating effect on tender plants. Thus it is important to identify the less hardy zones in the garden and plan accordingly. Watch out for these little frost pockets, and look for opportunities to direct warm winds toward heat-loving plants, to prevent cold wind tunnels from damaging tender plants, and to take advantage of (or avoid) wind's drying effects.

For example, you can deflect a frost using a white, south-facing wall and/or overhead cover. Many plants that are not otherwise hardy in a certain region will thrive up against a nice warm wall. Likewise, rock borders, brick paths, fences, trellises, and waterways can also catch, store, and reflect heat, divert or filter wind, and shelter tender plants.

Existing weeds provide useful clues about the soil and microclimate (see chapter 4 for more on this). Also, look at how the water moves through the garden, and look for opportunities within. Learn to recognize and note the special circumstances that any of the above elements impose on the site. Find several microclimates in your home and garden space, and try to identify their individual needs and opportunities.

Adjacent microclimates influence each other, especially along the edge. For example, a greenhouse not only is a warm, humid microclimate in itself but also creates varying microclimates on each side, below, and above. Thus you can create a warm microclimate along the south side of a greenhouse, using the space to grow heat-loving plants. If you put a dwelling on the north side of the greenhouse, it will benefit from the surplus heat and protect the plants from chilly northern winds. Likewise, you can look for a natural microclimate, such as a shady grove of oak trees, and use it to grow useful shade plants that would not survive in the sun of the garden.

Some people recommend following your pets around to find microclimates. On a cold winter day put the cat out and see where she goes; chances are you will find a warm microclimate where you can plant a winter garden or put a sensitive houseplant. On a midsummer afternoon notice where the dog seeks shelter from the heat, and you may find a cool, dark place to dry herbs or store fresh foods.

Further, within each microclimate, and again within the whole, there will be a wide diversity of niches, some of them filled with living creatures and plants, others waiting for a symbiotic opportunist or two to settle in. By learning to identify the specialized opportunities within a site, you can assess its potential and determine what steps to take when building beds, improving soil, and choosing plants. Knowing your niches and microclimates will help you make best use of your space, increase the range of plants you can grow, and thus multiply your overall yield.

Identifying Resources

When looking for a garden space, also keep an eye out for the other resources you will need, such as plants, seeds, tools, and soil-building materials. Start with the waste stream and work backward. Ask yourself: *How can we use all of this trash to make our lives more beautiful, more ecological, more interesting, more fun, safer, healthier, and more peaceful?*

By making good use of what is going to waste around us, we can drastically reduce the effort and expense required to start and maintain a garden. Dumpsters across the country are brimming with valuable resources, from organic food to old-growth lumber. Before you decide where, how, and how big to grow a garden, tap into the waste resources around you and develop a clear vision of what you really need. You will save time and money, plus interrupt the waste stream, which prevents pollution down the line.

It is important to learn to differentiate between useful surplus and true waste. That pile of old Styrofoam might seem like it would make good insulation but in reality may just disintegrate all over the garden—leave it at the dump where it belongs. Conversely, organic materials such as food scraps and dimensional lumber should always be diverted from the landfill and at least used for compost and firewood.

Don't overlook the people around you as a valuable resource. Ask your peers and neighbors for their opinions and ideas. They know, have, and do things that can benefit the community as a whole. Connect with them and share your ideas. See chapter 10 for more about how to connect with like-minded people in your community and beyond.

Free Plants and Seeds

In order to establish diverse paradise gardens, you will need as many different plants as you can find. This can be an expensive habit, especially if you buy starts at retail prices. Even small veggie starts can run a few dollars each, and perennials and trees can cost twenty dollars or more. This is a last resort for most of the gardeners I know—we prefer to start most of our plants from seeds or cuttings, salvaging the rest from the waste stream.

Seed samples aren't expensive when you consider that each sample, at about three dollars, usually contains at least a hundred seeds. It is important to support small-scale seed companies, but if you are really broke, most of them will give you last year's stock for free or at a big discount, especially if your garden project is geared toward community benefit. When stored correctly, seeds can last hundreds of years, so these outdated packets are a real score. See the resources section for a list of seed companies that frequently donate to community garden projects.

Seedlings can take a long time to grow, however, and often it makes more sense to bring in larger, more established plants. You can propagate these yourself with cuttings gleaned from local areas. You can also find a wide diversity of plants going to waste all around you; with a little nurturing these will thrive and flourish in your garden.

It is quite possible to grow a large, diverse garden without paying a single dollar for plant material, by getting donations, salvaging composted plants, and connecting with local garden clubs and seed exchanges, all of which I will elaborate on below. Before you know it you'll have your own surplus of plants to give away or sell to raise money for your projects.

Donations

Most places that sell plants end up with heaps of unsold merchandise every fall. You can connect with these businesses and secure donations for your projects. Also solicit donations from local gardeners, landscapers, and farmers. Many of them will have surplus and are happy to share. Post flyers and Internet ads describing your project and mentioning that you need plants and seeds. This is especially effective if you can get a local nonprofit to sponsor you, so that donors can benefit from the tax write-off.

Just as it is important to respect the earth, it is also important to respect the sources of our donations. This means always being courteous to workers, respectful to paying customers, and honest about where the donations are going. Food Not Bombs once lost a valuable organic bread source because some new volunteers went in for the weekly pickup and were rude to the bakery employees. Another time a volunteer was caught shoplifting at a health food store, and we lost twenty-five pounds of organic food a week for several months until we could repair the relationship with the store. Avoid wasteful behaviors like these and your work will be that much more effective.

Salvage

For a variety of reasons, some places would rather throw extra plants away than donate them. It is easy enough to get these out of the dumpster after hours. Cruise the back alley behind local garden centers and see what you can find. Also visit local farms and ask if you can pick through their compost for starts. I have seen truckloads of tomato plants thrown away because the farmer deemed them unfit for market, but they would have been fine for home gardening.

Find and visit the local organic-waste dump. Most cities have at least one place where landscapers and anyone else can bring truckloads of yard debris and dump it. If you don't know where it is, call the folks at a landscape company and ask them where they take their debris. You can also invite those landscapers to dump debris at your place (see chapter 4 for more on this).

These piles are rich in useful resources. Besides mulch and compost materials, you can often find caches of living plants. A friend of mine once came home from the dump with a pickup truck full of chrysanthemums and lilies—about two thousand dollars' worth of living, beneficial perennials! Just as one person's junk is another's treasure, so can one gardener's weeds be another's flowers.

Garden Clubs and Seed Exchanges

The other gardeners in your neighorhood are one of your most valuable resources. By connecting with them you can gain access to the wisdom of the ages, and through seed and plant exchanges you can exponentially increase the diversity of your garden and your bioregion. Look for flyers at local nurseries, or do an Internet search to find out about local garden clubs and seed exchanges. You may never have to pay for seeds and plants again!

Before you are ready for plants and seeds, though, you will need to build garden beds, establish paths, and accumulate necessary tools such as shovels, digging forks, buckets, wheelbarrows, tarps, and more. Let's examine some strategies for finding the other materials you need to turn your yard into a garden.

Tapping the Flow

When I was about ten years old my dad had some pet rabbits in the backyard of his suburban house in Long Beach, California. We couldn't afford commercial rabbit food, so once a week, Dad took my sister and me around to the dumpsters behind the local supermarkets. He would jump into the dumpster and toss out lettuce, carrots, potatoes, apples, and an assortment of other fruits and veggies. We girls would cringe in the alley, putting the vegetables into a box and hoping none of our friends saw us.

Later, when cooking for Food Not Bombs, I realized that much of that "rabbit food" of my youth was served at our own table as well as given to the rabbits. Further, many of our other possessions, such as the furniture, my first computer, and many of Dad's tools, also came out of local dumpsters. I hadn't realized it at the time, but my father was an accomplished urban scavenger, putting the Greater Los Angeles waste stream to good use for his family and friends.

As a child I was embarrassed or disgusted to eat food out of the trash, but now I am proud to be a trash digger. Dumpsters are an undertapped but rich, diverse source of free food, from fifty-pound bags of bread to delicacies such as organic almond butter and chocolate truffles. Sometimes if a single jar breaks, people will throw out the whole case. Other products have expired sell-by dates but in fact are good for several days or weeks after.

And it doesn't stop with food. The waste stream is also rife with nice clothing, furniture, electronics, and expensive building materials such as oak boards and power tools. Sometimes the best finds are not immediately recognizable as useful resources. For example, a pile of pallets might not look like your new bathhouse, but many pallets are made of good hardwood lumber and can be disassembled, de-nailed, and reused to make beautiful, sturdy buildings.

Other examples: Cardboard makes great mulch or insulation; an old speaker head can be turned upside down and used as a magnetic holder for hand tools; metal scrap can become fencing; old fabric can be made into rag rugs or patched together to make a quilt or curtains; broken bikes can be parted out and pieced together anew; inedible food scraps can be taken home in buckets and used for compost or sheet mulch. Be creative and make note of where the good spots are, so you can revisit them later.

You can get excellent free resources out of the trash in all kinds of places, from urban business districts and residential neighborhoods to rural farmsteads and wild places. Here are some places to start.

Business Districts

The city is tremendously rich in waste resources. Every dumpster, every house, every alley has something interesting, something useful, something worth finding. People in cities all over the world cherish these found items, make art with them, make tools, and live better through their resourcefulness.

Look for alleys behind stores, restaurants, factories, and distribution centers. This is where the big dumpsters live, and useful merchandise goes right in with the trash. Bring gloves and a flashlight, park on the street, and walk down the alley to the dumpster. You may have to climb in and open up bags to get at the good stuff, so be careful and clean up your mess, or you might find the same dumpsters locked next time.

Look behind places that sell food, including restaurants, stores, and warehouses. You will find edible food and good stuff like buckets and pallets. For other items, think of where you might go to buy them, then see if you can get them from those places, or from where they got them, for free. Free items might be cosmetically challenged or somehow defective, but they could still work just as well for your purposes as the same things at retail value.

If you are looking for a particular item, such as carpet for sheet mulch or canvas tarps, let your fingers do the walking: Look in the phone book or online for local merchants, and check behind the stores after hours. The same places will often be willing to donate surplus materials to a community project—it usually doesn't hurt to ask.

One person's trash can be another's tasty treat!

Sometimes you will discover a regular source of food or supplies; we frequent a well-known salsa dumpster and regularly get good organic bread and condiments from another place. In circumstances like these, it is essential to be respectful of the facility. Chances are, you are not the only person who frequents that spot, so don't ruin it by making it a nuisance for the associated business by leaving a mess, making a lot of noise, or harassing the employees.

Don't limit your investigation to the trash can. While you're out, look for stuff piled up in alleys and on curbs. I have found many good-quality garden tools that were left behind thrift stores for donation. Taking these items is technically illegal, but it's still a great way to find good stuff. I personally don't have any problem with taking things from a donation site, as long as the stuff is used for a good cause. I do think it's a little weird to take free stuff and then sell it for profit, but, hey, that's what the stores are doing, whether directly or indirectly. Many stores use the money to run social programs, but again, if you are using the goods to generate community and increase ecological integrity, then no harm done.

The choice is yours; just know that most large chain thrift stores have loading docks or unlocked donation bins that fill up with good stuff every night, and especially on Sunday. The same stores also often have huge dumpsters full off great stuff that didn't sell quickly enough. Check it out—but don't get busted!

Residential Neighborhoods

Cruise residential streets the night before trash day, or go postsale scavenging after a sunny weekend. On Friday or Saturday morning check out the newspaper, drive around, and make a list of yard sales. Then drive by on Sunday night, after the sale is over, and look for piles of stuff put out for the trash or with a sign that says FREE.

The best time of the year for residential trash digging is after the winter holiday consumer frenzy, when people are cleaning out the old as they integrate their new possessions. This is especially effective in upscale neighborhoods, where people are more likely throw stuff away than to donate it. In college towns we celebrate "Hippie Christmas" in mid-June when college students move out and go home, leaving piles of furniture, clothes, books, computers, and more in the dumpsters behind their apartment buildings.

Residential neighborhoods are also a great source of plant material. You can usually harvest a few seeds or take some cuttings without any problem, especially if the parent plant is hanging over a back fence or other out-of-the-way site. Of course, it rarely hurts to ask, so introduce yourself to that neighbor with the fabulous jasmine and get some cuttings for your garden!

Urban Gleaning

Sometimes what you need isn't in the trash at all but is hanging from the trees above. A single plum tree can yield hundreds of pounds, and most urban fruit trees drop more on the ground than the property owner can deal with. Look for plums, cherries, apples, figs, and more in your neighborhood, and see if you can have some of the fruit.

Besides trees, most cities also host a plethora of edible and medicinal plants, from blackberries down by the river to wild echinacea in a vacant lot. Develop a map of these local resources and harvest what you need. However, some urban sites can be very toxic, so use your powers of observation to make the good choices.

Most rural homesteads have piles of great stuff.

Gleaning Rural Surplus and Farm Junk

Gleaning usually refers to getting free food from the leftover harvest at local farms. Many counties have gleaning programs in place, or you can just call around to local farms and ask whether they have any surplus. This is but one of many ways to make good use of the resources going to waste in the countryside near you.

Often you can also glean some useful junk. Don't be afraid to ask about that pile of cedar boards or that cool old bathtub out by the barn. Most rural homesteads have piles of great stuff that has been lying around the place for years, and the owners are often happy to let you haul it away for little or no money, or in exchange for a few hours of weeding time.

Rural Wildcrafting

Let's not overlook the vast and wonderful diversity of food, medicine, and other resources in the wild and semi-wild places outside town. The forest, the ocean, the desert: All these environments are rich in materials that can help build closed-loop systems in town.

Wildcrafting is a useful skill that can bring wonderful mushrooms, edible fruits, and medicinal herbs to the table. Native seeds can also be found in the wild, then cultivated and perpetuated at home to be used for restoration and regeneration later on. The shore brings even more good stuff: seaweed, driftwood, oyster shells—all this and more can be harvested and used to enhance your compost, mulch, and garden beds.

However, it is very important that taking from these places be a last resort, when you absolutely need something and cannot find it or a good replacement through other means. There is precious little left of our natural resources, and we would do well to carefully safeguard them. Never take more than a little from any natural site; your impact should be invisible. It is best to engage in the proper training with a local naturalist before taking anything at all. You will learn much about the local ecology and help ensure that your impact is a positive one.

Cyber Scavenging

Another way to find and distribute free stuff is through the Internet. Almost everyone has heard of eBay—an excellent way to sell unwanted items to the highest bidder. There are also many sites that cater to people giving stuff away for free. Yahoo! has an assortment of "freecycle" lists for cities around the world. Also check out craigslist.org, tribe.net, myspace.com, and the like for good local connections.

Filling the Gaps

If you can't get what you need for free, you still have several good options besides buying retail, such as barter, borrowing, and buying at a discount. Many small businesses and individuals are open to bartering; you can trade for labor, materials, crafts, or anything else of value to the person you are bartering with. Look for local directories of alternative resources such as natural health care, used building materials, organic food, home services, and so forth, and make contact with the individuals who have what you need.

If you need a certain tool for a specific purpose, often the best idea is to borrow it from someone. Some communities have tool libraries where people pool their resources and share them around the neighbor-

The Free Box

A free box can be a cardboard box in front of the house, put out for a few days until the stuff is gone, or an established space in the community to which people take their surplus and look for what they need. If your neighborhood doesn't have a free box, build one in an unused side yard or the local park.

Build a big wooden box, big enough to hold larger items but not so large that you can't reach to the bottom. Drill holes in the bottom for drainage, in case something spills or rain gets in, and if you want to get fancy put a simple roof over the box. Post a sign that says FREE BOX and make a note asking people not to leave trash or toxic waste such as motor oil.

People will gather at the free box, giddy over the plethora of good free stuff, and will bring their surplus clothes, furniture, plants, and other items there rather than throwing them out or giving them to a thrift store. Relationships will begin, and resources will flow.

I recommend having a volunteer "free-box monitor"—someone who stops by once every couple of weeks, pulls out the trash and recycling, and takes stuff that no one has claimed to a thrift store or shelter. This role usually falls, by default, to the house that hosts the free box, but it is better when rotated among neighbors, to keep one person or household from burning out.

Alternatively, ask the folks at the local dump if they will host a space that can become a free store. I have seen several of these in city dumps, and they work well at keeping functional goods such as clothes, furniture, and building materials out of the landfill and in use.

Recycle unwanted items through a local free box.

hood. See chapter 9 for more on organizing resource exchanges and lending libraries.

The last thing you want is to waste any of that hard-earned money, and even if you absolutely must buy something new, with all of the discount resources available these days, it is foolish to pay retail for most items. Before you buy anything look again at what you need it for, and consider whether you might just do without it. If you really must have it, then try to find it secondhand.

Thrift stores resell used goods at a discount, making them available to people who can't afford them new or who would prefer to recycle. Many stores operate social services with the proceeds. Also, if you have a lot of large stuff that you need to get rid of right away, most thrift stores will pick it up from your house and even give you a tax receipt. Still, it makes more sense to distribute goods directly to the people who need them rather than through a third party that will charge money for them, so do consider taking your surplus goods to a local free box instead (see the sidebar on page 47).

Yard sales are another option. They are also an excellent way to get rid of stuff and make a little money—sometimes a lot of money. I had a yard sale in which I sold surplus furniture, clothes, plants, kitchen supplies, and an assortment of other items that were not necessary to my home system. I made seven hundred dollars; enough to pay my rent for three months. I gained more space at home, distributed goods to community members in need at a fair price, and also gained an opportunity to take some time off work and focus on my volunteer projects.

Closing the Loop

As you establish and maintain a paradise garden, you will probably be surprised at the overwhelming abundance generated by your efforts. If you do not distribute or recycle these surpluses, they will become pollution and degrade the ecological integrity of your project. Conversely, if you give them away, you increase the yield and efficiency of your own system while simultaneously building community and preventing or reducing waste and pollution. There are few better ways to inspire the neighbors than by giving them fresh organic fruits or extra seeds and other resources.

Getting and giving away stuff for free is the root of a gift economy—one in which surplus resources, rather than going to the landfill, flow among community members in a collective effort toward a better life for everyone. A gift economy helps enable us to withdraw from the consumer paradigm and exist on our own terms while providing for our own needs. So give away your surplus and you will simultaneously build community, improve the natural environment, and make room for new ideas.

This also applies to garden space. If you already have a garden space but live in an area where many of your neighbors do not, consider sharing space with someone. Many people have enough energy and plenty of excellent ideas but do not have access to land or a space on which to grow. If you don't have extra land but do have an indoor space such as a garage or workshop, why not offer it up to a community group for workshops and events? If you do not want to organize something yourself, perhaps others would like to host events at your space.

Small activist groups may want to host a benefit show or an event to raise money for their project, but without the capital to rent a space they're unable to do so. A bookseller in Eugene lets people hold events like this at her bookstore in the evenings while it's closed. If the event is free, the space is free; if there's a door charge, she charges a nominal percentage. It works out for her because it brings in new customers, and it works for the community because it gives them a place to have dance classes, meetings, and workshops, as well as to gather and share information.

Now that you have a good idea of how and where to look for garden space, how to make the most out of that space, and where to find the supplies you need without spending a lot of money, you are ready to start developing your paradise garden. The next few chapters will move through some of the elements of a paradise garden, including water, soil, plants, and seeds, and will give you plenty of project ideas.

If I have my way, you'll read this whole book before you actually do anything in the garden. If we are to build gardens and communities that will endure, we must first learn to weigh our options and assemble resources into the appropriate ecological design, rather than hastily throwing together projects that will do more harm than good to the natural environment. So read through, make notes, and develop a cohesive, ecological plan.

3. The Water Cycle

Water—the ace of elements. Water dives from the clouds without parachute, wings, or safety net. Water runs over the steepest precipice and blinks not a lash. Water is buried and rises again; water walks on fire and fire gets the blisters. Stylishly composed in any situation—solid, gas, or liquid—speaking in penetrating dialects understood by all things—animal, vegetable, or mineral—water travels intrepidly through four dimensions. . . . Always in motion, ever-flowing (whether at steam rate or glacier speed), rhythmic, dynamic, ubiquitous, changing and working its changes, a mathematics turned wrong side out, a philosophy in reverse, the ongoing odyssey of water is virtually irresistible.

—Tom Robbins[1]

A Finite Supply

We know that 70 percent of Earth's surface is water. We also know that our own bodies have a similar composition, varying from 70 to 90 percent water, depending on age and body type. I don't need to convince you that water is perhaps the single most essential element to life. It's obvious, right? Three days with no water, we die. Just a few hours without it and we start to experience headaches, muscle pain, and irritability.

Plants, which are also 70 percent water, provide the other human essential: food. The second step to building a paradise garden is to establish a holistic on-site water cycle. As you establish and improve your garden, you will need to plenty of fresh water to get the compost steaming, the seeds sprouting, and the fruits ripening.

Watering can be as simple as turning on an automatic sprinkler system and forgetting about it, but water usage should not be an arbitrary choice. Even in wet regions it is vital to conserve water in the home landscape and beyond. Huge portions of the world's population live without access to clean water, and even in the wealthy United States most of us filter our drinking water. Fish and aquatic plants are dying, underground aquifers are drying out, and though water is as finite on this planet as oil, human water needs increase with every new-born child. We use and abuse the global supply as if there were no tomorrow. If we do not shift from mindless consumption to mindful conservation, today, there may indeed be no tomorrow, for our species or any other.

Because water is so crucial to any garden, and in such short supply, I recommend designing the rest of the garden around a water system that makes sense for the ecology in which you are working. Many gardeners instead try to adapt their water system to their landscape and lose money and ecological integrity in the process. But a paradise garden requires an integrated home water cycle that reflects and cooperates with nature.

This book is about solutions, not problems, but because the global water situation is so tenuous I feel it is worth devoting a few pages to exploring the very real, and in some cases truly sinister, reasons why. Sadly, not enough people are taking the issue of water conservation seriously, and unless we educate ourselves, quickly, we may find ourselves up a dry creek without a clue.

Fortunately there are solutions to these issues on all scales, from recycling in the home and garden to organizing watershed stewardship coalitions. The second half of this chapter is devoted to these solutions and includes an assortment of ideas for making your home water cycle conservative, yet beautiful and abundant.

Why We Should Worry

It may seem ridiculous to be worried about water when there is so much of it around, but only about 0.05 percent of the water on Earth is fresh water that is accessible and available for human use.[2] More than 97 percent of Earth's water is salt water, and another 2 percent is ice. Groundwater, freshwater lakes, and streams represent less than 1 percent, and the rest is in the soil and atmosphere. All statistics aside, the point is: Even though it seems like there is water everywhere, the finite supply available to humans is simply running out.

Irresponsible use, pollution, and climate change have caused the depletion of giant

It may seem like the Earth has plenty of water, but a limited supply is available for human use.

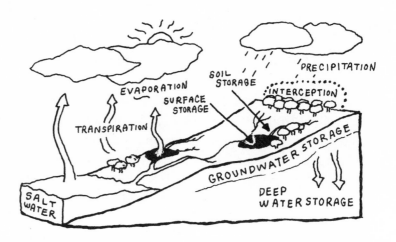

underground reservoirs, such as the Ogalalla Aquifer under the mid-western United States. Some of these once vast reserves have been building up since the Pleistocene epoch, more than two million years ago,[3] and we cannot hope to replace them in the foreseeable future. The proverbial glass is now far closer to empty than full, and if we are to survive we must learn to live with less and change our attitude toward water from one of casual consumption to one of reverent conservation.

Primitive people used about a gallon of water a day for drinking, cooking, and washing. Today in the United States the average person uses, per capita, *twelve hundred gallons each day* for basic needs such as food, washing, and drinking. This does not include the hidden water uses in energy, material goods like clothes and cars, and industry, such as the sixty-five thousand gallons it takes to make a single ton of steel.[4]

Only a tenth of the water used in the developed world goes to municipal and residential situations, but the consumer choices made by that minority tenth are reflected by larger industrial and agricultural impacts. The negative impacts of consumer culture on global water supplies include scarcity, pollution and environmental degradation, and oppression through corporate control.

The worst culprits are the pulp and paper industry and the food and beverage industry, followed closely by chemical, pharmaceutical, and textile companies. This translates to newspapers, wafer board, conventional agriculture, beer, sugar, coffee, cosmetics, cleaning supplies, drugs, cotton, and polyester—all bought and paid for by consumers like you and me.

Once water is used for industry and conventional agriculture, it becomes polluted and salinated (salted), and hence unavailable for human use. But it does not go away. Think of what happens when you put a tiny bit of soap into a fountain. It quickly spreads through the water, which soon bubbles over the edges. You have to turn off the fountain and drain it to clean out the soap. But we cannot turn off the global water cycle. Toxic waste spreads easily through world waterways, polluting all the varied ecologies it meets. And because we dump it all the time, every day of the year, the damaged ecologies never get a chance to recover from the overload of poison.

As a result more than a billion people lack access to clean drinking water, and whole ecosystems are going extinct. If we substitute the word *safe* for *clean*, the number jumps closer to three billion, or nearly half the global population.

Diarrhea caused by drinking unclean water kills more than two million people—mostly small children—every year. Other grim conditions include intestinal worms and trachoma, which causes blindness. And

The average American's lifestyle consumes or pollutes about 1,200 gallons of water every day.

don't forget the two hundred million people with schistosomiasis, which causes liver damage, seizures, and paralysis, all from having a dirty water supply and no way to clean it. It is possible to repair damaged waterways and build natural filtration systems, and I'll get more into these solutions later, but often these options are not available to the economically disadvantaged communities I'm talking about here.

Throughout history whole societies have committed ecological suicide using the very same tactics we employ today: namely, a highly productive agriculture based on short-term profits, a dependence on hierarchical systems for essential resources, and an arrogant disregard for environmental stewardship. The current trends of depleted groundwater, climate change, and destruction of the aquatic environment (so necessary to renew the water cycle) tell us that we too travel down the very same road of ancient civilizations before us, toward extinction. But first—and soon—will come the day when clean water is still available, though only to the elite few who can pay the price.

One out of twenty people relies on privately owned water for life.

Access to good water should be the right of all living things and was guaranteed by the United Nations Declaration of Universal Human Rights. Yet that isn't stopping corporations from privatizing and profiting from public water supplies around the world. International players are calling water the "last infrastructure frontier for private investors."[5] The race is on to garner a controlling interest in water and, thus, the world economy.

In much of the world already, pure drinking water is available only to those who can afford it. This means that about 12 percent of the global population—the economically privileged—uses more than 85 percent of the water, and, to add insult to injury, trade agreements such as NAFTA and the WTO make it virtually impossible for local communities to prevent the export and exploitation of their community water supply.[6]

Today one out of twenty people relies on privately owned water for life, and billions more depend on government-controlled, municipal sources.[7] Our vulnerability in this position is beyond just having to keep a job to pay the water bill. Ask yourself, *Who controls my water supply? Who makes and sells my filters? Who owns the source? If I have the money, what will I drink? If I can't pay, how will I live?* Start asking these questions now, and don't let the wild water near you fall into the wrong hands.

Even in the United States, where we currently enjoy relative economic privilege, millions of people filter their drinking water, and most of us don't even know what toxins we're filtering out, let alone whose responsibility they are. Frankly, even if we choose to ignore the death, disease, and destruction caused to other places by our lifestyle here, if we do not clean up our act, quickly and globally, even the United States will suffer dearly for a lack of clean water.

The Monsanto Company views the global water crisis as a multibillion-dollar business opportunity. We see big problems—it sees big money. Monsanto's Robert Farley admits, "Population growth and economic development will apply increasing pressure on the natural resource markets. . . . These are the markets that are most relevant to us as a life sciences company . . . in which there are predictable sustainability challenges and therefore opportunities to create business value."[8] Monsanto foresees profits of sixty-three million dollars by 2008 for water ventures in India and Mexico, and other companies are riding the dusty bandwagon to the tune of more than three hundred million a year in these two countries alone.[9]

While companies such as Monsanto pursue global domination under the guise of sustainable development (an oxymoron?) and global security, the hard truth is that monopolizing the water supply is a recipe for social and ecological devastation. Privatization may seem to provide opportunities for project funding, system improvement, and increased distribution, but real-world examples show that political corruption, economic exclusion, and environmental degradation are the more likely outcomes.[10]

We should address the problems of scarcity and pollution as crucial points of action rather than opportunities for profit and exploitation, and protect and conserve our regional water supplies as if our lives depended on it, which they do. We must not allow the greed of the corporate regime to usurp our lifeblood in the name of free enterprise and property rights.

Beyond human consumption, we must also consider the water supplies that nourish the plants, animals, fish, and connected ecosystems on which we depend. Ultimately we must put the power back in the bioregional communities to which it belongs and develop a whole-system ecological approach to watershed stewardship.

Options for Survival

There is a wide range of things that we can do to conserve and protect our water supplies, from organizing community coalitions to implementing ecologically sound practices at home. Many local communities are beginning to take action, but no current system in the world provides a model for perpetual water security. We must make these models for ourselves and develop bioregionally based, long-term plans that use a variety of strategies to ensure a wet and fertile future for humans and other living things.

Just as we must create and act upon our own individual and community visions for peace, we must also design and develop localized, closed-loop systems for water. Ecology teaches us that everything is connected, and the water cycle provides ample proof of this. Everything we do has a ripple effect on everything else. If we work to conserve and protect our local and regional water sources, we will influence the whole and contribute to healing the larger cycle.

Here are ten top strategies for saving our water and ourselves. They are in no particular order of importance—we must do them all, and more, if we are to reverse the tide of scarcity, pollution, and corporate control that threatens us today. Each of these could constitute a whole book in itself, but I will just touch on them here. Check the resources section for more information.

Ten Things We Can Do to Save Water

1. *Eat Organic Food and Support Local Organic Agriculture.* Organic methods don't use harsh toxins that pollute the water. Organic farms and gardens emphasize mulch and other soil stewardship practices, which means less erosion and/or salination of the soil, and less runoff and damage to waterways. Local food means shorter distance from farm to table, which translates to less pollution from fossil fuels. If it is difficult to find local organic food, there's another good reason to grow a garden. Also, see chapter 10 for ways to find like-minded people near you.

2. *Reject Corporate Globalization and Control Industrial Water Use.* Don't buy corporate water, and fight the corporate takeover of your local waterways. If they've already moved in, kick them out by organizing local coalitions and fighting for local control. We can promote corporate accountability by monitoring industrial pollution levels, interacting with business leaders, and refusing to support wasteful and polluting companies. On a political level constitutional amendments establishing water as a basic human right and endangered natural resource can protect supplies and ban corporate control. Also, think of the nonhuman species and their needs, and fight companies that threaten nature. If we pay attention and share information, we can create an atmosphere of collective concern and mindful stewardship—a necessary tool in the face of blind and powerful corporate greed.

3. *Regenerate Native Habitats.* Healthy riparian zones are essential to long-term water supplies. With our help damaged systems can regenerate themselves exponentially faster than if left on their own. Volunteer with a local restoration project to stabilize banks, clean up pollution, and replant native plants. Ask around through local environmental groups, or start a new one in an endangered area near you.

4. *Develop Watershed Stewardship Coalitions.* Work together for change. Local watershed management coalitions, made up of scientists, environmentalists, farmers, and other local citizens, can develop long-term, ecological strategies that include restoration, conservation, and harsh penalties for wasting and polluting water supplies. These coalitions can also work on related issues such as energy, overpopulation, and climate change and can establish bioregional networks to find and implement solutions. See chapters 9 through 11 for more on community organizing.

5. *Use Renewable Energy.* Ride a bike instead of driving to work. Invest in solar or passive solar electricity, heat, and water heating. Reject dam-based hydroelectric energy, which steals water from connected ecosystems and destroys essential fish habitat.

6. *Eschew Packaging.* Processed industrial foods take too much water to produce, package, and distribute. The biggest culprits are sugar, soy, and all types of meat, but anything packaged in paper or plastic caused major water damage before it got to you. Choose local produce and unpackaged bulk foods, and store them in reusable bins in your kitchen or pantry. Beware of "bulk" items that came to the store in a plastic package that the merchant threw away before selling you the bulk product. This is just another marketing scheme and generates almost as much waste as individually packaged items.

7. *Buy Less of Everything, and Reuse What You Can.* Beyond policy changes and community collaboration, personal choices are the key element to ecological living. The embedded water costs associated with each of our consumer choices (food, transportation, clothing, building materials, et cetera) amount to more than four hundred *billion* gallons each year in the United States alone. This is an unfathomable waste. Our culture teaches us to ask, *What can I buy?* Instead we should ask, *What can I avoid buying?* When you must buy something, choose recycled and secondhand materials. You will save water as well as money while rescuing useful items from the waste stream.

8. *Use Water-Efficient Appliances or Get Rid of Them Altogether.* Choose options such as front-loading washing machines and water-efficient toilets and showerheads. Fix leaks and drips. Evaluate your electric and water usage and eliminate or downsize any appliances you don't really need. For example, use a clothesline instead of a dryer, or build a draft box and get rid of your fridge.

9. *Save and Recycle Paper, Glass, and Metals.* The pulp and paper industry is the number one polluter of world waterways. Limit your contribution to the oceans of filth it creates by insisting on recycled paper and conserving as much as you can. Glass and metal recycling also saves water, but it is best to limit your consumption first. Plastic recycling is a hoax—don't buy it. All phases of plastic processing cause water pollution, ozone depletion, and cancer. Avoid it.

10. *Establish an Ecological Home Water Cycle.* The best way to contribute as much as we can to global water solutions is to design and implement a holistic personalized water system, at home and in our communities, that includes graywater usage, rain catchment, and water-efficient agriculture and land use. By emphasizing sincere stewardship and prudent conservation of this most precious resource, we teach by example and gain greater control over our personal supply.

Not only will all these actions save huge amounts of water, but they will also contribute to an overall improvement in the ecological integrity of your life and community. Consumer choices—what you buy—are by far the most important aspect of water conservation, and your choices are woven through every aspect of your home water cycle. Try not to get overwhelmed—just do what you can and share what you learn with your community.

We will examine lifestyle and consumer choices more in chapter 8. For now let's focus on the last item on the list: "Establish an ecological home water cycle." The home is the place over which we have the most control, and recycling water there will help ensure personal supply and send a ripple effect through the global situation.

The Home Water Cycle

A typical home water cycle goes something like this: Water comes in, from a well or municipal pump system, and is piped to the kitchen, bathroom, laundry room, and several places in the yard. We use it once, then send it to the sewer. Rainwater from the roof runs down the drainpipe and then into either the sewer or the storm drain. Except for drinking water, water quality rarely matches usage, meaning we use clean water when we don't need it, and household graywater (once-used water tainted only with soap and food residues) goes straight to the sewer, with our poop, to become pollution.

An ecological home water cycle looks quite different: Rainwater is directed from the roof into barrels and/or cisterns and from there into the house, where it is filtered for drinking and washing and then drained into

An ecological home water cycle saves money and promotes a healthy planet.

a living filter, or "slime monster," which cleans out soap, germs, and other residue. The cleaned graywater then runs into a pond, where it mixes with surplus rainwater that ran off when the household storages were full.

When the pond overflows, it irrigates the garden via an intricate system of ponds, dams, and swales and eventually percolates into the soil, where it is available for deep roots and soil communities. (Even the toilet water can be recycled, through a blackwater system, but because that takes so much more energy than recycling graywater, I don't recommend doing blackwater at home. Instead try eliminating toilet water altogether by composting human waste.)

Within each stage of any cycle, there are opportunities to influence the cycle (see the sidebar on pages 62–63). If we see that a cycle is out of harmony with nature, then we can make subtle changes to shift it toward the right direction. Conversely, other changes may disrupt the natural flow and throw the whole cycle out of balance. We should make the smallest changes we can to achieve the greatest benefit to the whole, and we should always watch for opportunities to achieve better balance with nature. As we ponder this concept of whole-cycle design, we can look to the way water flows through our home and garden as an example of how everything is (or should be) connected.

An ecological home water cycle saves money, reduces waste and pollution, and increases the fertility of the garden. Keeping rainwater and graywater on-site adds a dynamic, visually spectacular element to your space and invites a new diversity of life to reside there. You will need to invest some time and money to get it flowing, but I can think of few worthier investments than personal water security.

In the next few pages we will explore the elements of an ecological home water cycle. These include water-wise gardening, graywater usage, rain catchment, and combining them all to recycle, cleanse, and conserve water as much as possible. With the information here you can experiment with just a few strategies—or revamp your whole system. Whatever you choose, you will be that much closer to doing your part to conserve the world's water. Let's start with the garden . . .

Water-wise Gardening

Just a few simple strategies will make a big difference in how efficiently your garden uses water. These include deep mulching, appropriate irrigation, using microclimates, and contouring, which includes building swales and ponds along and around garden beds to catch and store water.

Mulching

Water wisdom in the garden goes right back to the soil stewardship discussed in the preceding chapter. The greater the water-holding capacity of our soil, the less we will need to irrigate. All kinds of mulch and compost increase the soil's ability to catch and hold water, as do cover crops, compost teas, and other soil-building strategies. Mulch keeps the surface of the soil from drying out and insulates plant roots and fragile soil communities. Deep trench mulches create underground reservoirs that provide surplus water for deep roots. Mulches also help prevent erosion because they act as a sponge to catch water and filter it into the soil.

Irrigation

Many gardeners advocate drip irrigation or soaker hoses, which squirt water low into the garden beds via networks of plastic tubes. Such irrigation systems use less water than overhead sprinklers, but I don't recommend them. The plastic is ugly to look at, is toxic to produce, photodegrades in the sun, and becomes a pile of useless plastic

Cyclic Opportunity

Natural cycles, such as planetary orbits, seasonal changes, and women's menses, are all around us. Most are predictable, and we can learn them through observation and pattern recognition. Because cyclic patterns are everywhere and inevitable, it is crucial that we include them in our garden plans. Just as you would plant according to the seasons, you should also make other decisions based on the cycles and patterns you observe around you.

Many cycles seem like loops, but most are actually spirals—never coming back to the exact same point, but overlapping into similar experiences. Though her orbit is mostly predictable, Earth never returns to exactly the same spot in space twice, and neither do any of her cycles.

In every step of a cycle there are opportunities to mimic, divert, or interact within that cycle. In ecological design we use this principle of cyclic opportunity to divert energy, initiate new cycles, and open niches in space and time. This results in higher yields, new opportunities, and a more ecological and efficient system overall.

In ecological paradise garden design we consider nine primary cycles, looking to them for opportunities and ripple effects. These are: Water, Soil, Seeds, Cosmos, Society, Wilderness, Self, Chaos, and Waste. I'll come back to these again later. For now the point is that each of these cycles is rife with opportunities to improve the ecology and fruitful yield of our gardens and community projects. Here are a few strategies to get you started.

Divert the flow: The first strategy of cycling is to divert the flow (of energy, materials, water, and so on) as many times as possible between the source and the sink. Look again to water: If the well is the source, and the sewer is the sink, then how many times can we use that water before it is unavailable for further use?

We can drink the water and then recycle the pee onto our garden. This would be a relatively short cycle, but still better than just flushing the pee away. In addition, we can use the water to bathe or wash dishes and then run the resulting graywater through a living filter and into a pond. Then we can use the pond to grow water plants and fish and use the plants and fish to feed our animals and ourselves. We can use the fish and plant waste to fertilize our garden and use the pond

waste within just a few years. In addition, the long, stiff tubing doesn't lend well to the organic, nonlinear shapes of a paradise garden, and the water doesn't get to all the plants.

On the other hand, recycled garden hose, found easily at any thrift store, is flexible, not stiff like drip tape, and can be perforated with a nail and snaked around the garden to provide conservative and attractive irrigation exactly where you need it. Still, ground watering like this will often exclude plants on the periphery, and sometimes hoses seem to interfere with, rather than enhance, the beauty and efficiency of the garden.

I prefer and recommend overhead watering, but this doesn't mean running a sprinkler in the middle of the day in full sun. This is the worst way to water the garden, because most of the water evaporates before it ever hits the plants, and the drops that make it onto a leaf then magnify the sun and burn the plant. Instead, water in the morning or early evening, when the sun is low in the sky, and direct the water at the soil and plant roots, rather than the leaves. Water deeply and less often,

water to flush an outdoor toilet. The toilet water can again be filtered through a living system and later used to irrigate fruit trees. Thus the same gallon of water can stay on a site for months or even years, with just a bit of protracted thought and ingenuity.

We can also divert the flow of energy, materials, and information and use them to supplement our work. For example, recycling and dumpster diving make use of materials that were headed to the "sink," or landfill in this case. We can divert human energy away from idleness and toward our gardens by creating opportunities for participation.

Remember that if you divert the flow from one point, you may change the cycle farther on. If you take water out of the stream, the person downstream may have less. That's why it's crucial to take as little as we can, reuse as much as possible, and give back what we take in another form, at another point in the cycle.

Encourage natural succession: For example, we can plant pioneer species, those that stabilize soil and provide habitat for successive species. By planting pioneer species in a barren location, we need care for the pioneers only for a short time, and then nature will take its course. The pioneers will shade the area, draw moisture and nutrients into the soil, and spur new cycles of life. Thus alders will give way to dogwoods and willows, birds will come and spread seeds of new plants, animal and soil communities will grow and change, and the whole system will perpetuate itself, while we are free to focus on other projects.

Community projects also spawn a form of natural succession. Each project may inspire dozens of others, which will inspire more, and so on. If we construct our efforts to allow others to expand upon them in their own way, we start new and self-perpetuating cycles of action and change.

Generate new flows: Your own energy is essential. We haven't discovered the secret to perpetual motion yet, but we can keep pushing the carousel around with every new use of a resource. Keep on the lookout for wasted energy, and catch and recycle whatever you can. Every time we add a link to the cycle we create a yield, in the form of either material or energetic gain. By finding, creating, and using cyclic opportunities, in the garden and beyond, we turn waste into resources and save time, money, and energy.

rather than shallowly and frequently, and double-check any odd corners of the garden to make sure marginal plants are not being excluded.

Microclimates

Some areas will need much more water than others, as will some plants. Identify the varied microclimates on your site and choose plants that will do well in those conditions. In a wet spot group together the plants that need more water, and grow those that love dry soil somewhere else. Make use of tree drip lines and moist, shady spots that allow you to grow shade lovers in sunny, dry zones. Look for drought-tolerant varieties and grow them in dry beds to strengthen the trait, then save their seeds and grow them again.

Remember that changing the water cycle will change the adjacent microclimates, so consider this when developing your system. Use the placement and flow of water to help you create the environments you want, where you want them.

Contouring

Build a network of ponds, swales, berms, and contoured beds to cycle water through the garden and keep it on-site as long as possible. Without these soil catchments surplus water will run right down any slope available and off into the gutter before you have a chance to use it. Contours catch that water and keep it, and they add depth and dimension to the landscape.

Contours create edges that are unique microclimates, where you can grow a whole new range of plants (see the sidebar at right). Contouring also helps prevent erosion. In a 1969 Ohio survey of soil loss under various treatments, corn grown in plowed, *sloping* rows lost between seven and twenty-two tons per acre of topsoil, while corn grown in plowed, *contoured* rows lost only two to three tons per acre. Corn grown in *un*plowed, *heavily mulched*, contoured rows lost none.[11]

Contoured gardens usually include swales, which are shallow ditches in contour that catch water and filter it into the soil. To build a swale, dig a trench one to three feet deep and one to five feet wide, on contour—not on a slope—so the water does not run down the swale but sits in the swale and percolates into the soil. Direct water to the swale via drainpipes, downspouts, dams, and ditches. Build garden beds above and below the swale—and also on contour. The bed below the swale will

Use the diggings from the swale and additional organic debris to build a berm on the uphill side of the swale to create useful microclimates.

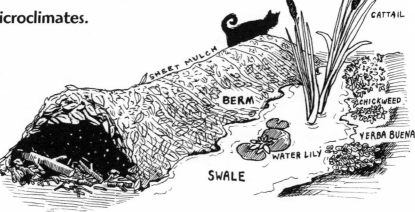

Fringe Benefits

As you establish garden beds and water flows through your landscape, you will create and discover new microclimates. At the edge of each microclimate, in the zones between zones, you will find your fringe benefits—a wonderful phenomenon called the edge effect. Look for examples in your yard and around your natural surroundings—you will find plenty. These margins, fringes, and edges host a greater diversity and offer more opportunities than either of the areas they connect, and we can learn to recognize, create, and use edges to maximize the diversity and efficiency of our gardens.

The Malay Archipelago in the South Pacific is an excellent example of the edge effect. On Bali 87 percent of the plants and animals are similar to those found in Asia, but the remaining 13 percent are species native to Australia. On the next island,

Lombok, just fifteen miles away, the ratio drops to 73:27, and within a hundred miles the Australian natives dominate. So these few islands in the margin between Asia and Australia enjoy twice the biological diversity of either neighboring ecosystem.[12]

In the garden, if we intentionally make use of the spaces between, we can maximize diversity on all levels. We will be able to grow certain species with more success, provide habitat for more beneficial insects, and increase our yields exponentially.

Building edges into ponds creates niches for fish and plants, and adding edges to buildings creates more storage and/or workspace. The list of examples goes on and on. The point is, recognizing and using edges will prove useful throughout the design and maintenance of your system, and the home water cycle is an excellent place to practice.

require much less watering than the bed above it, because of the water percolating into the soil, so plant accordingly.

Most swales have a berm on the downhill side, built from the dirt dug out of the swale. You can also build up the berm with tree prunings, cardboard, leaves, scrap wood, or any other organic matter. Alternatively, you can build just the berm on slope or on contour, without the swale, to slow runoff velocity and/or direct the flow of water and thus encourage soil infiltration.

Berms also slow and direct other flows, such as wind. Windbreaks like this decrease evaporation and, therefore, the need for water. In addition to berms, other types of windbreaks include fences, trellises, buildings, and hedgerows, all of which should be included and carefully placed in a whole-system design.

Swales, berms, and contoured beds become even more useful when connected to one or more garden ponds. Depending on your scale and design goals, these ponds can be as small and simple as a few washtubs placed strategically around the garden, or as elaborate as a large-scale swimming pond, stocked with fish and edible water plants. We'll come back to ponds in a minute.

Graywater

When we think of wasted water, we often think of drips, leaks, and spillage, but the real waste in our homes is the (average) 150 gallons per day of graywater (once-used wash water) that drain to the sewer along with the toilet water.

We are, quite literally, throwing the proverbial baby out with the bathwater every time we pull the plug in the tub and watch all of that almost-clean water go down the drain. You can do the math yourself, but even if you limit your household consumption to only 100 gallons a day, that adds up to 36,500 gallons per year—enough to grow several hundred pounds of food and turn any yard into a lush paradise garden.

Twenty years ago it was the accepted norm to throw food scraps into the trash along with landfill waste, but now millions of people compost this rich and valuable resource. When I was a child we threw all our glass bottles in the trash, yet now recycling is common practice throughout most of the world.

Using graywater, while certainly not a new practice, will undoubtedly become much more popular in the years to come as water scarcity becomes more commonplace. And while it is still illegal in many cities due to health concerns, if properly processed, graywater adds an abundance of water and fertility to an otherwise much drier environment. The regular influx of living, moving water adds diversity, reflects light, creates edges and microclimates, and enhances the ecological integrity of your landscape.

My first graywater experiment entailed removing the trap from below the bathroom sink and putting a five-gallon bucket under the drain. When we needed to flush we would just open the cabinet, grab the bucket, and dump the water into the toilet. The rush of water triggered the toilet's flush system, and away it went to the sewer.

This system can be installed by anyone with a pipe wrench and a bucket and makes perfect sense: You use the toilet, wash your hands in the sink, then use the same water to flush the toilet. This uses far less water than a regular flush and adds a second round to the sink water, which is of course plenty clean enough to wash out the toilet bowl and carry the contents away. Just be sure not to leave the bucket full of graywater for more than two days; it will ferment and turn to blackwater, which is toxic.

Where to Put the Pond

Here are some important things to consider when establishing a pond. Take the time to draw a simple map of your site and work through each of these steps. Imagine the pond in several places and choose a spot high on the site, with good access and drainage. Maximize the edge principle (see the sidebar on page 65) and start small, keeping in mind the connections between the pond and the other elements of your garden. This process will help you avoid time-consuming mistakes and will create a working record of your ecological home water system in progress.

Hidden pipes: You can usually get a map from the city of existing pipes, and many places require a pond permit for anything with a holding capacity of more than a hundred gallons or so. You definitely want to avoid any accidental fractures caused by digging in the wrong place: These can be very expensive mistakes.

Access: Does the flow of graywater run across a major throughway in your yard? You may need to build a small bridge. Also, there needs to be a simple way for the water to get from the house to the outside system, so unless you want to install underground pipes the first section of the system should be relatively near the source.

Viewpoints: Where will you see it from, and who else will see it? If you are bending local laws, your outlets from the house should be well obscured from potentially disapproving neighbors. On the other hand, you may want a nice view of the pond from your office or kitchen window, or to put the graywater system out in the open to demonstrate how beautiful and efficient it really is.

Nearby trees: Shade and leaf fall will greatly affect the water garden. Some water plants prefer shade, while others need sun. Some trees, such as ginkgo and cherry, will drop beautiful leaves and flowers into the pond, adding aesthetic value to the whole. Others, like pine and black walnut, may fill the pond with acidic or discoloring debris, and you will spend more time cleaning the pond than reflecting on its beauty. Also consider that while installing the system, you may disturb the roots of nearby trees, and some plants, like bamboo, have running roots that can destroy a pond liner if they are growing nearby.

Reflection of images in the pond and light into the windows: You probably do not want a double view of the yucky concrete building next door, but you can use the pond to reflect a nice tree or send light into an otherwise dark window.

Safety: Even a small pond could drown a child or a chicken. Place the bog and pond in a location where you (or your children) won't slip into it, and well away from the chicken yard, if you have one. Chickens are terrible swimmers—I have known full-grown roosters to drown in only a couple of feet of water. Alternatively, you can cover the surface of the pond with a screen or grate. This not only keeps anyone from falling in but also protects fish from would-be marauders such as raccoons and opossums, which will destroy even a well-built pond trying to get some dinner.

Drainage: This is the single most important factor in placing water features in a landscape. An ideal system will store water as high on the site as possible, then direct it into the varied functions as it naturally moves downhill. The pond should be able to receive and conduct water from and into the whole. Pumping water uphill is expensive and, in a well-designed system, unnecessary.

The best way to avoid the health risks involved with graywater is to build a "living machine" to cleanse and neutralize it. This living machine—or slime monster, as some people fondly call it—will filter your graywater, direct it into the landscape, and use all those yummy germs from your body, laundry, and dishes to feed the hungry communities in your soil.

Designer John Todd builds living machines that recycle large quantities of graywater from cities like Burlington, Vermont, where he built a sewage treatment plant in a greenhouse near Lake Champlain. Living machines use sunlight for fuel and, like natural ecologies, have the ability to self-organize, self-design, self-repair, and self-replicate.

Todd views waste as "resources out of place" and sees excess sludge as a sign of an incomplete design. His project at Lake Champlain turns raw sewage into pure water in just over two days. Home to more than four hundred species of plants, the greenhouse looks more like a botanical garden than a treatment plant and combines waste treatment with fuel production, educational opportunities, and cash crops such as flowers and other beneficial plants.

This type of system, if implemented in cities worldwide, could quickly repair degraded environments and reduce the human damage to the planet by 90 percent. To do this will require a major political and economic transformation that may seem far-fetched but is not out of reach. We have the examples and information—we just need to put them into action.

On a home scale you can build a small slime monster that will filter and cleanse your household graywater. Here's how:

Step One: Establish the Pond that your graywater bog will flow into. In general, your pond should be high on the site and designed so the overflow runs into your contoured garden bed/swale system. Vary depths and emphasize edges to create diverse microclimates, which will come in handy later. A pond provides rich sludge that is great for compost or mulch, so design yours so that you can scoop out the bottom when needed. There are many variables to building a pond—more than I can cover here. Refer to the resources section for some good references, and design a pond that fits well with your style and situation.

All ponds can and should host a diversity of plants and animals. Just like natural waterways, the water environments you create need biological balance to thrive. To achieve this balance, add plants and fish. Read up on local water ecologies and try to establish one that will thrive in your climate.

For fish, start with gambusia, koi, guppies, or common feeder goldfish. These will eat mosquito larvae and add life and movement to your pond. Larger ponds can be stocked with trout or catfish, which, given proper conditions, will reproduce and provide food for years to come. Refer to chapter 5 for some great water plants.

It is a common misconception that home ponds need an electric pump to circulate the air. What ponds in nature have such technology? A well-designed ecology, with plants, fish, and plenty of edge, will circulate and balance itself. In addition, if your pond connects to a system that consistently adds graywater or rainwater, the frequent influx will keep things moving.

A pond provides rich sludge that is great for compost or mulch.

If you choose not to have a pond, then set up the graywater bog so that the overflow runs directly into your garden system. Personally, I prefer a pond. Ponds are beautiful and relatively easy to build, and they create valuable habitat. Even a small pond can hold hundreds of gallons. They are worth more than their volume in long-term benefits to the garden.

Some graywater systems utilize a series of several ponds, connected through constructed swales, ditches, and waterfalls. As with every aspect of the garden, each design should be site-specific and well suited to your individual tastes, needs, and available space. If you don't have the space or resources for a garden pond, try using a large barrel or bathtub for a container pond. I have several of these in my greenhouse, each thriving with its own little ecosystem.

Step Two: Build Your Slime Monster. You can use a bathtub, a wine barrel cut in half lengthwise, or just a shallow pit dug into the ground. Create a two-inch opening two-thirds of the way down on the side of the container for an outlet and insert a tight-fitting pipe, which will drain to the pond. Situate the monster near the place where your household water will exit, and make sure that your container is below that exit so the water can drain in easily. (Don't worry about the plumbing yet— we're almost there.)

Line the pit or container with plastic. Anything will do—an old tarp, recycled greenhouse plastic, trash bags, what have you. Put a two-inch

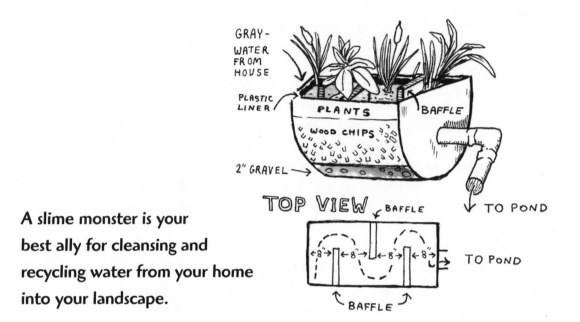

A slime monster is your best ally for cleansing and recycling water from your home into your landscape.

layer of gravel and rocks in the bottom to hold down the liner and create air pockets.

Now place baffles in the container, eight to twelve inches apart, to slow the water flow (see the illustration). Nestle the baffles in the gravel so they don't fall over. Fill the gaps between the baffles with wood chips; on the top plant rushes, cattails, irises, horsetail, canna, comfrey, reeds, and other water-loving, nonedible plants.

Step Three: Feed the Monster. Now that you have a way to receive the water, you are ready to open the floodgates. Because graywater is illegal in many cities, many people choose not to reroute the plumbing but to catch the water in buckets and pour it into the slime monster by hand. This works fine for the able-bodied, but it can become tiresome or impossible when dealing with bath- and laundry water, which is easy to reroute from the sewer to the slime monster with a couple of Y-joints from the local hardware store.

Home plumbing is a field of its own, and I will leave the details to you. There are plenty of do-it-yourself plumbing manuals around if you get confused. In general, make sure to cap off any open pipes to prevent leaks, and unless you are ready for a blackwater system, keep the toilet water out of the graywater flow. Set up a small screen between the house outlet and the slime monster to filter out hair and debris. Clean the filter often and throw the sludge into the compost.

Again, graywater may be illegal in your neighborhood, so be discreet to avoid inspections and fines. Even just for aesthetic purposes, it is a good idea to hide the outlet behind an attractive shrub or garden sculpture. This will also prevent any nosy inspectors or neighbors from alerting the water cops.

Now that you have your very own slime monster, take good care of it. Like all pets, it needs love, attention, and plenty of water. Never let the monster dry out, and scoop out and replace the wood chips if they get really rotten—usually once every couple of years. The living community of plants, insects, and microorganisms will filter all the soap and pathogens out of your graywater before sending it into the garden, and the slime monster itself will provide a unique microclimate for unusual bog plants.

Rainwater

The other big waste of household water is the thousands of gallons that wash off the roof and into the street every time it rains. In many places rain catchments are the main source of residential water. Even in modern cities, much of the municipal water comes from rain, but why wait for the city to catch it and pipe it back to you when you can catch it yourself from your own roof, driveway, or other impervious surfaces?

It is easy and inexpensive to set up simple rain catchment devices all around your home and garden, and to link these with your home water cycle. This involves three steps: catching the water, storing it, and directing it into the landscape. Catching the water is easy. Find recycled gutters at construction sites where people are remodeling or reroofing their house, or make simple ones out of long wooden boards. Attach gutters to the edge of the roof and direct the downspouts into your swale or storage tanks.

Be sure to keep your gutters clean of leaves and debris—scoop them out a few times a year, and use the contents for mulch. I have also seen a "gutter" made by attaching a taut cord or chain to the edge of the roof. The water runs down the chain in the direction of its slope. Check around your neighborhood and surf the Internet for more ideas about rain collection.

Build a basic rain catchment system using old honey barrels.

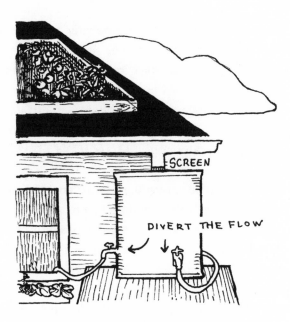

Storing the rainwater can present bigger challenges, but none you can't solve with a little thought and flexibility. First, determine how much rainwater your roof can catch in a year using the following formula: Let F represent the footprint of the roof, which is not the surface area but the area, in square feet, of ground that it covers. Multiply F by the average rainfall (R), in inches per year, and divide the product by 12. This formula gives you the number of cubic feet per year of water that your roof will catch. To convert cubic feet to gallons, multiply by 7.5. In other words, $7.5(FR/12) =$ gallons per year of rainwater will hit said roof. Thus, a thirty- by forty-foot house in an area with an average annual rainfall of fifty-five inches will catch about 41,250 gallons of water per year.[13] Wow! Where will you put it all?

The key to storing rainwater is in diversifying the directions you send the water as it runs off the roof, and storing it in varied catchments that suit its intended purpose. Drain one section into clean barrels near the kitchen to use for cooking; direct a second section into a tank near the bathing area; and drain another section directly into the garden, to be stored in ponds and swales. Set up small storage containers where they are needed, using the nearest surface to catch the water. For example, install a small gutter on the roof of a dog- or chicken house to drain the rainwater into a trough for the dog/chickens to drink.

Unless you live in a desert region, where rain is very scarce, you do not need to store the entire annual rainfall. Your varied catchments need hold only enough water to last between rains. You may still want to build a small cistern for household water—an excellent investment for your home and not as expensive as you might think. Some friends built an eight-thousand-gallon cistern under their driveway and used a solar pump to bring the water into their home. This lasts them all summer, and the overflow goes to their pond and then filters out into the garden.

If you can't build a cistern, no problem: Use food-grade fifty-gallon plastic or steel barrels, which can be found for free or purchased cheap from food distribution warehouses. Look for those that used to contain honey or syrup, rather than fats or oils, and clean them well with soap and hot water before using them. Also, most old motor homes have large plastic water tanks that can be removed with just a few hand tools—check a local junkyard. These work especially well because they are rectangular and can be easily attached to the side of a building.

For increased storage link together multiple containers with hoses, and install a spigot at the end. Retrieve the water in buckets, or mount the whole system up high and use gravity to direct it straight into the household plumbing. Remember that water weighs about seven pounds per gallon, and even a small containment system can weigh hundreds of pounds, so be sure to build sturdy supports and anchor everything to the ground.

You can also use patios, sidewalks, and your driveway to catch water. The next time it rains, find the best place to tap the flow, and install a gutter or pipe to direct the water away from the storm drain and back onto your landscape. If you are building a patio or walkway, think ahead and angle it slightly so the water flows to where you want it.

While graywater tends to be very alkaline because of soaps and skin cells, rainwater is usually more acidic due to pollution and other factors. It is best to combine them by draining both into a central pond where you can achieve a more balanced mix before sending the overflow into the garden.

Again, I strongly recommend establishing swales, berms, and contoured garden beds *before* rerouting the household water onto the landscape. This will give the new influx of water somewhere to go and will fill your garden with life and diversity. Otherwise any pond overflow will just take the path of least resistance, which may work out fine, but could also cause serious erosion problems. Even a single swale, combined with plenty of thick mulch in the garden beds below it, will make a big difference in how well your garden holds water.

Drywells

If you are not quite ready to establish such an extensive water system, or if you just don't know what to do with a particular corner of the roof, try building a simple drywell under the downspout. Normally water gains momentum on the way off the roof, and by the time it hits the ground it is moving too fast to soak into the soil before running off.

Drywells use turbulence to dissipate energy in runoff water and therefore encourage deeper percolation into the soil. The average house needs only a nine-cubic-foot drywell at each downspout to prevent erosion and greatly increase soil percolation.[14] Here's how to make one:

Just below the downspout, dig out a hole three and a half feet deep and three and a half feet wide. At the bottom of the well, in the direction(s) you want to water to percolate, insert a two-inch perforated pipe a foot or two into the soil. Now line the sides with recycled brick or concrete blocks and drive a few pieces of rebar vertically into the bottom of the hole, to hold the walls in place.

A basic drywell is easy and inexpensive to build and recycles roof runoff back into your soil.

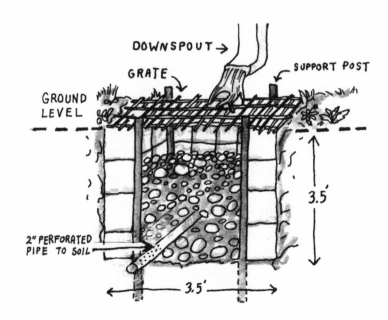

When you've finished the walls, fill the bottom two-thirds of the well with gravel and large rocks, being careful not to clog or disturb the pipe outlets. Place a grate across the top to filter out leaves and keep anyone from falling in.

Whether you build a single drywell or implement a home-wide ecological water system, you will be surprised at how quickly your landscape will respond. With careful planning and a focused effort, these strategies will turn even an arid landscape into a green oasis, will save you hundreds of dollars a year on your water bill, and will help steward your watershed resources.

Sharing Water

Nature shares water in many ways. From above and below, through our skin and our mouths, we drink, we pee, we swim, we bathe, we kiss, we make love. Water flows through, under, above, and around us. When we share water with one another, we deepen our connection with natural water cycles and strengthen our bond with the earth.

Here is a water-sharing ritual that a friend showed me. He said, "When people share water in this way, they become ecstatic." He was right.

I was a little scared at first to just let someone dump water on my head—the natural inclination is to duck or try to avoid getting wet. But it was a hot summer day at the Oregon Country Fair, so I figured what the heck. Here's how it went:

First, I bowed my head and he poured water on my crown—just enough to dampen my hair and run down past my ears. Then he passed the water to me, bowed, and let me pour it on his head.

Next, I tilted my head back and opened my mouth while he poured in the water until it began to overflow. I gulped it down and, again, returned the favor. Then we kissed. Just a nice, trusting kiss between fellow earthlings: water-kin, as it were. Simple and sweet—try it with a friend today!

4. The Living Soil

Gardening is healthy, it's interesting, and it promotes diversity. It gets you out of the box watching television and being an audience; always being catered to, pandered to, and ripped off while your resources are squandered. As a gardener, you can fulfill a destiny: The divine is closer to you in the garden than anywhere else. That's not true if you spray poisons and you kill every bug and you discriminate, but if you have a touch, and you get into the flow of the beauty of nature, you have a chance to feel the illumination that comes with love and peace and goodness.

—Alan Kapuler[1]

The most important components, beyond climate, of any self-sufficiency gardening program are the soil or ground in which you will grow your garden and the plant and animal populations that you encourage to or discourage from living there. To be effectively self-reliant, whether by choice or necessity, your goal should be a healthy, well-balanced garden environment which is self-sustaining, that is, does not require the purchase of commercial soil amendments, pesticides, herbicides or beneficial insects.

That may seem an impossible goal in a culture programmed to *buy* solutions to all of our problems, but it is not impossible if you will work intimately *with* Nature, using what is commonly known as organic gardening techniques, to build a healthy, non-toxic garden environment. [Thus,] building a self-sustaining garden environment that can support the goal of food self-sufficiency may require some adjustments in thinking.

—Geri Welzel Guidetti[2]

Full of Life

The word *human* comes from the same roots as the word *humus*, meaning "earth," and in fact our bodies do contain many of the same elements and microorganisms as fertile organic soil. To build a garden that will effectively nurture us, we need first and foremost to nurture a healthy soil community.

For many years soil studies focused primarily on minerals and rocks, but now scientists understand that the soil is a life force that is constantly moving and renewing the ground beneath our feet. In his revolutionary book *The Soil and Health*, Sir Albert Howard wrote, "The soil is, as a matter of fact, full of life organisms. It is essential to conceive of it as something pulsating with life. . . . There could be no greater misconception than to regard the earth as dead: a handful of soil is teeming with life."[3]

Whole communities thrive within every gram of topsoil, including arthropods, fungi, algae, roots, nematodes, protozoans, worms, springtails, and a billion different kinds of bacteria. As they move through the soil, eating, breeding, interacting, dying, and decomposing, they create a complex web of life that makes it possible to have clean air, clean water, healthy plants, and moderated water flow.

Some microorganisms store or "fix" nitrogen and other nutrients, making them available to hungry plants. Others moderate soil structure by secreting substances that enhance aggregation and porosity; this increases water filtration and the holding capacity of soil and reduces erosion and wasteful runoff. Leaves and roots can produce exudates, which provide food for bacteria and fungi. Protozoans move soil around, and nematodes eat disease-causing organisms. These critters interact with the rest of the soil community, feed on one another, and in turn nourish the plants and bring them to fruition. The plant and soil communities support each other in constantly pulsating, ever-evolving, living ecologies.

This is, of course, a simplified description of complex systems, and typically the more complex a soil community, the more ecologically sound it is. In general, perennial polycultures, such as those described in this book, will support a much more complex soil ecosystem than annual monocultures such as a potato farm or a cornfield.

Dr. Elaine Ingham, an accomplished soil scientist from Oregon, finds that a balanced, complex "soil food web" will suppress disease-causing and pest organisms; make nutrients available for plant growth at the times and rates plants require; decompose plant residues rapidly; produce hormones that help plants grow; and retain nitrogen and other nutrients such as calcium, iron, potassium, phosphorus, and more. She emphasizes the importance of bacteria and fungi in particular, noting our own dependence on the six million bacteria on every square centimeter of our skin.[4]

The soil is a living, dynamic system.

Soil health is linked to our own health, and soil communities bear remarkable resemblance to the flora and fauna in our own guts, with many similar microorganisms. Just as we must maintain a diverse, thriving intestinal community to be healthy, we must also cultivate a diverse, thriving soil ecosystem.

Unless agronomy is your passion we needn't dwell too long on the science. We need only understand that the soil is a living, dynamic system, affected by every action we take, for good or ill. Throughout history we find examples of societies that thrived and rose to power on fertile native soil, then waned and perished when they failed to adequately steward that soil.

When we build soil we build community in more ways than we know, and when we destroy soil we destroy our chances at a thriving global community. In short, engaging in responsible, proactive soil stewardship will help guarantee the abundance and long-term fertility of our gardens—and in turn our communities. In order to achieve this it is important to establish soil cycles that perpetuate their own fertility, and to grow our crops with the surplus nutrients created by such a system. This will become easier over time as the soil and the ensuing gardens expand and mature.

If you really want to geek out on soil science, check out the resources section for a list of excellent books and websites. In the meantime this chapter is packed with soil-building strategies that will diversify your soil community and help guarantee a long-lasting, healthy, and abundant ecological garden.

Starting or Expanding Garden Beds

Generally, if an area will yield lush green grass, then it will yield a lush, diverse garden. There may be exceptions to this rule, but I have seen none. Every time I witnessed or helped with a lawn conversion the resulting garden was lush and abundant, and the owners were thrilled to let the lawn become a thing of the past. If you have a lawn space and are ready to turn it into a garden, I am here to tell you how fun and easy it really is.

Whether you choose to garden the whole yard or just a section of it, remember that good care of the soil is the key to your success. The next few pages will describe some excellent strategies for pioneering or expanding garden beds in ways that are good for the soil. They will work well on almost any site, so experiment with them all and see what works best in your particular situation. Use a variety of methods to increase the deep diversity and long-term fertility of your soil, and it will reward you with a lifetime of health and abundance.

Before you start building and improving soil, however, you should assess the soil that is already there and try to determine which strategies would work the best.

Meet the Neighbors

The best way to improve soil is to diversify the living community within it. How to do so depends on what is already there and what the soil needs to achieve optimum balance and fertility. There are a number of good ways to help determine these needs, from simple pH kits to expensive laboratory soil analysis. These store-bought solutions are effective in some settings, but unnecessary for most home gardeners.

Before you go out and spend money on soil test kits, go out into your garden and look at what's already growing there. For centuries organic gardeners have relied on the plants themselves to indicate soil conditions, and many common weeds can provide excellent clues for how to improve your soil. By learning to recognize weeds, we can learn about our specific soil conditions and begin adding specific types of organic matter that will help provide what the existing soil lacks. We can also plant relatives of the wild plants that will thrive in the same soil conditions, or we can replace unwanted weeds with our preferred cultivars. (See the sidebar on page 80.)

Also, take some time to meet the varied critters who live in your topsoil. Depending on where you live, your topsoil is probably anywhere from half an inch to six feet deep. The topsoil is the most biologically active zone in the soil, and you improve it every time you mulch. Plant

Weeds and What They Tell

Weeds are weeds only from our human egotistical point of view, because they grow where we do not want them. In Nature, however, they play an important and interesting role. They resist conditions that cultivated plants cannot resist, such as drought, acid soil, lack of humus, mineral deficiencies, as well as a one-sidedness of minerals, etc. They are witness of man's failure to master the soil, and they grow abundantly wherever man has "missed the train"—they only indicate our errors and Nature's corrections. Weeds want to tell a story—they are nature's means of teaching humanity, and their story is interesting. If we would only listen to it we could apprehend a great deal of the inner forces through which nature helps and heals and balances and, sometimes, also has fun with us.

—Ehrenfried Pfeiffer, *Weeds and What They Tell*[5]

This chart will help you learn to recognize and respond to what the weeds are trying to tell you. These recommendations are not absolute; they're just representative of common patterns. Don't rely on this or any book to guide you, but let these clues help lead you to the appropriate action for your specific situation.

Weeds	Soil Conditions	Ways to Respond
Sorrels, docks, fingerleaf weeds, lady's thumb, horsetail	Soil pH is acidic or increasing in acidity	Add nonacidic organic matter (no conifer chips), plant cover crops, improve drainage, add lime
Field mustard, pennycress, bindweed, quack grass, false chamomiles	Formation of surface crust or hardpan	Till less, plant deep-rooted cover crops, mulch thickly
Lamb's-quarter, buttercup, pigweed, teasel, thistle	Overtilling and overcultivation	Let beds lie fallow, mulch, plant perennials, improve drainage, reduce impact, increase natural flows
Sweet peas, clover, other leguminous weeds	Soil is sandy or alkaline, is too well drained, or needs nitrogen	Add compost, maintain a thick mulch, create water and nutrient banks using hugelkülture and trench mulches
Wild lettuce, lemon balm, self-heal, cleavers, English daisy, groundsel, chickweed, plantain	Soil pH is balanced to slightly acidic, soil is well drained and fertile	Plant a garden and keep giving back what you take through mulch and cover crops

roots and biological activity also reach deeper, into the subsoil, where surplus moisture and nutrients are stored.

To get a nice view of your soil strata dig one or several small test pits, a foot wide by several feet deep. Use a flashlight to observe the varied levels of activity and changes in color. You will see an obvious switch from topsoil to subsoil. The topsoil will be dark and active and the subsoil will be lighter in color, heavier, and denser. Some sites have deep native topsoil while others have little or none, with bedrock lying just below the surface.

Take a handful of topsoil and squeeze it between your fingers. Does it clump together and stick to your fingers, or does it crumble and blow away? The best soil is somewhere in between: spongy and light, with a diversity of textures, colors, and creatures. Look deep into the clods and try to see how the varied creatures interact. If you can't find anyone living in your topsoil, then the strategies in this chapter will change that. If you already have good soil, teeming with life, then these methods will help you keep it that way.

Look back at the test pit and measure the depth of your topsoil with a ruler. Make note of your measurements and then fill in the pit or plant a tree there. Do this after each year of paradise gardening and you will see your topsoil getting progressively deeper, more diverse, and more full of life.

Bed Design

There are many things to consider when deciding what shape your garden beds will be, including contour, function, and efficient use of the

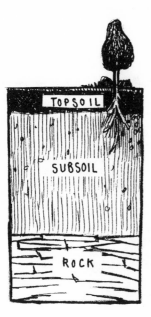

Your soil strata will vary and change according to climate, geography, and past and present gardening techniques.

available space. Millions of people grow gardens in boxes, but the rectangle is almost absent in nature—perhaps we should take heed and try something that makes more sense.

As we saw in the preceding chapter, the shape of your garden beds should adhere to the flow of water through your site. Build beds on contour and you will save water and prevent erosion. But don't limit yourself to long, curving rectangles either. While straighter beds are easier to maintain with machines, if you are working on a hand scale you should design your garden in patterns that make more ecological sense.

From a geometrical perspective, the best way to make use of a given space is with three-way branching patterns. Nature uses branching patterns to distribute nutrients in plants and trees and to drain and distribute water across the land. Warm-blooded animals also use branching patterns to transport blood and nutrients though complex vein and artery systems.

In the garden, branching patterns use the least amount of path, minimizing travel time and maximizing bed space. Try a Y-pattern that uses 120-degree angles in sets of three—it sounds a little complicated, but you will end up with a visually spectacular and highly efficient garden layout.

Later, when you plant the beds, think again of branching and intersecting patterns, and space your plants accordingly. Straight rows are the least efficient use of space, so get creative and see how your space expands! By layering patterns into your design at each stage of the work, you enhance the fractal nature of your garden and thus its ability to thrive on multiple levels.

Just a few of the many ways to use 120-degree angles and keyhole patterns to maximize garden space.

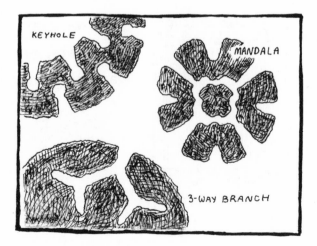

The Breakfast–Lunch–Dinner Theory

While you are building garden beds you may also want to start a few seeds. When growing plants from seeds, whether annual veggies or perennials, I subscribe to the Breakfast–Lunch–Dinner Theory.

It goes like this: Start seeds in their "breakfast," meaning in a neutral medium with plenty of aeration but not too much fertility. I like to use a mixture of perlite, vermiculite, and/or pumice, with a little bit of sifted compost or topsoil.

When it comes to making potting soil it is hard to avoid buying the structural ingredients such as perlite, vermiculite, or pumice. Still, a big bag will last several years if you use it sparingly. Try to find local sources, preferably from your own site, and recycle old potting soil by spreading it out in the sun for a few days and mixing it back in.

When the seedlings have a few pairs of true leaves, transplant them into a slightly richer potting soil, or "lunch." You can make a new mix similar to the above, but with more compost and less of the fillers, or just use the same mix and stir in a tiny bit of 3–1–1 fertilizer (see page 93). Some gardeners use jauche (nettle tea), compost tea, and biodynamic preparations in their potting soil—try them all and see what you like. Again, be sure not to put too much fertilizer in the lunch mix, because it can burn the baby plants. Never add fresh manure to any potting soil—always compost the manure first, or save it for sheet mulching.

Finally, the garden beds in which the starts make their permanent home should provide a rich, fertile "dinner." The Breakfast–Lunch–Dinner Theory doesn't actually lend itself to human nutrition—eating our richest meal at the end of the day is a recipe for indigestion and obesity! Still, this system works well for starting and establishing new plants in the garden, so remember it when you need it.

Be sure to consider human flows as you shape your garden beds. Pay attention to where people already walk through your site and shape the beds accordingly, rather than trying to get the people to conform to a new path.

Also, place beds in locations relative to what you want to grow. For example, build an herb spiral next to the kitchen door and you won't have to run all the way out to the garden for a quick sprig of rosemary. Put another garden bed near where children play and grow flowers for them to pick.

Chapter 5 will give you even more ideas about bed design as we look at the many approaches to polycultural gardening, such as alley cropping and using hedgerows. For now let's move on to soil-building strategies.

Compost Here Now

You can build compost anywhere, from a bucket in the kitchen to all over the front yard. Rich compost is worth more than its weight in gold in terms of garden success, and some form of it is essential for building

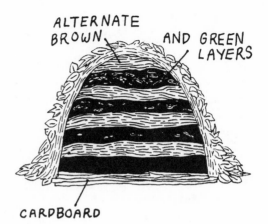

ALTERNATE BROWN AND GREEN LAYERS

CARDBOARD

Alternate between green and brown layers and use many materials to build compost.

soil. Some people build it in a shady corner near the kitchen door, then transport the finished compost over to the garden areas as needed.

I prefer to build compost right on top of the garden, in large, steaming piles that break down quickly. I then spread these piles around and plant into the resulting beds. This saves me from schlepping the wheelbarrow back and forth, and the big pile on the ground kills off the grass so I don't have to dig it out. Here is my method:

Mow the grass and punch some holes in the ground with a digging fork. If there are big, knobby weeds like blackberries, grub them out and shake the soil off the roots onto the bed. If there are a lot of rhizomatous weeds, such as bindweed, ivy, or some grasses, this and other sheet-composting and mulching methods may not work. These weed roots will just snake back and forth under the mulch/compost pile and form an impenetrable mat that eventually competes with your garden plants. See chapter 5 for more on how to deal with these extreme situations.

If all you have is regular grass and nonrunning weeds, you're good to go. Once you've aerated the soil and gotten the big weeds out, spread a layer of unwaxed cardboard on the area you want to turn into a garden. This space can be as large as you've got the materials to cover, but an area that's about four feet wide and six to eight feet long is a good size for starters. I don't recommend going any smaller than three feet by five—the pile won't break down well enough or be easy to contain in such a small space. Try another technique for the little spots.

Soak the cardboard well with water and build your pile on top of it, alternating brown and green layers. The recommended ratio is twenty-five parts brown or carbonaceous material to one part green or nitrogen-rich material. "Brown" items might include straw, wood chips, cardboard, dried leaves, vacuum dust, fabric, paper, dryer lint, or small branches. "Green" stuff might be fresh-pulled weeds, feathers, food scraps, seaweed, fresh leaves, hay, or any kind of manure. Don't use plastic, paint, or anything with nasty chemicals; take those to a toxic-waste disposal site. Glass can be reused as a building material, but it doesn't make good compost for obvious reasons.

Build up the pile as high as you can get it while still maintaining a sturdy form. Be sure to water each layer well before adding the next. If it gets too conical on top, dig a pitchfork into the center and pull material out to the edges so the pile is the same height all over—usually about five to six feet when freshly built.

Cover the pile with a protective shell of leaves, straw, or regular garden soil to keep the right critters in and the wrong critters (like rats) out, and aerate it periodically by stabbing the butt end of your pitchfork into the pile a few times. It is important that compost stay moist—though not dripping wet—so water it occasionally if needed or cover it with a tarp if it's raining too much.

Some people turn their pile every few days, while others prefer to let it take its own sweet time. To get the most out of your pile, use the biodynamic compost preparations described later in this chapter. A compost pile like this will take three to six months to break down. You can tell when it's ready by the fresh, woodsy smell and dark, spongy texture.

Now you can use the finished product to top-dress any neighboring beds, and when the pile is low enough to suit your design, spread it around and plant it up. Don't forget to set aside a little of the best compost for your potting soil, sifting it first—use a piece of hardware cloth to make a screen that fits over your wheelbarrow. Always be sure to add a layer of mulch over any compost you spread in the garden, so the light and air don't kill the compost critters before they have a chance to do their magic in your garden beds.

Mulch Much

Mulch is organic matter that you put on top of your garden beds and pots, up around the base of the plants. It can be anything from leaves, compost, or straw to cardboard and newspaper. Nature mulches herself naturally with every falling leaf, so mulching is one of the best things you can do for your soil because it keeps moisture in, protects soil critters, and can help stifle unwanted weeds. Mulching is fun and easy; I would much rather walk around the garden tossing mulch onto the beds than swing a hoe or crawl around with a weeding tool.

Maintaining a thick perpetual mulch will reduce work and increase soil health. It will prevent erosion, add diversity to the soil community, and provide nutrients for the plants. An extra-thick mulch can prevent freezing in the winter and keep the soil from drying out in the heat of summer. Mulching provides an important outlet for surplus yard debris such as leaves, uprooted weeds, and bedding straw if you have animals. Mulch can also provide habitat for slugs, and it doesn't really prevent aggressive perennial weeds such as couch grass or bindweed. Still, the good outweighs the bad in most situations, so don't let these small drawbacks deter you.

The fastest and easiest way to convert a lawn into a garden is by sheet-mulching it. Sheet mulching works in much the same way as the compost method I described above, except that you don't build the pile as high and you spread it over a larger area. You can sheet-mulch the whole yard and design garden beds later, or you can build mulch in the shapes of the beds and leave grass paths between. Here's the basic procedure:

Mow the grass as low as possible and use a digging fork to punch in some aeration holes through the area where the mulch will go. Lay sheets of corrugated, nonwaxed cardboard over the bed areas and run a sprinkler over them for a couple of hours.

When the cardboard is soaked through, cover it with about two feet of debris. Because the piles won't be built as high as compost piles, it is better not to use funky, rotty stuff like kitchen scraps—save those for the compost piles. Instead use straw, dead leaves, newspaper, and wood chips, and layer in manure and fresh chopped-up weeds to heat it up. Layer the bumpy, ugly stuff on the bottom, using the same 25:1 brown-to-green ratio as you would for making compost.

For the final layer, use something that you find aesthetically appealing. No one wants to look at a front yard full of cardboard, but if it is hidden then it will serve its purpose without ruining your view. Some people use landscape cloth, carpeting, or plastic under their beds,

Use sheet mulch to quickly convert lawn space into lush garden beds.

DEAD LEAVES AND STRAW
WEEDS
NEWSPAPER
FOOD SCRAPS
STRAW
POOP
CARDBOARD

but I don't recommend these materials for any sort of food garden because they are ugly and often toxic and can create a potential nightmare for any future gardeners who try to dig or till and come up with a truckload of twenty-year-old shag carpet.

You can plant right into a fresh sheet mulch. Sow seeds and plant small starts into the top layers, or punch a hole through the cardboard to make room for the bigger roots of trees and perennials. If weeds come through, pull them out or just mulch right on top of them. When you want to add new plants, push some mulch aside and stuff them in.

Alternatively, you can use cardboard or an old piece of carpeting to cover an area temporarily, killing off grass and weeds, then pull it up and build garden beds. This saves hours of weed- and sod-removing labor. Unlike polyester carpeting, cardboard biodegrades quickly, can be tossed into the compost when it gets too soggy for reuse, and doesn't leave fuzzy little plastic things all over the garden.

Where to Get Mulch and Compost Materials

I recommend stashing large piles of mulch all around the garden, in unused corners or in future garden beds. Here is a short list of places to get free mulch and/or compost materials for your garden beds and stockpiles.

The City

Many cities offer autumn leaf-collection programs in which they pick up yard debris from residential curbsides and take it to a central dumping site. That debris, which is usually a lush mix of leaves from all over the city, is often available to the public. In Eugene, where I live, you can sign up on a list and the city will actually deliver the leaves to your driveway, free of charge. In other places there are dumping yards where locals can bring a truck and load up. Ask your local parks department what it has to offer. It may also have debris from park maintenance, such as grass clippings and tree prunings, or even extra plants. The only problem with these options is that you cannot guarantee the materials will be free of toxins. Alas, it is a toxic world, and we can only make best use of the resources we have available. Strive for balance and your garden will respond accordingly.

The Curb

Most people, especially in the suburbs, do some form of yard maintenance, which generates debris. In places where the city does not pick up yard debris from curbsides, people often send it to the dump. This is a terrible waste, some of which you can thwart by picking it up yourself first. Ask the homeowners or don't; sometimes it's really not a problem to just cruise around and load stuff up. Try going out on a warm Sunday afternoon when everyone's been out mowing all day. People will usually thank you for the favor, and you will have better soil. You can also make arrangements with neighbors beforehand and have the truck ready for them to dump into. Or just put a sign in your front yard that says NEIGHBORHOOD LEAF DROP-OFF and see what shows up.

Tree Services and Landscapers

Most arborists and landscapers generate truckloads of organic matter daily, and many will even pay you to let them dump it at your place. More often they'll chip it up and leave it for free. If they won't chip it and have only large debris to offer, maybe you can build a "hugelkülture" (see p. 90) or use it for firewood. Just look through the yellow pages and on the Internet, call around, and make notes of what you find. It won't take long to accumulate a list of great resources. Most landscapers also have tons of surplus plants that were pulled out of one landscape but will survive if planted into another. Ask them to drop off a few of these leftovers when they bring the chips.

Restaurants and Grocery Stores

All types of food merchants have food waste that usually goes into the trash. Choose the organic sources first, asking them to save their food scraps in buckets (which you can provide, if need be). Most places are happy to accommodate. Other places just fill up dumpsters out back— big metal gold mines of garden fertility. Pull up a truck and shovel it in, and don't forget to wear rain pants and rubber boots so you don't slime your clothes.

Trash and Recycling

Food places aren't the only spots in town with dumpsters full of compost and mulch materials. Look in alleys, behind the mall, in school and church parking lots, and all through residential areas for useful garden and soil-building materials such as cardboard, bags of leaves, bricks, newspapers, and more. You will probably find lots of other fine stuff as well—many people make a good living from just finding stuff in the trash and putting it to use.

Fairgrounds and Event Sites

Every year the Oregon Country Fair uses bales to mark off parking areas in a big field during the event, which lasts for only three days. The bales then rot in the field until the following year, when they are replaced by fresh ones for the next event. So each year after the fair we take the farm truck down to the site and load it full of free straw and hay bales. We usually get enough to supply our needs for the year, a truckload or two, which is about two hundred dollars' worth of good, barely used hay and straw. Look around at local events for materials like this that are in temporary use and may go to waste, then ask the organizers if you can take them, or just drop by at dumping time and see if you get lucky.

Dairies, Hatcheries, and Ranches

Look for local sources of manure and bedding materials from places that keep animals. Visiting these places can be a difficult but enlightening experience, and I strongly recommend that you choose ones that meet organic standards and that treat their animals very well. Ask around or look in the phone book, and don't be afraid to ask the farmer/rancher about the living conditions of the livestock.

Hugelkülture, Large Debris, and Trench Mulching

Large debris, such as branches, stumps, and rotten or scrap lumber, can be buried to provide underground habitat, store surplus water, and reserve nutrients for soil communities. Hugelkülture (pronounced *HEW-gull-cool-tour*) involves digging a shallow pit in the shape you want the garden bed to be, then piling in debris to ground level. Use wood up to two inches in diameter, and try to break up the pieces so none is more than three feet long or so. Then add a foot or so of soil and mulch on top, and fill the resulting garden bed with plants that like well-drained soil.

The hugelkülture area will seem to need extra water, but below the surface it will act as an underground sponge, catching and holding water to share later with nearby areas. As the buried wood decomposes, it may tie up soil nitrogen for a while, so it is best not to plant heavy-feeding annual vegetables (broccoli, cucumbers, squash) in a hugelkülture for the first year. Instead try potatoes, tomatoes, beans, or salad greens, and don't forget to add some good perennial fruits and berries. Hugelkülture works great for starting perennial beds in odd-shaped, sunken, or infertile areas, and it helps generate a closed-loop system by providing an on-site outlet for large debris.

Turn unwanted large debris into garden beds with hugelkülture.

Similar to hugelkülture in principle is a technique that I call trench mulching. Trench mulching also catches and stores water in the soil, but instead of digging pits, you dig trenches about two feet deep. The trenches need be only as wide as the wood you plan to bury, and unlike hugelkülture you can trench-mulch with wood of any diameter. Cover the trench mulch with a thick layer of garden soil to bring it to just above the ground level, and then plant it.

This technique works especially well around the edge of an orchard or garden area, and the large chunks of wood will hold water for many years to come. However, larger wood ties up more nutrients during decomposition, so stick to cover crops and other plants that need less nitrogen to grow.

Tilling, Plowing, and Double-Digging, Oh My!

Plowing damages soil communities in several ways. It kills fungi and chops up larger critters such as worms and beetles. Heavy machinery compacts the soil, which leads to waterlogging, erosion, and anaerobic conditions. Disregard of these facts by industrial farmers has left us with only about 5 percent of the original topsoil in the United States, and it has been said that the plow is to the prairie what the chain saw is to the forest. Just a few years of overtilling can destroy topsoil that nature took thousands of years to build, and once the soil is damaged it is difficult to repair.

You cannot improve soil just by mixing it all up—the nutrients in the subsoil become available only gradually as soil life works its way down. If you mix in too much of the heavy, clayey subsoil, many of the organisms that thrive in your topsoil will die. The best way to increase the depth of your topsoil is to build community—that is, add organic matter, such as mulch and compost, to the surface and let the critters do the rest. It is possible to dig or till garden beds, in moderation, and still maintain a wonderful tilth, but a single mistake can take many years to repair, so be very careful in this regard.

Tillage is a huge topic among farmers and gardeners everywhere, and I won't get into all the different types of equipment out there. Generally I recommend using no-till techniques such as mulching and composting, especially in urban settings. Still, in some circumstances— especially in large areas with fertile soil—it makes sense to till or dig beds to more fully tap into the resources there. Thus, here are a few pointers that will help you avoid big mistakes.

Not Too Wet

Soil tilled when it is too wet can become overly compacted, can lose valuable water-holding capacity, and will be more likely to erode when the wind and rains come. If water pools on the surface, or if the soil's muddy enough to clump together, it's too wet. Wait.

Not Too Dry

Dusty topsoil will blow away in even the gentlest breeze, so make sure there is some moisture in the soil before you turn it. To be worked up properly, the soil should be moist but not soggy, should hold together but not clump, and should not be dry enough to blow away—think *dust bowl* and avoid it! It should remind of you chocolate brownie batter, and you should be able to squeeze water through it like a sponge.

Not Too Often

Some gardeners become addicted to tilling and want to run the machine over every little weed that pops up. As with all technology, use tilling as little as possible. Manual weeding is good for your body and better for the soil.

Not Too Deep

The rare occasion calls for deep tilling, or subsoiling, but this is a call best made by experts. Just try to knock back the weeds and get some fluffy soil to add mulch and seeds to; you'll be on your way.

Mulch or plant cover crops quickly onto bare or tilled ground, or the weeds will sprout and try to cover the naked soil. Some gardeners till often, incorporating weeds and mulch into the soil and building fertility that way. Others prefer to till only when first establishing an area and maintain a deep mulch from then on. Still others will till up an area every few years and mulch or hand-work the area, or leave it fallow between. Experiment—though cautiously—and try to find a balance so that you are creating the least amount of disturbance for the greatest beneficial effect.

There *is* a small-scale technique called biointensive gardening, developed by organic gardening experts Alan Chadwick and John

Jeavons, that involves double-digging fluffy beds by hand, then maintaining them with deep mulch and cover crops. This technique is an excellent way to grow a lot of food on a very small plot of land.

I rarely double-dig anything myself, preferring naps in the hammock and less strenuous approaches like sheet mulch to such hard work. Further, it is essential to accompany double-digging with the other strategies in biointensive agriculture, such as cover crops and detailed rotations, so don't just go out and excavate a huge hole without learning the technique. I do not include instructions here, but if this interests you be sure to read the books by John Jeavons, listed in the back of this book.

Maintaining and Improving Soil

Once you've established garden beds you'll need to consistently add organic matter to the soil to replenish the nutrients used by your crops. In a closed-loop system the rule is one calorie in for one calorie out, and in a truly beneficial system you should improve the soil even beyond just replacing what you take. Here are some good strategies for maintaining and improving organic soil.

Fertilizers and Amendments

Many farmers and gardeners use manufactured "organic" fertilizers and amendments as their primary tools for building soil. These inputs, usually made of mining and meat industry by-products, can indeed boost a yield and help create a lasting fertile soil. However, while fertilizers can help provide a short-term fix for this season's deficiencies, they should always be accompanied by a long-term soil-building strategy that includes several or all of the other strategies described here.

For giving plants a light boost, try a simple 3–1–1 mixture of fish meal, rock dust, and kelp, respectively. You can use this mix all over the garden: when transplanting, as a side-dressing, and mixed into potting soil (see the sidebar on page 83). I am not big into fertilizers, preferring good old-fashioned compost, but the 3–1–1 seems to work really well and is relatively low-input. To determine what is best for you and your soil, ask around to find out what works for the other organic gardeners near you.

When choosing to buy fertilizers and amendments, think of where the resource comes from and try to tap into the waste stream wherever possible. Again, if we embrace the goal of creating a self-perpetuating ecosystem, we will see purchased fertilizers and amendments as last resorts, to be used only when other options are not available.

Jauche

Pronounced *YOW-kuh*, and also known as nettle tea, jauche makes a great fertilizer for young plants. Stinging nettle regulates iron for plants and can help prevent or eliminate pest invasions. Add two pounds of fresh nettle greens to two gallons of lukewarm water. Let this sit and steep for twenty-four hours, then sieve and spray on leaves. Use the leftover sludge as a mulch around perennials. Spray as often as twice a day for diseased plants, or dilute and use periodically for a general health boost. Many gardeners make similar concoctions using comfrey, mullein, tomato leaves, and other plants, with varied effects. Try some and see what works for you.

Compost Tea

Made by aerobically fermenting finished compost in water for twelve to twenty-four hours, compost tea boosts fertility on both organic and conventional farms. Proven to overcome and prevent disease and to increase the diversity and vigor of soil communities, compost tea is an essential component of a truly ecological agriculture. Store-bought brewers can be very expensive, but it is important to make the tea correctly. Consider going in on a brewer with a local garden club, or find a local source of surplus compost tea. A garden center near you probably has extra tea available every week when it cleans out the brewer.

If you don't want to mess with big machines, make your own cold-water tea brewer with a five-gallon bucket and a small pond pump (solar-powered is best). Fill the bucket with rainwater and dangle an old sockful of compost over the edge, so the sock acts like a tea bag. Submerge the pump and turn it on. In twenty-four hours your tea is ready to use.

Or make humus tea. The rich, spongy soil generated on the wild forest floor is called humus, and it is the absolute best-quality soil around. It is easy enough to build humus at home through composting, mulching, and the other methods described here. If you can mindfully harvest some good humus from a natural area nearby, then bring home a bucketful, dilute it with fresh water, and sprinkle it on your soil and compost piles. The microorganisms you import will enhance the diversity of your existing soil community and speed up the beneficial processes.

Biodynamic Compost and Soil Preparations

Often described as "homeopathic fertilizers," these magic potions are much more than herbal remedies. In 1924 clairvoyant scientist Rudolf Steiner gave a series of lectures to the farmers of Europe about the most ecological, sustainable ways to grow food. He put forth the following recipes—infusions of plant, animal, and cosmic energy—and claimed they would help restore balance to the soil and promote optimum fertility on the farm.

Since then biodynamic compost preparations, joined by three field and foliar sprays, have proven themselves time and again as highly effective, organic inputs. Biodynamics is a whole field of agricultural study, but the preps are useful to organic gardeners of all sorts. These preparations are usually identified by the numbers 500 through 508, as indicated below. I will do my best to describe, briefly, each one:[6]

500: Horn Manure. Made by filling a cow horn with cow manure and burying it over the winter, then digging it up and mixing a small handful into five gallons of water and stirring for an hour (see below) as the sun sets. The liquid is sprinkled on the soil and around the farm or garden using your fingers, a paintbrush, or a small broom. This promotes root activity, stimulates soil life and increases beneficial-bacterium growth, regulates lime and nitrogen, helps in the release of trace elements, and stimulates seed germination.

501: Horn Silica. Made by filling a cow horn with ground quartz and burying it over the summer, then digging it up and mixing it with water, stirring for an hour (see below) as the sun rises, and sprinkling it on foliage, branches, and buds. Horn silica enhances light metabolism of plants, stimulates photosynthesis and the formation of chlorophyll, and influences the color, aroma, flavor, and keeping qualities of crops.

502: Yarrow. Made from yarrow flowers stuffed into a stag bladder and hung in the sun for the summer. The flower substance is then removed from the bladder, and a teaspoonful is put into a hole in the compost pile. Preparation 502 assimilates potash and sulfur and helps plants attract trace elements.

Embrace the goal of creating a self-perpetuating ecosystem.

503: Chamomile. Made from chamomile flowers stuffed into a cow intestine and buried over the winter. The little sausages are then dug up, and the substance inside is added to a second hole in the compost pile. This preparation assimilates potash and calcium, allows plants to take in more nutrients, stabilizes nitrogen, and increases soil life.

504: Nettle. A pouch is made from peat moss, filled with stinging nettle leaves, and buried over the winter. The decomposed nettle is removed and added to a third hole in the compost pile. Nettle helps plants access remote nutrients and balances iron and nitrogen.

505: Oak Bark. Made by filling a cow skull with white oak bark, burying it over the winter, and then digging it up and adding the resulting substance to a fourth hole in the compost pile, 505 helps combat harmful diseases and moderates the whole compost ecosystem for optimum health and performance.

506: Dandelion. This preparation is made by stuffing dandelion buds into a cow mesentery, burying it over the winter, and then digging it up. Add 506 to the fifth and last compost hole. This stimulates a relationship between silica and potash and attracts cosmic forces into the soil.

507: Valerian. Make this final compost preparation by squeezing valerian flowers through some cheesecloth into a brown glass and fermenting for one year. The juice is diluted with water and stirred for ten minutes (see below), then sprinkled on the top of the compost pile after the other five preparations have been inserted into their respective holes. This seals the pile and stimulates the effective use of phosphorus by the soil.

508: Equisetum Tea. Another kind of jauche, this tea is used to treat and prevent fungal disease. Combine one part equisetum (horsetail) with ten parts water. Bring to a rolling boil, then reduce the heat to a fast simmer and let simmer for fifteen to twenty minutes. Turn off heat, cover, and leave for seven to fourteen days in the dark to ferment. The fresh lemony fragrance tells you that it's done. Dilute 10:1 with water, stir for twenty minutes (see below), and sprinkle over the leaves of fruit trees, squashes, tomatoes, grapes, and anything else that is susceptible to blight, powdery mildew, rust, or similar problems.

Use a similar recipe to make a tree paste: Prepare equisetum tea as above and mix with cow manure, clay, and diatomaceous earth. Paint from the base of the tree to a foot out on the first few branches to protect the bark from sunscald and disease.

Stirring the Biodynamic Preparations. Place a portion of the preparation into a five-gallon bucket of rainwater or piped-in water that has been left out for a day to allow the chlorine to evaporate. Using your arm, a wire or wicker whisk, or a stick, begin moving the water around in a circle. Keep going at a steady rate until you see a strong vortex form in the water, spiraling down like a mini tornado into the bottom of the bucket.

Now switch directions, breaking the vortex and starting over in the other direction. Keep going back and forth like this for as long as the preparation calls for. The valerian compost preparation mentioned above needs to be stirred like this for only ten minutes, but the two field sprays (horn manure and horn silica) require an entire hour of continuous stirring. Stirring the preps is most fun when done by a team of two or three people, handing off the bucket when arms get tired, and it is a great way to spend intentional time with your fellow gardeners.

Animal Inputs

Some people like to mix up manure teas by tossing some good organic poop into a barrel, adding a bunch of water, and letting it sit for a day or so before diluting it and dousing the soil with it. Manure and manure tea are valuable additions to any compost pile or sheet mulch and are the primary input relied upon by many organic farmers and gardeners around the world.

It is helpful to use manure of all kinds, but do not become dependent upon it or any other single component for soil building; also, as with all

Stir biodynamic preparations into a vortex, then break it up and switch directions.

inputs, always apply sparingly. Alpaca and rabbit manure can be used relatively fresh, whereas cow, chicken, and horse manure should be composted for at least a year before being used. Again, use on-site or recycled sources wherever possible. Most dairies and chicken farms are happy to get rid of surplus manure, and many will even dump a load into your truck for you with their tractor.

Manures and other animal inputs such as feathers, eggs, and dairy products, as well as the animals that produce them, add value, richness, and fertility to an ecosystem. Realistically, no piece of Earth can thrive without some sort of animal influence, and no whole-system design is complete without using the surpluses generated by the animals on-site.

We love our chickens and geese; they add character and entertainment to the homestead, eat weeds and slugs, and sift and manure our mulch for us before we add it to the garden beds. Interacting with these and the other animals on our farm brings us closer to nature and brings our farm closer to a closed-loop fertility cycle. See the sidebar at right for more about barnyard birds.

Some people, however, are deeply disturbed by any sort of domestication and/or use of animals and animal inputs, for various reasons. There are many farms and gardens that thrive without animal inputs at all, such as Bountiful Gardens in Willitts, California, where folks advocate using one-third of agricultural land for growing plants to build compost, which

Build a predator-proof chicken tractor and move it daily to keep birds healthy and minimize negative impact in the garden. Include a shady spot, a nesting box, and a roosting perch.

Pros and Cons of Barnyard Birds

Adding domestic birds to a garden, whether urban or rural, brings in life, fertility, and beauty. These benefits can help bring an average garden closer to paradise, but they are sometimes offset by the (often unforeseen) difficulties with these birds.

Most birds provide delicious eggs, valuable manure, beautiful feathers, and hilarious entertainment, but some types might be more trouble than you think. Birds are smelly and dusty, and even a small flock will ruin a nice garden within a few minutes, given the opportunity. Before you make the commitment to a flock of your own, visit local farms and gardens that have had birds for a while. Also see the chart below for pros and cons.

Type of Birds	Pros	Cons
Chickens	Comfortable in a small coop or "chicken tractor." Hens are nonaggressive. Good meat and eggs. They will weed an established perennial garden or spread mulch. They are tamable and trainable, and smarter than given credit for.	Very noisy—even the hens, from dawn to dusk, all day, every day. They scratch up baby plants if let loose in a young garden. Easily killed by natural predators.
Ducks	They eat slugs and snails. Eggs are rich and delicious. Ducks are funny to watch and quite sociable, and they come in at least as many varieties as chickens. They need a pond to thrive and add a nice aesthetic to any garden.	Ducks are loud and quite stupid, so it can be difficult to get them to go where you want. They love to eat salad and will trash your garden badly. Also very vulnerable—heard of a sitting duck?
Geese	Beautiful, graceful birds, geese are my favorite. The young goslings are very easy to tame and make great companions. Goose eggs are edible and very rich, and the hard shells last forever when painted.	They poop *a lot*, so if they're free-range, you've some cleanup to do. They can also be aggressive if not handled when young and have been known to bite—hard.
Turkeys	One bird makes a lot of meat, if you're into that sort of thing. The feathers are big and beautiful.	Big, mean, and ugly. They will chase children and demolish the garden. Not recommended.
Guinea fowl	Great meat birds because at four months they can weigh several pounds. They are beautiful birds, with almost iridescent feathers at maturity. Baby guineas are sweet and make funny noises, but . . .	. . . grown guinea fowl make a hellish screeching sound similar to that of a busted fan belt on a car, and they will sustain it for hours. Spare yourself (and your neighbors) the turmoil, unless you have a very large site and can keep them far away.
Pheasants	Stunningly beautiful, very wild, relatively low-impact when left loose in the garden because they prefer bugs to plants.	They often run away, and male pheasants can be very violent toward chickens and other birds.
Quail	Said to be delicious, though I can't see how such a small morsel could be worth the trouble. Their call is sweet and supercute.	Impossible to tame and so tiny that they usually run away or get eaten by predators.
Chukars	Similar to quail but larger and more beautiful, with a wonderful call. Chukars offer great ambience.	Like quail and pheasants, chukars will not put eggs on your table, and they are wild and vulnerable.
Pigeons	Great poop; very compatible with a small garden setting. Beautiful and interesting to listen to.	They can breed like rabbits and may move into an area where you don't want them.
Peacocks	Fabulous in so many ways—who doesn't like the idea of peacocks drifting about the yard? The feathers are valuable for many uses, and they will breed readily given enough room.	Again, very difficult to tame—our peacocks went feral and live high in the conifers on the outskirts of our farm. We hear their calls in the sunset . . .
Emus	Even more fabulous, and highly prized for their feathers, meat, and oil. Easily adapted to temperate climates and very tamable.	Untamed emus can be vicious and have claws that could kill a dog or human. Get young ones and treat them right.

will replace the nutrients lost to crops. Like many of the strategies in this book, this works very well in some circumstances and is impractical in others.

A growing number of gardeners use only the waste products produced by the humans on-site, namely urine and humanure. Urine and humanure are local, basically renewable resources that do not involve the processing, packaging, and transport that even the most benign organic fertilizers require. Using human waste is a highly effective yet controversial soil-building technique, made less intimidating with just a little information.

For starters, urine is totally sterile. I've heard that if you have ringworm or athlete's foot or sustain an injury in the wilderness, you should pee on it. In the garden fresh urine can be diluted 1:10 with water and poured on the soil or compost pile; a single human produces enough urine to fertilize about three thousand square feet of garden soil a year.[7] Don't put it directly on the plants, because it may burn the leaves, and in fact urine has been used by some people at full strength as an effective weedkiller. Use urine as fresh as possible to avoid the foul odor that comes after a few days of fermentation.

As for feces, also known as humanure, they should be collected and composted in a separate compost pile for a year, after which they can be added to fruit trees or perennials as a mulch. Obviously you will get a much higher-quality product if you choose a vegetarian, organic diet. With some basic precautions such as frequent handwashing and long-term composting, our own solid waste can become a free, nutrient-rich input to the garden. See the resources section for references to more information about integrating human wastes, safely, into your whole-system design.

Vermiculture and Vermicomposting

Earthworms might be the hardest-working creatures on Earth, and a natural agriculture is dependent on their constant churning, eating, and releasing of soil and organic matter. Their manure, or castings, is rich in essential plant nutrients as well as a plethora of microorganisms and is one of the best fertilizers there is. A simple worm bin will fit under the kitchen sink, makes a great educational tool for children and adults alike, and is easily built from recycled materials such as an old wooden dresser. Detailed information about the varied methods of vermiculture

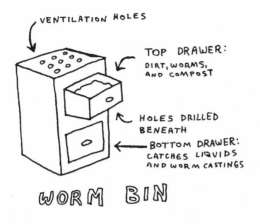

VENTILATION HOLES

TOP DRAWER:
DIRT, WORMS,
AND COMPOST

HOLES DRILLED
BENEATH

BOTTOM DRAWER:
CATCHES LIQUIDS
AND WORM CASTINGS

WORM BIN

An old wooden nightstand can be easily converted into a compact and productive worm bin.

(growing worms) and vermicomposting (using worms to make soil) is readily available on the Internet and at public libraries.

Cover Crops, Pioneer Plants, and Detoxifiers

An excellent way to improve soil and build long-term fertility is by planting cover crops, which suppress weeds and add organic matter to the soil. If you leave an area of bare soil, nature will cover-crop it on her own with a diversity of wild weeds, so why not plant beneficial soil builders instead? The best cover crops are polycultures—mixtures of plants that interact with one another to provide the optimum soil-building performance.

Start with a nitrogen fixer, which works with bacteria in a symbiotic relationship to fix atmospheric nitrogen and make it available to other plants. Most plants in the bean family (Fabaceae) have this ability, such as clover, fava beans, vetch, and kudzu. Other plants that can fix nitrogen include alder, autumn olive, sea buckthorn, and ceanothus. Add a grass like rye, millet, or oats to send roots deep into the soil, break up any hardpan, and bring nutrients to the surface. Feel free to mix in some good habitat and forage plants, such as buckwheat and wildflowers, to encourage bird and insect populations and provide flowers for the table.

As the cover crops mature, mow them a few times to increase the vigor and soil-building power of the plants. Add the mowings to the compost pile or use them for mulch. When you are ready to garden the area, either mulch or till it up and fill it with your garden plants, or just work up small sections and insert the new plants, leaving a living mulch of mowed cover crop all around.

If your soil is especially bad or you have problems with erosion or toxicity, consider adding some pioneer plants, which grow well in damaged soils and can help establish a garden space in an otherwise barren area. Pioneers stabilize and improve soil and, once established, provide shade and habitat for successional plant and animal species. Many pioneers are trees, which you can later cut down and use for fuel, construction, or chip mulch. Some useful pioneers are sycamore, alder, birch, poplar, and nitrogen fixers like tree lupine, locust, and buckthorn.[8]

Toxic areas need to be cover-cropped before being used to grow anything edible. If you suspect toxicity or are unsure of the history of the

A reliable cover-crop recipe includes annual rye grass to improve soil structure and fava beans to fix nitrogen. Mow it a few times while it grows, then till it in or mulch over it and plant your garden.

site, add detoxifying plants to the cover-crop mix. Sudan grass and alpine pennycress are fine detoxifiers, as are many kinds of mushrooms.[9] Pumpkins are also good; you can grow jack-o'-lanterns and carve them up for Halloween. Don't eat detoxifiers, for obvious reasons. When you grow pumpkins or other types of squash for food, do so on clean, fertile soil to avoid ingesting any toxins they may pull up.

Crop Rotations and Fallowing

Monocropping, or growing too much of the same thing, can damage soil by depleting too much of one nutrient or harboring disease and pest populations. Because disease-causing organisms can survive in the soil long after the plants have died, and because different plants use different nutrients, it is important to rotate the types of plants you grow through different parts of the garden.

This is especially true with annual vegetable crops, which are often heavy feeders and can rapidly deplete a fertile area unless a diversity of crops are rotated through. It is equally important to let every piece of ground go fallow (lie unused), or to plant it with cover crops, for at least one growing season every few years. Taking good notes each season helps facilitate good crop rotations, and Eliot Coleman's book *Four-Season Harvest* includes excellent recommendations for specific rotational patterns to use.

Seeds as Fertility

Every inch of topsoil contains hundred of tiny seeds, from the gamut of common weeds to the welcome volunteers that seem to come from nowhere, offering a tasty surprise. Adding seeds to your garden soil is one of the best ways to enhance the fertility of your garden. If you save seeds, put the chaff and leftovers from cleaning them into the compost or use them as mulch, and you will see a rapid increase in the diversity of volunteers that come forth. If you have leftover seeds from the season's growing, empty the packets into your compost or make seed balls, using the recipe in the next chapter.

Above all, remember that there is no one best way to build soil—you must combine and vary your methods according to your specific conditions. Take the time to learn about these conditions and to develop a soil-building strategy that meets your needs. Apply different techniques according to their function and relative location and application, and use varied combinations to optimize opportunities to make your garden grow.

Dirt Worship

We know that organic soil depends on vast, thriving communities of insects and macro- and microorganisms. Yet thousands of products line the shelves of every superstore in the world to help us kill plants, bugs, and bacteria.

Because we fear germs, weeds, and wildness, we poison everything around us, and ultimately ourselves, in our quest for health, purity, and control. Just walk into to any conventional garden center and you will be bombarded with the sickening smell of industrial poison.

If you want to garden you have to get dirty.

Nature, which we are of course a part of, is packed with germs, bugs, and living creatures, all of which have an essential place in holistic, healthy cycles. On our own skin and inside our bodies live thousands of species of bacteria—reproducing, dying, consuming one another, and supporting the bodily functions that keep us alive. If we were to sterilize everything (and don't think Clorox isn't trying), we would surely perish.

Likewise, if we nurture a thriving ecosystem wherever possible, we too will thrive. When we encourage, rather than discourage, the growth of plants, animals, insects, and bacteria, we immediately increase our ability to thrive on planet Earth. We can begin to heal our relationship with nature when we overcome our fear of the dirt.

If you want to garden you have to get dirty. Many nonorganic gardeners try to avoid this—at great expense to themselves and the soil community. They wear gloves and knee pads, spray weeds from ten feet away, set up intricate self-watering systems, and occasionally toss some fertilizer or mulch from a plastic bag onto the soil. People fear the dirt, but rarely will dirt make you sick. On the contrary, exposing ourselves to a diversity of life makes our bodies and immune systems stronger, better able to fight disease.

It is totally possible to grow a lush organic garden without straining your back, but the first step in getting reacquainted with the land, organically, is to overcome our fear of dirty, yucky things and allow ourselves to get grubby with the grub worms. As we conquer our fears we open to nature, and dirty work becomes a real adventure.

Get Planted

Someone once told me that the knowledge of how to thrive on the land is free and available to anyone who puts her hands into the soil. This means we each have the natural instincts to thrive as a species, within the life-web on Earth. In this modern age of fast-paced electronic consumerism and global violence, however, many people have lost touch with their natural instincts. A fun way to regain some of these instincts and get reacquainted with nature is to let a friend plant you in the garden.

Dig a hole one to two feet deep (perhaps this will be one of your test pits from earlier). Now get in the hole with your bare feet. Feel the cool dirt beneath your toes and imagine sending roots deep and wide under the entire garden, all the way to the center of the earth and through to the other side. Use all your senses to hear, smell, taste, see, touch, and intuit the life in the soil. Wrap your mind around the idea that all life depends on this tiny community.

Now have a friend pile in soil all around your feet and ankles, or up to your knees if your hole is deep enough. She should treat you like any other plant—packing the soil in well but not too tightly, adding mulch on top, and watering you in when she's finished.

While she plants you, raise your arms to the sky and imagine your leaves and branches unfolding, expanding toward the heavens. Close your eyes and imagine blooming, setting seeds, wilting, and returning to the earth. When you've had enough ask your friend to dig you out and switch roles. It may seem silly, but this is a truly transformative experience if you give it the chance.

Your relationship with the soil will grow and change as your garden does, and as you become more in tune with the natural cycles of the earth. Now we come to the most colorful, fragrant, and delicious part of the garden—the plants.

5. Plants and Polycultures

First, know food.
From food all things are born,
By food they live,
Toward food they move,
Into food they return.

—Taittiriya Upanishad

Plants for the Future

When you say "garden," most people think first of plants, but all gardens ultimately depend on the quality and quantity of soil fertility and clean water. I don't recommend planting anything except cover crops while you're still designing the basic bed layout and water flow through your garden. I have seen many a garden die because the gardener didn't properly prepare the soil and establish a reliable water supply. Once you've established this basic fertile infrastructure, you are ready to put some plants in the ground!

Whether we live on a farm and grow our own food or live in an apartment in the city and have never planted a seed, we need plants. Plants provide almost all our food and vast amounts of our fuel, fiber, and medicine. Plants filter the air and water and help bind together the cycles of the earth.

Learning about plants inspires an instinctual, natural awareness that leads to increased creativity and mental and physical healing. Plants provide opportunities. The more diverse the plants, the more diverse the opportunities.

Biodiversity and Food Security

The average person in the United States knows over a thousand corporate logos but only ten species of plants.[1] Well, what if we ditch the corporations and learn how to interact with more of the nonhuman species around us? Could we then increase our capacity to steward the land, provide for our needs, and nourish the other species on Earth? You can reap great rewards by growing and knowing just ten species of plants—imagine the benefits of knowing and growing a thousand.

In nature you will rarely find more than a few square feet of just one kind of plant. But in conventional agriculture, and many home gardens, large patches of just one species, also known as monocultures, are the status quo.

The tragic Irish Potato Famine in the mid-1800s occurred because only two varieties of potatoes were growing in the whole country—both susceptible to potato blight, a disease that devastates crops. Both crops failed when the blight hit hard one year, leading to major food shortages nationwide. Farmers did not know or think to diversify their fields—they thought only of the potato that would allegedly provide the best yield, and as a result they lost it all. Ironically, just across the sea hundreds of potato varieties, many of which were probably blight-resistant, were growing all over North, Central, and South America.

There are many lessons to be learned from this type of tragedy: Don't grow just one or two varieties of anything, don't grow the same thing every year, and don't base your food security on just one, two, or even fifty species. If we embrace biodiversity—and more, seek out and perpetuate it—we will directly increase the longevity and quality of our own lives and those of our species.

By encouraging an ever-widening array of plants, insects, and micro-organisms, we can design and create gardens that are beautiful, diverse, functional, and teeming with life. Conversely, if we pillage the gene pool until only those species with immediate economic value remain, then we may destroy our chances of long-term survival on planet Earth.

The importance of diversity in our lives and gardens is apparent in everything we do, and by maximizing plant diversity in our own back-yards we enhance the diversity of our ever-connected planet. So far we have seen how to establish a diversified system for making best use of our water resources, and how to cultivate a diverse soil community. Next, we will see how to establish diverse gardens that will nurture us—and the earth—for genera-tions to come.

Your paradise garden should host as many different plants as possible. But not just any

plants. Many plants will easily outlive the gardener, and all, if left to their own devices, will propagate themselves in perpetuity, given the right conditions at the outset. Therefore, it is crucial to choose each plant and its placement carefully and with a vision of the larger, long-term ecological cycle. Plants are at the core of a healthy bioregional ecology, so let's look at the most ecological ways to bring them into your landscape and your life.

Plant Guilds and Polycultures

One of the most essential strategies for building long-lasting, low-maintenance paradise gardens is the use of plant guilds, or polycultures, which bring together plants that help one another to thrive. Though some gardeners differentiate between the two, with *guild* meaning a specific group of mutually beneficial plants and *polyculture* referring to the larger, diverse garden full of guilds, I will use both terms interchangeably here.

A well-planned polyculture will yield year-round, providing food, seeds, and compost crops for people, wildlife, and microorganisms alike. Because they are so diverse, polycultures tend to yield more and require less maintenance than monocultures, and they are much less susceptible to disease and insect infestation.

Typical vegetable gardens focus on annual or biennial plants, which die after a year or two, but a polyculture will contain from three to fifteen different plants and should include trees and long-lived perennials among the vegetables. This is more akin to nature's gardens, in which the older, larger plants shelter and support the tender annuals.

Like the rest of an organic garden, a plant guild works with nature rather than against it—mimicking nature rather than trying to overpower it. The guild, once established, will take on its own successive cycles, in which the inhabitants regulate themselves. You can then introduce new species when you choose, based on the ongoing needs of the whole garden.

Native tribes in North and South America have long practiced polycultural gardening, such as in the traditional Three Sisters corn-beans-squash combination. In this example corn is the staple crop, a heavy feeder that needs fertile soil. Beans fix nitrogen, add a second crop, and utilize vertical space as they climb up the sturdy cornstalks. Squash provides a third crop as well as a shady ground cover to keep the soil moist. Sometimes a fourth sister is added: cleome, also known as spider flower. Cleome is aromatic with a magnificent flower; these traits attract beneficial pollinators, and the spiny stems deter would-be marauders from ravaging the corn patch.

Revolutionary Japanese farmer Masanobu Fukuoka presents another classic example with his "Natural" farming technique. Fukuoka grows a mix of rice, barley, and clover on his farm and uses complex guilds in his orchard with hundreds of varieties of plants. He grows many varieties of evergreen and deciduous trees including nuts and fruits; adds soil builders such as clover, alfalfa, vetch, lupine, and soybean; and plants grasses and perennials below them, to shelter and support tender annual vegetables.

He also grows multifunctional shelterbelts, sometimes called hedgerows (see the sidebar on page 110), which provide windbreaks, produce food, and attract beneficial insects. He uses no fertilizer or pesticides and a minimum of labor and water, yet his fields yield as much (or more) grain every year as the farms around him. He attributes his success to the wildness and diversity of his gardens.

Fukuoka uses homemade "seed balls" to plant polycultures on large sections of land. These clay pellets are about half an inch in diameter and contain anywhere from three to a hundred varieties of seeds. The clay forms a protective shell to keep birds and insects from eating the seeds before they sprout. Fukuoka believes that we should sow seed balls everywhere, letting the plants decide where to thrive and where to give way to other species.

Use the recipe in the sidebar on page 111 to make your own seed balls. Fun to make with children of all ages, they are the fastest way to introduce a plethora of new species to home and neighborhood gardens, or to disperse and reestablish native plant species in environmentally degraded or barren sites in cities and elsewhere.

A third example of polycultural gardening is called alley cropping. Alley cropping involves growing carefully selected guilds—such as the Three Sisters example above—in lateral strips between orchard rows. Oregon organic farmer John Sundquist uses alley cropping to rotate

Multifunctional Hedgerows
by Jude Hobbs

Multifunctional hedgerows are an excellent strategy to include in an ecological garden as part of whole-system design for self-reliant living. Hedgerows consist of mixed plantings that may include trees, shrubs, low-growing plants, perennials, herbs, and vines. Hedgerows often grow along field borders, fence lines, and riparian zones in either rural or suburban settings. They enhance the beauty, productivity, and biodiversity of the landscape.

Hedgerows act as bank and soil stabilizers and conditioners; animal fodder; nectar sources for bees and other pollinators; habitat for pest predators, mammals, birds, reptiles, and amphibians; windbreaks, shelterbelts, and privacy and sound barriers; and a source of diversified income. In riparian zones hedgerows also provide shade areas that cool the water temperature. They are an ultimate opportunity for biodiversity.

Potential income-producing opportunities of hedgerows include fuel wood, craft materials (such as willow), medicinal herbs, floral materials and dye plants, and seeds, rootstock, and cuttings for propagation. The leaves, berries, nuts, roots, shoots, and fungi are wonderful food sources.

One of the most useful functions of hedgerow plantings is their role as windbreaks. Wind will be affected by a planting that is only three feet high as long as it is of 40 percent density and is sited perpendicular to the wind. It can also reduce home heating costs from 10 to 40 percent. Hedgerow windbreaks can typically reduce open-field wind speeds by 20 to 75 percent at distances of up to ten times their height.

The combination of function and beauty is an essential component of all landscaping. The location and size of the area to be planted will determine hedgerow design, but hedgerows are always longer than they are wide. In placement, a north–south planting direction is ideal but not essential. Whenever possible, arrange hedgerows perpendicular to prevailing winds. Although a single line of trees will provide some benefits, four or more rows of plants are best for windbreaks, water and soil conservation, wildlife habitat, and general biodiversity. When it works for the situation, place plants tallest at maturity in the center row, with shorter ones interplanted between and along the edges.

A diverse selection of plant sizes and characteristics is most beneficial. Through thoughtful observation, the design will match the site and plant characteristics. The elements that influence plant selection, again, are function, location, and size of a fully grown hedgerow. Planting hedgerows also encourages wildlife corridors. As an example, if you are interested in attracting birds, then include deciduous trees as the tallest plant in the hedgerow. Birds find it much easier to land in deciduous trees due to their open form.

Establishing a hedgerow is a long-term commitment. With proper planning and care, it will take approximately four to eight years to establish the planting and thirty or more years for it to reach maturity. However, it is worth the investment. Whether in a rural or urban setting, multispecies plantings provide beneficial opportunities for everyone.

vegetable crops through his diverse fruit-and-bamboo orchard. The orchard alone requires a significant amount of mowing, pruning, and mulching. So rather than grow his annuals in a separate field, he tills beds between the rows of fruit trees and sows seed mixes, with flowers, vegetables, and fiber plants.

How to Make Seed Balls

This is the recipe recommended by photographer and ecological activist Jim Bones, who works with schoolchildren to revegetate damaged natural landscapes. Together they collect seeds, make seed balls, and sow them during the rainy season. The plants take it from there.

Seed balls are the fastest way to plant a wide variety of plants over a large area, and they are great fun to make. Here's the recipe.

Seed mix: This may contain all the seeds for a complete habitat or just a few varieties for a specific combination of crops. Use from three to a hundred different varieties, depending on your goals.

Semi-dry, living compost: Do not use sterilized compost. You need the living organisms to help inoculate the soil. Choose your best stuff from the core of a finished pile and sift it. It is a good idea to mix in additional humus or bacterial inoculants to the compost before mixing up the seed balls.

Powdered red clay: A few pounds is plenty. Do not use gray or white clay—it lacks the important mineral nutrients present in red clay.

Mix one part seed mix, three parts compost, and five parts clay. Stir it around with your hands and make sure all the small clumps are broken up. When the mix is grainy and crumbly, add one to two parts water, a little at a time, until you get about the same consistency as cookie dough. Pinch off a small (half-inch) piece of the "dough" and roll it between your palms until you feel the ball tighten up as the seeds, compost, and clay lock together. Toss the balls onto a tarp and store in a sheltered area for twenty-four hours until dry. Now you can store the seed balls in a cool, dry, dark place for up to several weeks—but it is best to use them as soon as possible, because many of the seeds may begin to sprout immediately.

Seed balls contain anywhere from one to one hundred different kinds of seeds.

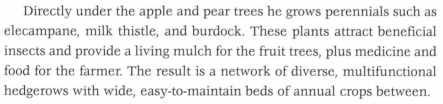

Directly under the apple and pear trees he grows perennials such as elecampane, milk thistle, and burdock. These plants attract beneficial insects and provide a living mulch for the fruit trees, plus medicine and food for the farmer. The result is a network of diverse, multifunctional hedgerows with wide, easy-to-maintain beds of annual crops between.

The benefits are exponential: First, by consolidating the plants, John uses less water and spends less time moving around irrigation equipment. Next, when he weeds the annual beds, he throws the weeds onto the adjacent perennial beds as mulch, which holds in soil moisture and suppresses weeds. Also, because he often lets the strips go fallow for a few years after each use, he is able to maintain soil fertility with a minimum of inputs. He brings in a few cubic yards of mulch a year and sometimes applies small amounts of rock dust, kelp, or compost.

What results is a multilayered rainbow of annual and perennial herbs, flowers, fruits, and vegetables, literally vibrating in the summer sunshine, with bees, hoverflies, hummingbirds, butterflies, and a dozen other types of pollinators. Any time of year there is something to eat, and when local schoolchildren come out for farm tours they see how one person can produce large amounts of good organic food.

Alley cropping is more diverse than a simple Three Sisters–style guild and less chaotic than Fukuoka's junglelike orchard polycultures. The linear alley beds keep the garden organized and allow for easy access for weeding and harvesting. Alley cropping works especially well in a large area, where there is plenty of space for the wide hedge-like rows. The wide paths and semi-straight rows make for easy maintenance, while the mixed crops and perennial fruits keep the row-cropped landscape diverse and interesting.

In a small space such as an urban garden, however, it makes more sense to incorporate these ideas into a tighter, curvier design that includes diverse perennial borders with patches of annual vegetables between. The hedges filter wind and sun for the tender veggies and provide mulch and compost materials. You can also use hedges to create "rooms" within the garden that make it seem like a labyrinthine jungle instead of a boxed-in yard. Alternatively, remove fences between individual urban lots and replace them with diverse "alleys" of fruits, nuts, and perennials.

Alley cropping combines traditional orchard row crops with polyculture techniques to create a diverse, easy-to-manage landscape.

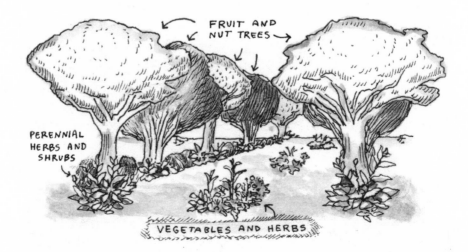

Function, Space, and Time

All these methods employ one important technique: the intentional assembly of plant communities based on the function, form, and life span of the plants. This creates an ecologically harmonious situation in which the plants, soil, gardeners, and related ecosystems all benefit at once. We can use the natural forest as a model for building guilds that layer functional niches within niches in space and time. When we plant several of these guilds together the result is a multifunctional, polycultural garden that thrives in low-maintenance perpetuity.

To understand this, think of the way a forest looks: Small plants and debris cover the ground so that no soil is bare. Larger plants and shrubs grow up against small trees, and tall trees fill in the gaps to create an overstory canopy that is rich in bird and animal life. Vines wrap around the trees and drip across the skyline. Something is always sprouting while neighboring plants die or go dormant for the season, and some kind of food is always available.

The entire forest remains moist and cool even on hot days, yet cold winds and killing frost rarely penetrate the dense growth, so the interior of the forest remains temperate, while sun-loving plants crowd the edges where there is more light. Every nook and niche has something to offer and is home to something or someone, so that every square foot reeks of life and diversity.

An urban application of alley cropping might include replacing fences between lots with orchard rows and planting gardens between.

The forest is nature's masterpiece—the climax toward which all landscapes strive. We can benefit from helping our own gardens toward this goal. By designing gardens that mimic a forest ecology, we can grow edible "food forests" that also yield fuel, fiber, medicine, and habitat and that stack functions, space, and time toward a highly efficient, low-maintenance, beautiful garden ecosystem. We'll start with stacking functions and then see how to stack plants in space and time.

Stacking Functions

To design a polycultural garden, start by filling the functional niches that your garden and lifestyle require. First, make a list of everything you want to grow, focusing on the plants that you need to live—what you like to eat, what flowers you like, what medicinal herbs you use, and so on. This will give you a good idea of what your primary crops will be.

The primary crop is the main thing you want to get out of this particular area of the garden, and its needs are what the rest of the plants in the guild will support. For example, in the Three Sisters guild the primary crop is corn, and the companion crops are beans and squash.

Next to the name of each primary crop, write down what it might need to thrive in your garden. This could include shade, nitrogen, mulch, protection from insects, or anything else that seems pertinent. Support plants, sometimes also called companion plants, can serve a variety of functions—see the list below for examples.

Some people include at least one plant for each function in every guild, while others make specific choices based on their observations in the garden. Remember also to group the plants according to light and water needs and the type of soil they prefer.

Sometimes it helps to make a slip of paper for each plant you have or want, with its function and form, and move the slips around on a map of your garden until it all makes sense. Later you can add successive crops, which will mature and ripen after the first crops are gone. Don't worry too much about how it will all fit together in time and space—we'll get to that soon enough. For now we are concerned with function. Don't plant anything yet; just start listing and assembling plants.

Below is a list of functions a plant or group of plants might serve, with common-name examples for each. Please refer to the resources section for a list of books that contain species lists and lists of specific plant com-

An example of a multilayer, multifunctional polyculture

binations. My purpose here is not to give you lists of plant names to memorize but to help you determine what you want the plants in your garden to do, and to show you how to choose what to grow accordingly.

The plants I recommend as examples are those with which I have a significant amount of personal experience, or which were recommended by experts. The majority of these plants are either perennial or self-seeding, so you need plant them only once; they will naturalize in the garden. This is by no means a complete list; there is no such thing.

For best results grow as many different species as you can find, and don't limit yourself to my (or anyone else's) recommendations. Assemble guilds with the plants you have rather than searching for the "right" plants to use. If you need something to fill a niche but can't find a certain plant, try using another species in the same genus or family that may serve the same function.

A quick aside: I do not include cultivation instructions for any plants. This is because each site, and each microclimate within each site, is so variable that it is impossible to say just how to grow a certain plant. I assume you have some basic gardening skills; if you don't, the resources section offers some excellent books to get you started.

Grow what interests you, and if it doesn't thrive, either move it or change the microclimate. If it dies, there could be any number of causes and influences. Regardless, it's worth trying to grow the plant again, or perhaps a similar one that fills the same niche. Some plants grow best in special climates, but most of the plants listed here are versatile and easy to establish and maintain.

I have also excluded the most common annual edibles, such as cucumbers, lettuce, and tomatoes, assuming that most people will list these as primary crops. I encourage you to mix these familiar annuals with plants that are new to you and grow them all within a fully integrated, multifunctional garden. You may choose to maintain a small, strictly edible kitchen garden up close to the house for those times when you just want to grab a quick salad, but even small gardens grow better with support plants. That being said, let's look at some of the functional roles plants in a polyculture might play.

Edibles

Food is the most common use of a primary crop, but most edibles also serve other functions, and you will find that there is much crossover among the categories here. Plants like to stack functions, and so should we. Most annual vegetables are easy enough to grow; also try perennial edibles such as fruits and berries. More examples: horseradish, rhubarb, pawpaw, kiwi, passion fruit, currants, figs, sea buckthorn, goumi, akebia, and asparagus pea. I have a keen interest in the ancient vegetable crops from the Andes, such as oca, yacon, mashua, canna, and ulluco. These plants come from the same places that gave us tomatoes, potatoes, and peppers, and most of them will do quite well in temperate climates, but they can be difficult to find. Still, it is important to diversify our gardens and diets as much as possible, as well as preserving the foods of other cultures, so it is usually worth the energy to track down unusual seeds and plants that interest you.

Medicinals and Aromatics

It is quite possible to grow and process all or most of our medicine with just a few carefully selected plants. We can grow remedies for colds, headaches, muscle pain, toothache, allergies, and stress, as well as fill our homes with wonderful incenses and potpourri. There are many excellent books on medicinal herbs, so here I will just name a few of my favorite ones, which no temperate garden should be without. These include spilanthes, garlic, echinacea, dandelion, ginkgo, hops, valerian, yarrow, jasmine, mullein, raspberry, and as many plants from the mint (Lamiaceae) family as you can find room for.

Ornamentals

There is no such thing as a plant that is strictly ornamental. Every plant, whether a magnolia, a gardenia, or Grandma's favorite daphne, fills a function other than just being beautiful. It may, for instance, create shade, wildlife habitat, and forage opportunities. Still, don't be afraid to choose to grow something simply because you think it is beautiful.

Some gardeners become obsessed with "practical" function and forget to include beauty and inspiration as essential components. Many edibles and medicinals are extraordinarily beautiful and make great front-yard landscape plants; these include artichokes, hops, blueberries, akebia, and passion fruit. And don't forget to include jasmine (aromatic), magnolia (soil builder/aromatic), rose (edible/medicinal), hawthorn (medicinal/habitat), and bamboo (fiber).

Fiber Plants

Fiber plants add functional diversity to the garden, as well as providing opportunities for moneymaking craft projects. Some fiber plants, such as bamboo, can provide stakes and trellis materials, while others are better for making baskets and sun hats. These include flax, nettle, willow, hazel, cattail, ivy, akebia, blackberry (said to be the very best by a basket-weaver friend), cedar, jute, hemp (illegal in some places but extraordinarily useful), kenaf, hops, vine maple, passionflower, and most tall grasses.

Nitrogen Fixers and Detoxifiers

Sometimes, such as in a cover crop, the purpose of the primary crop is to repair or improve the soil. An ecological garden should have a few areas in cover crops at all times to ensure that we give back what we take from the soil. You should also include in each garden guild at least one nitrogen fixer, such as beans, clover, or a tree legume like locust. You can plant guilds directly into a cover-cropped area by just mulching or digging a small section and putting in the new plants, while leaving the rest of the area in cover crops.

Mulches

In addition to annual cover crops there are many perennial plants that accumulate large amounts of leaf or root mass, which can then be harvested as mulch for neighboring plants. Include several of these in your overall garden design, but because they grow so big and so fast, give them plenty of room so they don't overwhelm smaller plants.

Comfrey is my number one choice: It is easy to grow from just a small root cutting; it can be cut down several times a year for mulch or compost; and it will grow back within a few weeks. It is beautiful and medicinal and makes an excellent summer hedge. Also try elecampane, clover, burdock, mullein, artichokes, sunchokes, nettles, and plenty of deciduous trees (for the leaves).

Habitat Plants

Habitat plants provide shelter and forage for wildlife and are often best placed in the outer edges of a garden, where they can delay and nourish any hungry critters who might otherwise eat your primary crops. Good forage plants include clover, hawthorn, blackberries, and sunchokes. It is also a good idea to create habitat within the garden: places for songbirds to nest, and places for snakes and toads to hide before they come out to eat slugs at night.

In the interests of giving back to nature and nurturing species other than our own, I encourage you to include a healthy dose of habitat plants in your garden design. Start with native species, asking local experts what they recommend. Plant a few coniferous trees, which live and provide habitat for centuries. Overall, the more lush and diverse your garden grows, the more it will become a natural ecosystem of its own, with you, the gardener, as just one of the many living species within.

Insectaries

Many gardeners have an inclination to eliminate every insect from the garden. However, if we strive instead to encourage a healthy and diverse insect population, the insects will mediate one another, and the garden as a whole will benefit. Many plants attract or repel some sort of insect, which means you can choose which insects to encourage or discourage in your garden. There are several common plants, known as insectaries,

Plant pollinator forage, like milkweed, to improve the ecological integrity of your garden.

that are known to be especially useful in this regard, and you should include at least two plants for this purpose in every garden bed.

The first type of insectary brings in ladybugs and predatory wasps that eat garden pests like aphids and cabbage moths. These include yarrow, dill, angelica, lovage, valerian, and most plants in the carrot (Apiaceae) and mint (Lamiaceae) families. Other plants, such as nasturtium, calendula, marigold, chives, and the entire onion family (Liliaceae), either act as traps for harmful insects or excrete substances that repel them.

A third category attracts pollinators like bees, butterflies, and hummingbirds. These plants usually have big, colorful flowers and work especially well when planted next to fruit trees or vegetables that flower around the same time. For example, tulips and other bulbs, when planted in an orchard, will bloom at the same time as the fruit trees and attract insects that pollinate the blossoms. Also, native pollinators such as hoverflies and mason bees like to visit dandelion, sweet pea, Oregon grape, camas, currants, and cinquefoil. Finally, always include the easy-to-grow pollinator favorite, phacelia. If you have issues with bugs or disease, add more compost or spray jauche, and be sure everything has enough—but not too much—water. Also, make sure you have plenty of air circulation in each garden bed.

The Eight-Layer Garden

Once you have assembled lists of the plants you want to grow together, you are ready to place each plant into the appropriate niche in space. To do this, think again of a forest. We can break down the spatial niches in a forest into eight basic layers: roots, ground covers, herbs and vegetables, shrubs, small trees, tall trees, vines, and water plants. By including all eight layers in our garden designs we make best use of available space and other resources and create a multidimensional, forestlike environment.

I will go through each of these layers briefly below, listing a few good examples to start with. Work through each layer on paper, keeping in mind the individual garden beds you will use, and add plants to fill niches as needed. Return to your plant list: Use it to make a chart for yourself like the one in the sidebar on page 121. Choose primary crops from each layer and support plants that fill the layers around. Using this formula, which layers function, form, and time together, will help you establish long-lived garden guilds that mimic and harmonize with natural cycles.

Layer One: Roots

All plants exist in the root layer, but some are grown primarily for their fleshy, edible roots and tubers. Roots are rich in minerals, amino acids, enzymes, and carbohydrates. Many of the plants listed below, such as sunchokes, burdock, and chicory, also produce copious amounts of aboveground foliage and fill more than one layer. Some plants have shallow roots, while others penetrate twenty feet or more into the soil.

As a general rule, assume there is at least as much growth below the soil as you can see aboveground. Try to space your plantings so that roots don't compete for elbow room but instead stack together as they grow down like the layers of branches and foliage above. My favorite root crops include beet, burdock, canna, chicory, daikon, garlic, groundnut, horseradish, oca, potato, rutabaga, turnip, sunchoke, sweet potato, and tulip.

Layer Two: Ground Covers

Ground covers provide a living mulch over soil that, if exposed, would dry out or cover itself with weeds. It is good to get ground covers established when the taller plants are still young and the sunlight still reaches the ground. Once established, most ground covers will spread readily and can be extended to other areas of the garden. Try planting a "napping lawn" of Corsican mint or white clover. Then stretch out on a summer day and enjoy the fragrant, cool leaves against your skin!

The plants listed here tend to be low-growing and will do well underneath perennial herbs and shrubs or around patches of annual vegetables and the other layers of the garden. It is quite possible, and highly recommended, to establish a semipermanent ground cover over most of the perennial garden. Try cinquefoil, clover, Corsican mint, crocus, erba stella, gotu kola, kinnikinnick, nasturtium, oregano, prunella, purslane, spilanthes, strawberries, thyme, violas, violets, and winter squash.

Niche Guide

Layer Function	1. Roots	2. Ground Covers	3. Herbs & Veggies	4. Shrubs	5. Low Trees	6. Tall Trees	7. Vines	8. Water Plants
Edibles	Potato Garlic Rutabaga Canna	Strawberries Sweet potatoes Chickweed	Violets Rhubarb Lettuce Alexanders	Burdock Kale Raspberries Blueberries	Gooseberries Pawpaw Peach Persimmons	Fig Mulberry Cherry Linden	Maple Passion fruit Kiwi Akebia	Lotus
Medicinals	Garlic Echinacea Dandelion Licorice	Spilanthes Wild ginger Mints Oregon grape	Yarrow Dock Mullein	Rose Wormwood Rosemary Raspberries	Magnolia Chaste tree Lilac Albizia	Magnolia Ginkgo Chestnut	Wisteria Hops Jasmine	Bacopa
Fiber Plants	Dock	Most grasses	Nettles Jute Hemp	Blackberries Bamboo	Willow Hazel Maple	Cedar Willow	Akebia Hops	Cattail
Nitrogen Fixers and Detoxifiers	Comfrey Licorice Astragalus Peanuts	Pumpkins Clover Alpine pennycress	Fava Nettles Squash	Oleaster Ceanothus Lupine	Locust Alder Golden rain	Catalpa	Kudzu Pole beans	
Mulches	Comfrey Sunchoke Potato	Ajuga ivy	Burdock Nettles Yarrow	Bamboo	Plum Apple Pear	Maple Empress	Blackberries Kudzu	Lemna Azolla
Habitat		Wood sorrel Cattail Foamflower	Waterleaf Lingonberries	Indian plum Serviceberries Snowberries	Rowan	Oak Mulberry	Honeysuckle Clematis	Water lily
Insectaries	Horseradish Daikon	Ajuga Nasturtium White clover Field peas	Yarrow Dill Marigolds Zinnias	Hydrangea	Lilac	Linden	Honeysuckle	Water hyacinth

Layer Three: Herbs and Vegetables

A large portion of our home remedies and summer annuals fit into this category. Many plants in this layer need partial to full sun, so design plenty of sunny edges around the garden to accommodate them. Most herbs and a few vegetables are perennial and live twenty years or more, but most veggies are annual or biennial, taking up space in the garden for only a short time. This makes them an excellent choice for planting next to perennial plants that are still young. The annuals will shade the ground and provide food for you but will die by the time the perennial needs the space.

A polycultural garden should include many kinds of herbs and vegetables, such as alexanders' greens, amaranth, arugula, beetberry, black-eyed Susan, calendula, cattail, chamomile, chives, cleome, columbine, comfrey, feverfew, good King Henry, jute, kale, lovage, marigold, milkweed, millet, Oregon grape, parsley, poppies, quinoa, sea kale, skirret, soybean, stevia, summer squash, sunflowers, tree collards, valerian, vervain, yarrow, and zinnias.

Layer Four: Shrubs

As with ground covers, establish shrubs when the trees are still young, because many of them need sun to get established. Once established, most shrubs will be relatively drought- and shade-tolerant and will help filter the wind through the low parts of the garden. This is important because though trees provide an excellent windbreak, if there are no shrubs, then the open space creates a cold wind tunnel, which can be rough on tender herbs and vegetables.

Trees and shrubs require less maintenance than annual vegetables, and some can produce hundreds of pound of food each year, with almost no labor once they get established. Most will benefit from regular mulching and pruning. Many of the fiber plants fall into this category, as do most of the small fruits. Try artemisia, artichoke, bamboo, blackberries, blueberries, ceanothus, chrysanthemum, currants, gardenia, goumi, honeysuckle, huckleberry, hydrangea, jujube, lavender, prinsepia, raspberries, rose, rosemary, salal, salvias, and wintergreen.

Layer Five: Small Trees

Here we find many of our large fruits, some nuts, and plants that supply countless other products, such as shade, mulch materials, wood, and wildlife habitat. Small tree crops are the heartbeat of permanent agriculture, and every garden should have at least one, if not several. Most small trees take several years to fruit but will usually outlive the gardener who planted them, providing food for many generations to come.

Layer function, form, and time together.

Start with apple, cherry, dogwood, elder, figs, hazel, hawthorn, pawpaw, pear, persimmon, plum, peach, sea buckthorn, strawberry tree, and willow. Be sure to get a "pollinizer," or mate, for fruits that need it, such as kiwi, akebia, peaches, figs, and some kinds of cherries, apples, and plums.

Layer Six: Tall Trees

Tall trees are the slowest-growing and longest-living layer, with some species living up to five thousand years. Be sure to plan for their size at maturity; grow short-lived herbs and vegetables in the space the trees will later fill. Tall trees provide wildlife habitat, lumber, erosion control, food, medicine, firewood, and windbreaks and create the essential canopy that helps shade and mulch the forest/garden floor. My favorites include chestnut, ginkgo, linden, magnolia, monkey puzzle tree, mulberry, oak, walnut, and yew.

Layer Seven: Vines

Vines add a junglelike feel to the garden and help maximize vertical space, which is especially good for cramped urban settings. The long stems can be used for basketry. If left untrellised, some vines will make a good ground cover. Or use the trellis to create a microclimate by placing it to reflect sun, block wind, or both. You can prune back vines every year or let them climb wild, toward the sun.

Most vines are shade-tolerant but will flower and fruit toward the top, where they can reach the light. Vine brambles make great habitat for spiders and other beneficial insects. Many nitrogen-fixing legumes are climbers, which makes them good choices for the vine layer. The list of beautiful, multifunctional plants for the vine layer includes akebia, bignonia gourds, Chinese yam, grape, hops, hyacinth bean, jasmine, kiwi, luffa, passion fruit, scarlet runner bean, schizandra, and sweet peas.

Layer Eight: Water Plants

Every garden should have at least a container pond, and if you choose to establish an ecological home water system, such as described in chapter 3, you will certainly need an assortment of water plants for your swales, ponds, and slime monster. These plants cleanse and aerate the water and provide shade, food, and habitat for fish, waterfowl, and humans. Try bacopa, duckweed, lotus, wasabi, watercress, water hyacinth, water iris, water lily, rushes, cattails, horsetail, canna, and some chrysanthemums. If you design each guild carefully, you will be able to include many different plants in every microclimate. Always keep in mind that the design of your system should be site-specific and make use of available resources. The plants and methods in this book, even if used exactly as described, will work on some sites and fail on others. Experiment with different ideas, techniques, and philosophies, then develop a system that works best for you.

Again, always be sure to give each plant plenty of elbow room. Clotted areas provide the moist, sticky conditions many harmful pests need to thrive, and when plants are too crowded they compete for nutrients, which weakens them and makes them vulnerable to insects and disease. So water, weed, mulch, and prune when necessary. The most common mistake gardeners make is planting things too close together—remember how big the plants will be at maturity, and make sure they have the space they need.

Layers in Time

Many people think of the "growing season" as being only from April to October or so, usually coinciding with the last and first frost dates in their bioregion. But plants grow and change throughout the year, and just as the natural forest produces food throughout the year, so should our home gardens.

Many gardens sit out the winter as bare ground, but this is neither aesthetically appealing nor productive. Sure, summer is the peak season for most gardeners, but in many climates you can have food and flowers year-round. Use niches in time, combined with niches in space and function, to deepen and diversify the productivity of your garden.

To incorporate time niches into the guild, go back to your list of primary crops and support plants, and add notes regarding harvesttime according to your own climate. Choose plants that fruit at different times of the year. For example, most nut and fruit trees yield in the autumn, when summer vegetables have finished, and brassicas (broccoli, kale, and their like) and salad greens grow well in the off-season, when deciduous leaves have fallen and summer shade gives way to cool winter sun.

Note where and when existing plants will yield room for the next crop, think ahead to what you might grow next, and write it down. Include plenty of plants that will perpetuate themselves by either dropping seeds in the garden or spreading underground, and include their future offspring in your long-term vision.

You can also extend the growing season for tender vegetables by using greenhouses and cold frames to protect plants from frost. Use recycled wood to build a simple greenhouse off the south side of your house and reap the rewards of having a sunny, warm indoor garden throughout the year. I highly recommend that you establish some sort of greenhouse space near your garden, and it is quite possible to do so with little or no cash investment. However, building greenhouses is a larger topic than we have room for here, so please refer to the resources section for more information.

Build a simple greenhouse off the south side of your house to increase your capacity to grow food year-round.

Make small mobile greenhouses, or cloches, from heavy wire mesh and clear plastic.

GARDEN CLOCHE

If you aren't ready for a greenhouse, or if you just want to extend the season at multiple points, use cloches—little miniature greenhouses that cover your garden beds and protect plants from frost. You can build a simple cloche out of some sturdy wire mesh and a piece of clear plastic (actual greenhouse plastic is best). Just poke the mesh into the ground along the edges of your garden bed to make a hoop over the bed, lay the plastic over the top, and weight it down with some rocks. Or cut the bottom off a few gallon-sized milk jugs and use them to cover individual plants. All types of greenhouses and cloches get good and hot inside, so water often.

Making Plants from Plants

As you develop your polycultural paradise garden, you will need to acquire and propagate a lot of plants. Set up a nursery area in a sheltered spot where you have daily access to water and use the tips below to multiply the plant material you bring home.

Almost every plant will grow from root divisions or stem cuttings and will make seeds from there. Look for cuttings throughout your neighborhood and in parks, nurseries, and botanical gardens. Most people will not mind or even notice a few snips here and there; some gardeners I know take a pair of clippers and a few envelopes wherever they go.

Here are a few tips for making plants from plants, using vegetative propagation:

Find or make a propagation box that is at least four inches deep. Mix up a rooting medium using nutritionally neutral substances such as perlite, vermiculite, or pumice. I like to mix all three. Some people just use sand or pea gravel. Experiment and see what works best for you. The medium should be light and fluffy. Don't use compost, because the microorganisms will think the cuttings are food scraps and try to decompose them.

The purpose of the rooting medium is to facilitate air- and water flow for the rootless cuttings and to make room for the new roots as they grow. It is usually not at all necessary to sterilize the rooting medium; you can even reuse it by just rinsing it out and spreading it in the sun for a few hours, then putting it back into the propagation box and starting again. If disease or rot persists, however, compost the old stuff and start fresh.

Mix up a batch of willow tea, which will help prevent rot and encourage quick sprouting. Gather some wild willow branches, chop them into two-inch sections, and stuff them into the bottom of a watering can. Keep the can full and use it to dip the cuttings in and water them as they grow. The willow cuttings in the watering can will also sprout, which is fine, but if the willow water starts to stink, make a fresh batch.

Take cuttings from plants that are dormant, usually more than two months before or after they flower. Once they have budded it is best to wait until after seeds mature to take cuttings. Avoid taking cuttings when the weather is very hot, as they will most likely wilt and die.

For stems, take cuttings that are three or four nodes long; remove the leaves from the bottom two nodes and trim the edges of the rest. Roots also have nodes, sometimes on tuberous chunks, in the form of eyes, and sometimes along the root itself, like little joints. Root divisions should also have three or four eyes or nodes. Most cuttings will keep in a moist paper towel or newspaper in the fridge for up to several weeks, but it is best to use them right away.

Make a hole in the rooting medium with something besides the cutting, such as a chopstick. This keeps the tender cutting from bruising on the way in. I stick the chopstick in, move the medium aside, then drop the little cutting in and gently tamp the hole closed. For root divisions bury the whole cutting (roots). For stems put the bottom two nodes below the soil surface and leave the trimmed leaves on top.

Always use a very sharp, clean knife or scissors for every stage of propagation. A little peroxide on a clean cloth works fine for wiping tools. Some people prefer alcohol, which is highly toxic to plants and should be well rinsed off before use.

Water the cuttings from below by placing the box in a reservoir of

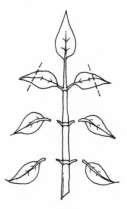

Most perennials are easy to propagate with four-node cuttings.

water, and mist occasionally from above with a spray bottle full of willow water. It is possible to make a humidity chamber using plastic and drip irrigation, but I don't find it to be necessary for most plants. Keep the cuttings evenly moist until new roots form, then transplant carefully into sifted compost.

Equality Begins in the Garden

macrocosms and microcosms

When I started working on this book I asked my mentor, Alan Kapuler, an expert organic grower, to name his top ten favorite plants. He said he didn't have any favorites, so I told him to list the ten plants that no temperate garden should be without. He laughed and told me it was like asking him to name his favorite finger. He said, "All of them," and then rattled off a list including crabgrass, barnyard millet, soybeans, and marijuana, indicating that the first two are essential to pull out and compost, while the last two are critical for health and nutrition.

He reminded me that, just as chemical poisons stall the natural cycles that build and maintain soil fertility, our own attachment to the idea that one plant is better than another stalls the creative cycle that builds and maintains fertility of thought and action. Again, the primary emphasis is on diversity. Use diverse strategies, experiment with diverse plant material, work with a diversity of people, and your projects, both in and out of the garden, will undoubtedly thrive.

By embracing diversity in our attitudes and in our gardens we can enhance the liveability, and longevity, of our communities and gain a deeper understanding of nature's message: All beings are equal and interconnected. Through developing a love and reverence for plants and other living things we can create peaceful, functional ecosystems, and thus welcome ourselves home, to paradise.

To Prune or Not to Prune?

If you grow fruit trees or woody perennials, you will need to decide how to care for them. It is always a good idea to mulch around fruiting shrubs or trees to provide them with nutrients lost in the harvest. But what about pruning? As you consider how intensively you want to manage your landscape, it helps to consider death as integral to the cycle of life. When we try to grow our food as naturally as possible, we feel a certain relief that we are following the ways of nature rather than attempting to dominate or control it.

When a plant sheds limbs, leaves, flowers, and seeds, a life cycle perpetuates itself. We humans are simply a part of that process, and we can benefit from tuning in to the cycle as a whole rather than trying to make it work for our needs alone. So when you're asking the question *Should I prune my grapes?* try to see yourself as the willing servant to the garden, not the master.

Trees prune themselves in a variety of ways. If a tree is too dense, disease may kill a branch. If the fruit load is too heavy, a limb may break off. Fire, wind, and floods are also natural agents of pruning. Left to themselves, trees often regulate themselves better than we do. In fact, most fruit trees will grow and produce quite well if never pruned. Often, the need for pruning is the result of unskilled pruning in the past. Fukuoka experimented with letting older trees go wild and found that the more a tree has been pruned, the more likely it is that it will need pruning in the future.

The reasons to prune are as many and varied as types of trees. The most common ones are disease prevention, fruit production, creating access to fruit, tree size, and aesthetics. Pruning removes dead or dying branches and allows for better light and air penetration, which improves the health of the tree and the quality of the fruit.

Some trees, such as figs and cherries, simply do not need pruning, and unless you need to repair damage from a windstorm or a bad pruning job, you can let well enough alone. A simple rule of thumb is to let the tree dictate its own form. By working with the tree's natural tendencies you can encourage a healthy, fruit-bearing tree that requires less work and pruning in the long run. Here are some basic guidelines to help you prune as naturally as possible.

Pruning Tools

You will need hand clippers for the small stuff, loppers for branches up to half an inch in diameter, and a small curved saw for branches up to three inches; if you'll be performing major surgery, a bow saw is helpful. I really don't recommend chain-saw pruning, and while long-handled or pole pruners can make it easier to reach those high branches, the novice pruner will always do a better job from close up. Get up in the tree and have a look!

Sharp tools are essential. Just like humans, trees heal much better when cut with sharp, clean blades. A sharpening stone should be included in your tool kit, and many people carry rubbing alcohol and a rag to wipe their blades between trees, preventing the spread of disease.

Timing

The most common time to prune is late winter/early spring. Spring pruning encourages growth, and fall pruning discourages growth. In the spring prune before the sap is running so that the tree does not waste energy growing branches that will just be cut off. Spring is the best time to work on the overall structure of the tree and encourage growth in desirable areas. This is the time for major surgery, while the tree has the entire growing season to recover. The tree will send its energy to the places where you made cuts to heal them, and often "suckers" will sprout from those points. This is why, if you go out to your apple tree in the spring and cut off all of the vertical suckers, you will just have to do the same thing next year.

Some results can be achieved only by pruning in the summer or fall. However, it is generally not a good idea to prune heavily just before a major frost, because the tree will not have a chance to recover in time to withstand the extreme cold. Late-summer or fall pruning allows the cuts to heal over before the strong push of spring and does not encourage suckering. This is a good time to remove those pesky suckers, and if you wait until after harvest, no fruit will be wasted. It is always a shame to cut off a branch that is loaded with little unripe fruits!

Making a Proper Cut

This is very important. It is possible to kill a tree with bad pruning, and the most common cause of this is a bad cut that becomes infected. For small branches, cut back either to the branch junction or to within one-quarter inch of a dormant bud. The new shoot will grow in the direction the bud is facing. Larger branches are usually cut back to the branch junction.

Cut right up to, but not into, the branch collar, which is the raised ridge in the bark near where the branch comes out of the mother branch or tree trunk. Cell division occurs rapidly in this collar, sending out healing tissue to cover the wound. Do not cut off any portion of the branch collar, but don't leave a big stub either. Try to find a balance.

Cuts should be clean. Tears in the bark of a tree are very vulnerable to infection, so it is often a good idea to make an undercut one-third of the way through the branch from below, then saw the rest of the way through the branch from above. If you do have a tear, try to clean it up by making a new cut.

Pruning Steps

1. *Stand back and observe the tree as a whole.* Repeat this step every three cuts to keep a perspective on the overall form. Yes, this means you may be climbing into and out of the tree several times during the pruning process.
2. *Take out the "D's," in order:* Dead, Dying, Diseased (moss and lichen are not disease, but fungus often is), Damaged, Dangerous (like limbs about to fall on the house), Doubling (two branches growing out of the same spot or rubbing on each other), and Deranged (bad angles, branches twisted around others). Stand back and look at the tree. If after removing the D's you have cut around a third of the tree, you are done. Wait until next year to make any more corrective changes.

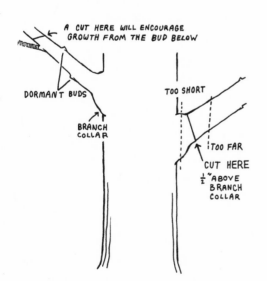

Use proper cuts when pruning to help keep trees from getting diseases later on.

3. *Choose your leaders, or main vertical structural branches.* These will form the basic structure of the tree and can range in number from one to five. Choose vigorous, healthy branches that will support good horizontal branches. Allow ample space between the leaders and remove any other vertical branches. Stand back and look at the tree.

4. *Choose your horizontals (branches growing from the trunk of the tree at an angle greater than forty-five degrees).* These form the "scaffold" of the tree and will support most of the fruit. Choose healthy branches with good fruiting spurs. Choose branches that give an overall desired shape and allow easy harvesting. The lowest scaffold should be at least three feet above the ground, for good airflow. There should be one to five feet between each level of scaffolding. Stand back and look at the tree again.

5. *Thin for air circulation.* Remove any horizontal branches growing toward the center of the tree. Take out up to half of the vertical suckers, leaving the ones that fill gaps in the tree. Remember that these branches will eventually be weighted down with fruit and will fall into a horizontal position, so make sure there is room for them. Again, stand back and look.

6. *Finally, prune twigs to encourage horizontal growth.* You can often change the direction of a branch by pruning back to a bud that faces in the direction you prefer.

Remember, never cut off more than one-third of the tree in any one year. This includes the trunk, so choose your cuts carefully. It is generally better to make a few large cuts than many smaller cuts, to minimize the shock to the tree. Be patient and watch how the tree responds to your cuts throughout the year, so that you can make better decisions next time.

Eat the Weeds

In addition to pruning you will also most likely need to do some weeding. Sometimes this feels like playing God—deciding who lives and who dies is no small matter—and sometimes it feels like war. But weeds are not the enemy, and a warlike attitude will not help us toward a peaceful culture.

Take a moment to ponder the relationship of these plants to other living things around, now and in the future. Your weeds provide forage and habitat for insects, birds, and animals, as well as shelter for the seedlings of other plants. They cover the bare soil and bring moisture and soil life closer to the surface, where they can do their good work. Weeds should be respected for their tenacity, persistence, and versatility and looked upon more as volunteers than as invaders.

Throughout its life every plant engages in a complex relationship with the ecosystem that produced it. We humans can benefit greatly by participating in this cycle rather than trying to dominate it. We may indeed gain much wisdom by following nature's tendencies.

We saw in the preceding chapter that weeds can give us valuable information about our soil conditions. In addition, many common weeds are edible and/or medicinal. These wild foods are rich in vitamins and minerals and can be eaten raw or cooked or processed into tea or tincture and used as medicine. Some are delicious; others are bitter and eaten to aid digestion.

Most of the common vegetables we enjoy in our salads, such as lettuce, carrots, parsley, and mustard, were once considered weeds. Their wild kin are what we call weeds today, but why not let them act as volunteer herbs and vegetables and participate in the evolving polycultures? What better plants for a paradise garden than these hardy, self-sown gifts from the soil?

On this, paradise gardener Joe Hollis writes, "We gardeners go on making the land say 'beans' (or 'roses,' or 'lawn') because that's what we do, what gardening is. . . . But could gardening be more of a dialogue, the land getting to say what it wants to, too? It says such interesting things, all year long: shepherd's purse, creasy greens, poppies, violets, lamb's quarters—the way to hear their message is to ingest them."[2]

Wild plants contain more nutrients than many cultivated varieties and can add new flavor to a tired-out recipe. See the sidebar on page 136 for a list of common edible weeds and their uses. Depending upon which part of the plant you use, you can prepare edible weeds in a number of ways. Often the sweetest parts are the new leaves, which can be steamed or eaten raw. Some roots, such as burdock and horseradish, are also good raw when peeled and grated.

If the plants are older, or tough or bitter, chop them up and dry them in a food dehydrator or on a drying rack like the one described in the next chapter. Mix in tastier herbs such as peppermint or fennel, and use the blend for tea. I like to make what I call Yum-Yum: Mix up stinging nettle, dandelion, and dock with your favorite culinary herbs, such as oregano, basil, parsley, and thyme. Toss in a few tablespoons of powdered sea salt and store the mixture in a jar with a tight-fitting lid. Sprinkle Yum-Yum in guacamole, salads, omelets, potatoes, tacos, pasta sauce, and more. This way you get all the nutrients in the wild plants without the bitter taste.

Some plants are deadly poisonous, so invest in a good book on wild edibles and be sure to correctly identify each species before you eat it. As with any new food, try just a little bit first, then wait a day or two to see whether you have an allergic reaction. Chances are, everything will be fine, but better safe than sorry!

Pull out poisonous plants and compost them in a nice hot pile for a few months. Compost neutralizes most poisons and toxins (except chlorine-based chemicals), so a few poisonous plants won't hurt anybody once they break down.

Invasion of the Garden Snatchers

So what about bindweed? What about kudzu? What about water hyacinth and butterfly bush, English ivy and quack grass? How are we supposed to grow wild, lush, diverse gardens, full of every kind of plant we can find, without some of them just taking over? From naturalists to conservationists to hobby gardeners and orchid thieves, the global debate over introducing, displacing, and cultivating tenacious nonnative plants rages on.

Most "invasive" plants are pioneer species that thrive on disturbed soil. By trying to eradicate them with poisons and machines we disturb the soil even further and encourage more pioneer plants to come in and try to repair the damage.

Of course we should conserve pristine ecosystems, but with our constant disruption of natural ecosystems, through growth and industry, humans create conditions for invasive plants to thrive. Unless we change our actions and attitudes toward land use in general, waging war on "exotic" plants is just another futile diversion from the real issues.

Nature and the plants were moving slowly around the earth, replacing one another, interbreeding, and feeding insects, animals, and bacteria, for millennia before humans existed. Our own lives now depend on the varied functions they serve. It is perfectly natural for plants to succeed one another, and our national resources would be better spent preventing the real threats to the wild earth—namely industrial development, resource extraction, and industrial pollution.

In the United States and several other countries narrow attitudes about successful exotic plants have led to widespread and potentially catastrophic eradication plans. In February 1999 the National Invasive Species Council formed. In 2001 it released the National Management Plan, and as recently as 2003 it introduced several new weed control acts to the House and Senate mandating the control and removal of thousands of species of wild, edible, and medicinal plants across the nation.[3]

California seedsman J. L. Hudson raised the alarm about a proposed "White List" several years ago. This White List, sometimes called the "clean list," "comprehensive screening," or "risk assessment," would contain only the handful of species approved for existence on U.S. soil. The proposed list excludes more than 99 percent of the world's fauna and flora, including many species native to North America, and does not allow for any new discoveries or introductions without a prohibitively expensive approval process.[4]

While it makes sense to want to protect native ecosystems, many of these new laws offer more benefit to herbicide companies than they do to nature. Not coincidentally, these chemical companies are behind much of the anti-weed legislation.

However, if each community takes the thoughtful stewardship of its own watershed seriously, there is no need for wide-sweeping government policy, and we can keep ourselves from the grips of the corporate profit-mongers who push such unnecessary legislation under the guise of environmental stewardship. We can develop localized, nontoxic removal programs and can find uses for the masses of food and organic matter produced by these plants.

I am of the opinion that the most invasive species on this planet is *Homo sapiens sapiens*, which, along with the cockroach, housefly, and carpenter ant, has spread across nearly every bioregion in the world, leaving pollution, disease, and extinction in its wake. I would much rather see a rolling green landscape of edible buckthorn, Himalayan blackberries, and brilliant, blooming morning glory than the vast expanse of concrete and wafer-board

Edible Weeds of the Northwest U.S.[5]

Common and Botanical Names	Parts Used	Nutritional/Medicinal Information	Comments
Alfalfa (*Medicago sativa*)	Young leaves, flowering tops, sprouted seeds, tea.	Vitamins A, C, D, E, and K, plus minerals.	Good steamed; common in Latin American cuisine.
Blackberry, raspberry (*Rubus* spp.)	Fruits are edible raw, leaves in tea or as a sprinkle. Jams are acidic and easily canned and stored.	Vitamin C, malic and oxalic acids, tannins.	Good tonic for overall health; dozens of edible relatives.
Burdock (*Arctium lappa*)	Leaves, roots, and stems. Good fried or in sushi; used for beer.	Calcium, magnesium, phosphorus, inulin.	Biennial. Harvest during the first winter.
Chickweed (*Stellaria media*)	Leaves, stems, and flowers are delicious any time of year.	Vitamin C, iron.	Contains saponin; wash well before eating. Nutty.
Cleavers, bedstraw (*Galium aparine, G. verum, G. triflorum*)	Young leaves in salad, fruit as a coffee substitute.	Contains asperuloside; used for weight loss.	Used to curdle milk; good for baby geese, as a tonic.
Dandelion (*Taraxacum officinale*; several other species are also edible)	Whole plant raw, cooked, dried, or in tea; roots as a coffee substitute. Flower buds in wine or pickled.	Proteins, starch, inulin, calcium, phosphorus, tannin, and vitamins A, B1, B2, C, and E, plus minerals.	Used since prehistoric times as a bitter to aid digestion. Four times as nutritious as lettuce.
Dock, sorrel (*Rumex* spp.)	Leaves, stems, petioles; best eaten as a sprinkle or as a tea with milk.	Rich in vitamins A, B1, B2, and C, iron, chlorophyll, tannins, and oxalic acid.	Many edible relatives; roots have been used as a blood purifier.
Horsetail (*Equisetum* spp.)	Whole plant; used in tea to treat fungal disease.	Plant is almost 100% silica.	Difficult to cultivate but easy to find.
Lamb's-quarter (*Chenopodium album*)	Leaves raw, steamed, or dried. Seeds boiled as a cereal; wash well to remove saponin.	Rich in protein, vitamins A, B1, B2, and C, niacin, calcium, phosphorus, and iron.	Many edible relatives, such as *C. quinoa* and *C. bonus-henricus*.
Lemon balm (*Melissa officinalis*)	Leaves and flowering tops are excellent for tea or tincture.	Used as a calming herb.	Loved by children and baby chickens alike.
Mallow, cheeseweed (*Malva* spp., especially *M. crispa*)	Flower buds, flowers, and unripe fruits raw, cooked, or pickled; very young roots and leaves raw, steamed, or dried.	Vitamins A, B1, B2, and C, minerals, and mucilage.	Flavor and edibility vary widely among species. Beautiful flowers.
Milk thistle (*Silybum marianum*)	Young shoots, stems, and leaves raw or steamed. Boiled roots.	Used as a liver tonic.	Crunchy seeds are good fresh off the plant.
Miner's lettuce (*Montia* spp.)	Raw leaves, stems, and seeds.	Vitamin C.	One of the best wild salads.
Nettle (*Urtica* spp., especially *U. dioica, U. urens*)	Young shoots and leaves steamed, raw, or dried. Leaves for beer and sun tea. Harvest only before flowering.	Very rich in iron and protein, also fats, vitamins A and C, chlorophyll, tannin, mucilage, and gallic and formic acids.	Makes a great pesto. Wilt or steam to take away the sting.
Pigweed, amaranth (*Amaranthus* spp.)	Young leaves and stems raw or steamed; seeds as a cereal.	Proteins, vitamins A and C, and minerals.	Some species' seeds pop like popcorn.
Purslane (*Portulaca* spp.)	Leaves raw, steamed, or pickled. Good in winter.	Vitamins A, B, and C; rich in iron and mucilage.	Adds a tangy bite to salads; good in omelets.
Shepherd's purse (*Capsella bursa-pastoris*)	Very young leaves and roots raw or cooked; seeds as a spice.	Tannins, organic acids, bursin, minerals, and flavonoids.	Used to stop bleeding and relieve kidney pain.

housing developments and homogeneous stands of genetically modified corn that threaten to cover the fertile earth today.

Nevertheless, please do think long and hard before introducing new species to a bioregion. If you're living in it, it's not a pristine ecosystem, but you probably don't want to be responsible for clogging a major salmon run with imported water plants or wiping out a natural orchid population with aggressive, nonnative vines.

Still, you also don't want to accidentally eradicate a useful herb that thrives in your garden, so as a general rule never pull a plant you don't recognize. Every pulled weed and every planted seed should be a result of prolonged, thoughtful planning based on careful observation and ecological ethics. This is especially important when working in or near wild or semi-wild places.

Generally, in urban or semi-urban environments the native ecosystem is covered with concrete, exotic ornamentals, and nonnative grass lawns. In this instance anything goes when it comes to plants. Grow as many different things as you can find; the better they survive, the better for everyone.

Discouraging Unwanted Plants

While I advise against totally eradicating any species from your garden, there will always be a few that try to take up more than their fair share of the space. There are several ways to remove these plants while still cultivating an attitude that embraces, rather than hates or fears, nature and diversity.

Try to see weeding as an act of mediation rather than expulsion, and embrace the notion that all species have equal rights to survival. Chances are, they are there for a reason. You may not be able to see this reason, but in the interests of biodiversity it is important to make at least a little bit of room for everyone.

Find out as much about the plant as you can. Ask yourself, *What's it called? Where's it native? What are its uses? What conditions does it thrive in?* Maybe there is a use for it that you didn't know or think of before. If not, most weeds will go away if you cover them with a thick mulch or just yank them out and toss them in the compost.

If you pull something out and it keeps coming back, replace the plant with a species in the same niche that you prefer over the weed.

For example, if buttercup is taking over, try another spreader such as strawberries, cinquefoil, violets, or gotu kola. Most plants need certain nutrients to thrive, and if we plant a lot of something else that needs the same nutrient, it may outcompete the unwanted plant.

If that doesn't work, try changing the microclimate. Make a shady spot into a sunny one or vice versa by trimming or planting some trees. Heat up the area by building a reflective, south-facing wall. Amend the soil to change the pH level. Drain a moist area or flood a dry one. Chances are, your unwanted plant will not continue to thrive in totally different conditions.

Biodynamic gardeners collect the seeds of undesirables and burn them, then scatter the ashes around the garden. This seems to work well when done every year, perhaps due to cosmic messages, or just to the fact that you are collecting the seeds rather than letting them fall to the ground.

Sometimes plants that are weeds in one garden are absent in another, and you might be surprised at how easy it is to find people who want the plants and seeds that you don't. It may be worth the effort to pot up some of those extra plants and take them to the next seed swap to give away.

Whatever level of weed management you choose, please never spray herbicides. They are carcinogenic to you and everyone else, run off through the soil to poison waterways, and radically upset the natural, successional abundance that your garden is attempting to provide.

Let's not forget an essential piece of the ecological garden puzzle: the seeds. You need seeds to grow plants, and in many ways seed saving is the key to maintaining a biologically and economically diverse and thriving community. The next chapter will discuss the whys and hows of this ancient and essential tradition.

6. Seed Stewardship

On a Seed
This was the goal of the leaf and the root,
For this did the blossom burn its hour.
This little grain is the ultimate fruit.
This is the awesome vessel of power.
For this is the source of the root and the bud . . .
World unto world unto world remolded.
This is the seed, compact of God,
Wherein all mystery is enfolded.

—Georgie Starbuck Galbraith[1]

The reason for alarm and concern about the loss of native strains is the irreplaceable nature of the genetic wealth. The only place genes can be stored is in living systems; either living branches such as the budwood of apple trees or in the living embryos of grain and vegetable seeds. The native varieties become extinct once they are dropped in favor of introduced seed. That extinction can take place in a single year if the seeds are cooked and eaten instead of saved for seed stock. Quite literally, the genetic heritage of a millennium in a particular valley can disappear in a single bowl of porridge.

—Dr. Garrison Wilkes, professor of biology
at the University of Massachusetts[2]

A Heritage Lost

Organic food might seem like a new fad, but many of the agricultural practices go back thousands of years. For millennia humans have been eating roots and berries, returning to their favorite harvesting spots every year. People weeded, mulched, built compost, and saved seeds, selecting the varieties that grew best in their fields. This was the beginning of traditional plant breeding, and today people all over the world still practice careful planning and selection to develop the crops that work for them.

Until just a few generations ago saving seeds was something almost everyone knew how to do. It was as much a part of life as eating and raising children. A vast diversity of agricultural seeds were grown and saved again and again, passed from mother to daughter and all around the community, carried in the pockets of travelers and traded for other species, different varieties, new kinds of food for next year's table.

In the past two centuries seeds have become another form of capital—to be owned, manipulated, and profited from, rather than stewarded and shared for the benefit of all. Now most farmers and gardeners get their seeds from seed companies and government agencies.

Many traditional varieties have been patented by corporations and profit-minded individual growers. This rush to the plate for the ownership of living heritage is an insult to the right of all living things to be free, and it is a fallacy at best when it comes to seeds. Most organic seed growers agree that the best varieties are always those bred locally, recently, and with specific bioregional conditions in mind. Each bioregion, each farm, each small garden plot will have its own unique circumstances and will produce the seeds that do the best in that microclimate.

The privatization of life on any scale should and must be resisted, and at this point one of the best ways to protect seeds from patent is to grow them, publish detailed descriptions online and in catalogs, and give them away or sell them to other growers. Once they are in the public domain they are still at risk of colonization by the corporate culture, but at least the good traits have been spread around for individual growers to use and develop.

In addition to privatization, many more species and varieties go extinct each year because of contamination from genetically modified organisms, the industrialization of agriculture, and widespread habitat destruction. We have lost most of the garden seed diversity it took ten thousand years to develop. For example, fewer than 6 percent of the garden bean (*Phaseolus vulgaris*) varieties listed by the USDA as commercially available in 1903 still exist today in the germplasm collection of the U.S. National Seed Storage Laboratory.[3]

This is typical of all vegetables. In the past hundred years, with the advent of large-scale industrial agriculture, we have lost about 95 percent of the garden seed diversity that was available in the early 1900s.[4] Even less is actually accessible to the public via seed catalogs and other commercial sources.

Hundreds of plant and insect species go extinct every day, and we can assume that the same trend is happening below the surface in the soil communities. Extinction is real, based on the disappearance of genetic material, and human life depends upon a deep diversity of non-human species to survive. In short, what we have is *all* we have as far as genetics is concerned. Barring any miraculous discovery of new genes flowing out of a magic spring somewhere, when it's gone, it's gone forever, and if much more of it goes then so do we.

Hundreds of plant and insect species go extinct every day.

Saving Seeds, Saving Ourselves

The National Plant Germplasm System (NPGS), a project of the USDA, holds seeds and other propagative material (vegetative cuttings and tissue cultures) for plants from around the world. Samples are made available to any qualified researcher, even backyard breeders and conservationists. The folks at the NPGS strongly encourage collaboration: They want you to characterize, evaluate, and otherwise document what you get, and to send them back some seeds after the harvest.

Sadly, many of these seeds are lost every year due to inadequate funding and irresponsible stewardship. According to the USDA's Agricultural Research Service, most of the seed samples brought into the United States before 1950 were lost "due to inadequate knowledge and lack of suitable storage facilities."[5] And now, because of poor finances, bad politics, and paranoia about "invasive" species, plant expeditions for the purpose of conservation and discovery are fewer, farther between, and more strictly regulated than ever.

Not that current large-scale conservation efforts should be overlooked. Indeed, because the future of public-access seed conservation projects seems surely doomed in the face of budget cuts, gene patents, and irrational politics, it is essential that we get as many of those seeds into the public domain as possible.

We must also acknowledge that such important work needs to be shared. It cannot be left up to a small fraction of humankind to safeguard the genetic diversity for all. Stewardship must occur on all scales, from neighborhood seed swaps to bioregional associations to international collaborations.

The seeds we have today are the foundation of tomorrow's world, and by saving them we save ourselves. If we embrace the need for conservation and integrate seed saving into our garden cycles, then we still have a fighting chance. Through saving seeds and sharing plants and information, we can begin to honor and perpetuate, rather than marginalize and endanger, nonhuman species and create a thriving natural culture.

All responsibility aside, I can honestly say that seed saving is one of the most rewarding experiences I have ever had. More than most things, saving seeds feels like it is worth doing. The finer arts of seed saving seem to be worth knowing, and the seeds themselves are certainly worth having, storing, and sharing. Seed saving is possibly the most important piece of the human ecology puzzle. Seed savers reap a natural education and a deep spiritual empowerment unavailable anywhere else. Homegrown seeds are free and tend to be more vigorous and naturally adapted to your garden site. So why not give them a try?

Conservation at the Grassroots Level

Luckily seed saving has managed to keep a few strongholds in the hearts and gardens of the people. Seed Savers Exchange (SSE) is an Iowa-based organization boasting eight thousand members who work together to keep traditional heirloom varieties from extinction and to develop new strains for the future. SSE lists more than eleven thousand varieties of garden vegetables in its annual yearbook, hosts an annual gathering, and offers a public online catalog.

Seed saving is an ancient art form that is crucial to our survival as a species.

Several nonprofit organizations access and distribute seeds with the express intent of protecting and perpetuating public-domain varieties. These include Native Seeds/SEARCH in Arizona, the Bay Area Seed Interchange Library (BASIL) in Berkeley, the Organic Seed Alliance, and Seeds of Diversity in Canada. Each of these organizations has its own angle, such as conserving native food plants, developing agricultural seeds, or perpetuating local food security.

Through facilitating the exchange of seeds and information, these projects mediate a flow of genetic resources into the hands of organic gardeners like you and me, enabling us to participate in conservation while growing lush, diverse gardens at home.

Kinship Gardening

Unfortunately, just saving the seeds of our favorite vegetable varieties is not enough. We must seek out and preserve as many different types of plants as possible, regardless of their perceived economic value to humans, and we must also preserve and renew the varied habitats they came from. This is where kinship gardening comes in.

In the mid-1700s Swedish naturalist Carolus Linnaeus classified the world's known plants. He did so based on what their flowers looked like. For the next 250 years all new plants were categorized according to their floral structure, but in the late twentieth century scientists were able to unlock many of the doors to the genetic mysteries in plants and animals. Using this new information, a team of the world's top ten botanists, called the Angiosperm Phylogeny Group (APG), began reevaluating the taxonomy of the plants based on their genetic structure rather than just their physical appearance.

Using the data from the APG, molecular biologist Alan Kapuler developed a series of detailed layouts that he calls kinship maps. These maps enable us to see which plants are botanical kin to one another and, when applied to garden design, provide a strategic plan for preserving plant diversity.

My first visit to Dr. Kapuler, aka Mushroom, in the early spring of 2000, changed my life forever. At the time he was research director for Seeds of Change, an all-organic seed company that he cofounded in

1989. I remember following him around the field; he had several different seed crops in full bloom at the time, and the field was alight with color and chaos.

As we walked through the two-acre field known as Brown's Garden, Mushroom waved his arms around, dropping names of obscure plant species and ranting about world politics. Inside a three-thousand-square-foot greenhouse along the edge of the field he had planted a kinship conservation garden representing five hundred species of rare and interesting plants. The kinship garden was a world in itself, where agave and banana, olive and jasmine grew among their botanical relations, and where a novice like myself could begin to see the relationships among kin.

Mushroom believes this concept of kinship is at the core of understanding how to conserve and perpetuate diversity. He says,

> The destruction of habitats continues worldwide at an inconceivably rapid pace. The more we explore, the more we destroy. The result is the loss of whole communities of organisms. Our gardens can become alternative environments for the refugees from the struggle for the earth. . . . The idea is to explore the fabric of life by planting gardens that have as many different kinds of plants as possible. Thus we achieve several things simultaneously: conservation, diversification, education, exploration, and discovery.[6]

Kinship gardening helps us learn the relationships of the plants to one another.

Kinship gardening helps us learn the relationships of the plants to one another, which in turn helps us realize the relationships of the plant communities to ourselves. By taking the time to examine the kinships in our gardens we can better understand what we are stewarding and can see what's missing. If we see each garden not just as a resource for our own needs but also as a storehouse for genetic diversity, then we integrate our work with the larger ecological community. The resulting gardens are not only diverse and essential but multifunctional and extraordinarily beautiful as well.

In addition to the kinship garden, Mushroom and his partner, Linda, maintain more than two acres of seed gardens in Corvallis, Oregon, and save and distribute hundreds of varieties annually. The Kapulers have a small seed company, Peace Seeds, which offers samples of new varieties and forgotten crops. They publish the *Peace Seeds Resource Journal*, packed with stories, reflections, and data from their many garden trials. At home they have a large room filled to the ceiling with about ten thousand species of seeds from all around the globe.

These are but a few of the many seed conservation projects worldwide, and an Internet search under "organic seed" will yield many fruitful leads toward excellent sources and contacts for your stewardship. Because conserving diversity means perpetuating it, each of these projects always has a huge cache of seeds that need to be grown out: I even have one myself, more than I can handle. Thus, even if it seems like enough people are dedicating their lives to conserving and perpetuating biodiversity, there will always be more to do.

Not everyone can grow and save seeds from several thousand species of plants—nor do they need to. There are 250,000 documented species of plants on Earth. If every gardener in the United States were to steward just *one* species, saving seeds every year and sharing them with her neighbors and children, then the world flora would be preserved three hundred times over. Once you start to diversify your garden, you may be surprised at how many species fit into each small area.

Seed Saving for the Home Gardener

Seed stewardship can take on many forms, from actually growing and saving seeds to making important connections between community members and the seeds they keep. Again, we'll start in the garden.

Seed saving can be as simple as pie or as complex as pi. There are many levels of expertise, from the casual gardener who saves her own lettuce seeds to the serious plant breeder who keeps meticulous records, hand-pollinates everything, and produces new varieties every year.

It is impossible to learn the finer aspects of this ancient art from just this short chapter or even a whole book, and I cannot overstate the importance of both intentional study and experiential education in this arena. There are some excellent books listed in the resources section. In the meantime here are some basic tips on selection, collection, processing, and storage. Also, refer to the sidebar on page 146 for some essential supplies you will need to get started.

Selection

To create an ecological agriculture, both at home and culturewide, we must first diversify our attitudes about what plants are valuable and why. In food plants perfect fruit, predictable yield, and high market value are the three most common traits people look for in what they grow, but what about cold and/or drought tolerance or pest and disease resistance?

Some GMO varieties are bred to resist pests and diseases, but this artificial resistance lasts only a few generations before the pests and diseases mutate and continue to find food where they always have. Further, genetically modified plants breed rampantly with wild and heirloom varieties and are contaminating traditional gene pools world-

---

Tools of the Trade

Before you start saving seeds you will need to add some new tools to your garden shed. Some people dedicate a room or even a whole building to processing and storing seeds and seed-saving equipment; others keep everything in a closet and take it out when they need it. Whatever scale you work on, here is a list of things you will need to start saving seeds. Most of these items can be found at a thrift store or yard sale, or perhaps in your own kitchen.

1. Strips of fabric to mark selected plants
2. Pencils and some cut-up old mini blinds for labeling seed trays, pots, and garden plants
3. Scissors for a variety of uses
4. Garden clippers for cutting seed heads
5. Bowls in assorted sizes for winnowing
6. Jars for storage and/or fermenting
7. Buckets, clean and dry, for storage, fermenting, and fan winnowing
8. Screens in assorted grades for separating seeds from chaff
9. Trays, cookie sheets, and cake pans for sorting and winnowing
10. Fans, with adjustable speeds, for winnowing
11. Tarps for collecting and threshing
12. Airtight containers, coolers, tubs, and buckets for storing seed containers
13. Seed containers: envelopes, small paper and plastic bags for storing individual varieties
14. Tape and paper clips for holding envelopes and bags shut
15. Camera for documenting varieties
16. Notebook for documenting varieties
17. Funnels for filling containers
18. Measuring spoons for scooping samples

wide. These heirloom/heritage varieties have proven their worth over many years, through insect and disease resistance, superior nutritional content, better yield and stature, and more predictable cold tolerance—yet today they are being rapidly lost.

An integrated organic agriculture, which includes beneficial polycultures, fertile soil, and naturally bred disease resistance, brings more lasting, ecological results. Traditional plant breeding, where quality comes from years of careful selection in a living garden, promotes lifetimes of food security and does not carry the unknown and potentially ominous threats of genetic engineering.

You need not be a geneticist to breed plants—anyone can do it. In her book *Breeding Your Own Vegetable Varieties*, geneticist Carol Deppe points out that all of our major food crops came from amateur plant breeders and notes that until recently, all gardeners and farmers saved their own seeds; this "amateur" level of plant breeding was all there was.[7]

When you save seeds you are selecting for certain genetic traits, whether you realize it or not. Perhaps you are inadvertently selecting the plants that have mature seeds at the time you happened to harvest them, or plants that resisted a disease that killed off the rest of the patch before you came along.

Thus the more careful and methodical you are about observing and documenting your seed-saving work, the more likely you are to develop and conserve traits that you specifically want and that grow well in your specific environment. See the sidebar on page 149 for more on this point.

There is no blueprint for the perfect plant. You will have to choose what traits you need for the niches you are trying to fill in your garden, your life, and your bioregion. Here is a list of some of the most common things that people select for:

- *Stress, pest, and/or disease resistance.* For example, if powdery mildew is common in your area, then select plants that resist it. If you select for the same disease resistance several years in a row, you will achieve what's known as horizontal disease resistance, which spans many genes and protects crops from several angles.
- *Vigor and size.* Big, fast-growing plants are generally healthier and contain more genetic strength.

- *Volume, length, and predictability of yield.* Choose the plants that fruit when you want them to, and for as long as you want them to.
- *Color, which often indicates nutrient content.* Purple fruits contain different nutrients than yellow ones. Select a variety of colors and you will ensure a diverse nutritional intake.
- *Nutritional value, which usually requires lab testing.* See above.
- *Storage value/shelf life.* Some onions store well into the winter, but others will mold within a few weeks. This goes for many different foods, and storage value often depends on genetic traits.
- *Ease of harvest, processing, or use.* For example, certain kinds of corn, wheat, and other grains are very difficult to thresh (remove from their seedpods) without expensive machinery. Look for plants that cater to low-tech processing methods, such as hull-less barley or easy-peel garlic varieties.
- *Diversity versus uniformity of individual plants.* Conventional agriculture breeds uniform fruits and vegetables that all look alike and can all be harvested at once. For home gardens uniformity means too much of the same thing at once and works against our goal of many-layered diversity. Look for plants that are different from the rest, and use those unique traits to develop new varieties.
- *Compatability with a particular microclimate, such as cold or drought tolerance.* For example, if your garden doesn't get much water, save seeds from the plants that thrive in the dry conditions. If you notice that a plant does well in an odd microclimate, make note of it and save the seeds for future use in similar environmental conditions.

Keeping good records is essential for good seed stewardship, from noting growing conditions and dates to maturity through keeping track of where the seeds go after they have been harvested and distributed. The more notes you have, the better you will be able to tell whether your efforts are successful.

You may not be able to tell whether a specific trait is actually from

genotypic (related to the genes) or *phenotypic* (related to the environment) conditions. This distinction will be important as you choose and develop varieties to suit your needs and resources. Documentation will help you recognize patterns in this regard, but in the spirit of spreading our eggs among multiple baskets, it makes sense to select for several traits at once; this helps ensure the genetic diversity of the offspring and makes up for conditions you may have overlooked. If you select for only one trait year after year, you may pigeonhole your plants and create a situation called inbreeding depression, which results in a loss of vigor and disease resistance and a decline in overall viability.

Some of this relates to whether or not the plant is naturally an inbreeder or an outcrosser, and here we stretch into scientific territory

The Butterfly Effect

Ecology teaches us that everything is connected, and that everything we do has a ripple effect on the cosmic whole. We demonstrate this principle with every seed we save, through something called pleiotropy. Pleiotropy occurs when multiple, often seemingly unrelated, physical effects are caused by a single altered gene or pair of altered genes.

Carol Deppe calls pleiotropy a genetic version of the ancient Taoist understanding that you cannot do just one thing. She goes on to quote Lao-tzu in saying, "The way the world works is like a bow, when you pull the string, the top comes down, the bottom comes up, and all the parts move."[8]

An example: A gardener saves seeds from a tomato because she likes the pink color. She doesn't notice that the tomatoes with that color also have larger flowers than the rest. The larger flowers attract a certain kind of butterfly, which begins to thrive in her garden as she continues to grow the pink tomatoes. That butterfly's larvae happen to be food for an endangered bird species, which happens to also eat a certain kind of garden pest, and so on.

In chaos theory we encounter a similar phenomenon called the butterfly effect, named for Edward Lorenz's theory that every flap of a bird or butterfly's wing could alter wind patterns around the globe.

Real-life examples of the butterfly effect can be found in:

The weather, in which small changes in tides or winds affect global patterns;

The stock market, where slight fluctuations in one market will send unpredictable ripples through another;

Psychology, when thought patterns are altered significantly by tiny changes in brain chemistry or environmental stimuli;

The natural sciences, where seemingly unexplainable phenomena continuously point back to initial conditions, such as when a plant displays characteristics that were present in a parent plant several generations back.

We can use pleiotropy and the butterfly effect to initiate chain reactions in our gardens. Every seed planted has the potential to become a population of naturalized plants, and every trait selected could prevail into future generations. Thus it is imperative that we be cautious, thoughtful, and inclusive in our plans and selections. The more thorough we are in our design of the foundations of a natural system, the more beneficial will be the resulting long-term effects.

that is best covered elsewhere. For now I'll keep it simple and say that the more diverse your selection criteria, the more diverse your seed stock will tend to be. To avoid inbreeding depression, grow large populations of plants for seeds and educate yourself about the individual needs of the species you are working with.

Choose and prioritize the selection criteria that make the most sense for you, and clearly label the plants that you intend to save for seeds while they are in their prime. Make notes in your garden journal. Later, when the seeds are mature but the rest of the plant is in decline, it will be hard to remember which plant had that brilliant orange flower or which was the most vigorous before the gophers wiped out most of the patch.

Throughout the growing season go through and remove, or "rogue out," what you don't want, including any diseased plants or plants that are clearly failing to mature. Most of these are fine for compost, but if they are severely diseased, burn them.

Some advanced plant breeders cultivate "cesspools" of pest populations and diseased plants and test out the resistance of their varieties there. This practice can be very risky for backyard gardeners, though, and is perhaps best left to more experienced seed growers.

I have heard some organic growers argue that it is okay to use pesticides, herbicides, and chemical fertilizers on seed crops, to keep them from spreading seed-borne diseases and/or other weaknesses. When we dose the plants with pesticides, however, we breed pesticide-dependent varieties and pesticide-resistant pests. Seeds selected for optimum performance in organic conditions, after exposure to the pests, diseases, and other influences typical to these conditions, will produce plants that thrive through a diversity of challenges.

Collection

Collect seeds in the afternoon, when there is no dew on the plants. Pods should be as dry as you can get them with the seeds still inside. You can either cut the pods into a bag or a clean, dry bucket or just lean the plants over the container and shake the seeds into it.

Some plants have evolved for optimum seed dispersal, which means that often by the time the pods are dry enough to harvest the seeds all shatter onto the ground, blow into the wind, or get eaten by birds. To cut back on losses of this kind, cover maturing pods with a shadecloth to keep out birds and block the wind, or spread a tarp on the ground to catch dry seeds or mature fruits as they fall. You can also cut the plants just before maturity and dry them on a rack indoors, in a cool, dry area (see the sidebar on page 152).

Sometimes almost mature pods can be harvested and dried indoors. Label seed envelopes or small pieces of paper as soon as you bring the seeds in, with as much information as you can fit. Include date of harvest, date of planting, traits you selected for, species and variety names, area in the garden where it grew, where you originally got the seeds, and anything else that seems relevant. Let this paper follow the seed crop into storage, and you will always have the information at your fingertips.

Threshing and Winnowing

Most seeds mature within a protective coating called chaff. To process seeds for storage and replanting later, you must first remove the chaff; otherwise it will rot in storage and cause the seeds to go bad. To remove the bulk of the chaff, cut the plants down and fold them up in a clean tarp. Stomp and dance on the tarp, which will break open the pods and separate the seeds from the chaff. Be careful to avoid getting a lot of dirt and other contaminants into the seeds.

Now you can pour the broken-up seed/chaff mixture into a bucket and screen or winnow it. An assortment of screen sizes on hand will help you either catch or sift out varying sizes of seeds. Winnowing, or blowing off the chaff, can be done by blowing over the seeds while

Sift seeds through a screen to help remove the chaff.

Winnowing removes chaff and debris.

Build a Seed- and Herb-Drying Rack

Build a simple yet effective drying rack for seeds and plants with recycled window screens, wooden slats or branches, and some old bicycle tubes. To make a trilevel rack, which will provide approximately twenty-seven square feet of drying space, you will need eight two-inch by three-foot straight branches, six full-sized bicycle tubes (for twenty-six-inch tires or larger), and an assortment of old window screens no larger than three feet long on any side.

Cut the tubes in half lengthwise to make twelve long strips. Then tie the strips to the end of the slats. Tie each tier together, slide the screens on, and suspend the rack from the ceiling in a cool, dark, well-ventilated room, using four metal hooks.

For very small seeds, line the screens with newspaper or cardboard to keep the seeds from falling through. For larger seeds, just spread them out on the screens and keep the birds and rodents away. Most seeds take about two weeks to dry, but this will vary greatly according to climate, ventilation, and other factors.

This rack also works great for culinary and medicinal herbs. Just wash them, remove the stems, and, if you prefer, chop them up. Then spread them out and check back in a couple of weeks. See the drawing at right for details.

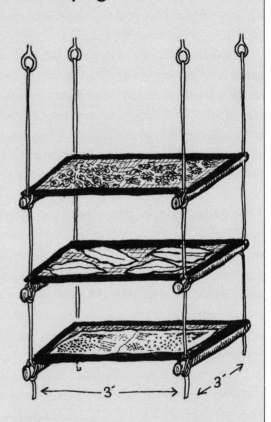

Build a multifunctional drying rack out of recycled bicycle tubes, window screens, and branches.

rotating them in a large bowl, or by pouring them from one container to another, letting a fan or just a gentle breeze gently blow away the chaff.

The most viable seeds will always be the heaviest, and thus will fall straight down, while the lighter seeds—those with less genetic material—will float farther on the wind. Select only the heaviest 10 percent or so for storage, and dump the rest of the seeds and chaff into the compost or spread it around the garden where you want that type of plant to volunteer.

Floating and Fermenting

Sometimes, as with plants in the onion family (Liliaceae), the chaff is wrapped around the seeds in a way that makes it very difficult to remove. Try pouring the partially cleaned seeds into a bucket of clean water. The chaff and nonviable seeds will float, and the good seeds will sink to the bottom. Now pour off the stuff on top, strain the seeds, and dry thoroughly (see below).

Many plants, including tomatoes, squash, and strawberries, make seeds within fleshy fruits and must be wet-processed. To do this, harvest the fruits when they are very ripe but not rotten and squish the seeds out into a glass jar or recycled container. Add a small amount of water and set the jar aside for a week or so to ferment.

Within a week the slimy protective seed coats will rot off, a thick skin of mold will form on top, and the mature seeds will sink to the bottom. Don't let them sit too long or they will rot (or sprout) and die. Fill the container to the top with water, pour off the mold, rinse the seeds a few more times, and strain out the remaining liquid.

Drying

All seeds, even if they seem totally dry at harvest, should be fully dried on a rack or in an electric dehydrator before storage. An electric or solar dehydrator with a thermostat control works best—run it overnight on the lowest setting, no higher than ninety-six degrees. If you choose to use a drying rack, let the seeds dry for at least two weeks, and be sure to shield your drying area from mice and birds, who will feast on your harvest if given the chance.

Short-term fermenting removes slimy seed coats and helps eliminate seed-borne disease from wet seeds like those of squash, melons, and tomatoes.

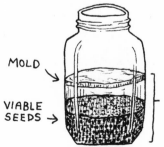

MOLD

VIABLE SEEDS →

WATER

Storage

Store seeds in the opposite conditions from those in which they will sprout. This usually means cold, dry, and dark. I store my seeds in bags and envelopes inside insulated picnic coolers (available for a few dollars at any thrift store) or in recycled five-gallon buckets (find them for free behind any restaurant) with tight-fitting lids.

Oregon seed grower Frank Morton recommends using stackable plastic bins, available for a few dollars each at most hardware stores. He puts the seeds themselves in ziplock bags with a labeled seed envelope inside. When the supply in the bag dwindles to the point that the rest of it will fit in the envelope, he knows it is time to move the seeds into the "grow next" pile. He also uses the big bins for winnowing and transporting seeds and for storing fresh-harvested seeds temporarily until they can be processed.

Some seeds should be stored in a freezer for best results. These include peas and fava beans, which are susceptible to pea weevils, whose larvae will die if frozen. Also freeze seeds from members of the onion family, such as onions, leeks, and chives, which are particularly short-lived and last much longer when frozen. In general the longevity and viability of your seeds will be largely dependent on storage conditions, so don't overlook this important aspect of stewardship.

The best way to learn how to select, collect, process, and store seeds is by working alongside someone who has been doing it or years. Look around for local seed savers, and visit and interact with as many of them as you can. You will find that some are strictly by the book, with specific policies about isolation, selection, record keeping, and varietal purity. Others are all about mixing it all up, developing

Store seeds in a cool, dry, dark place and they will stay fertile for many years.

new varieties every year, and literally tossing everything into the wind when it comes to genetics. Some of the most devoted seedgeeks, like Mushroom, will tell you to trust your instincts, that it is easy, that you should just "do it again and again, don't worry about reading the book. Forget about it. You get the seeds, you plant them, again and again, and that's it."[9]

Remember that we can protect diversity only by keeping it alive, and most seeds will perish if stored for more than a few years. You must grow and save them again every few years, and/or distribute them to others who will grow them. This massive, perpetual cycle of work and rebirth is daunting for even the most avid seed saver, and even large-scale intergovernmental conservation programs have failed to come up with an adequate plan for regenerating the vast quantities of disappearing species and varieties. Still, every saved seed holds the potential for centuries of food, so do what you can and hope for the best.

Other Ways to Steward Seeds

If we are serious about an ecological life, we must save seeds. For some people, however, this is just not possible right now. Luckily there are several other important aspects to seed stewardship. First, we can educate ourselves and others about biodiversity and genetic conservation to help build awareness and promote relevant products and programs. Next, we can participate in local land conservation, habitat renewal, and community-supported organic agriculture projects. Finally, organizing community seed exchange events and connecting like-minded people with resources and opportunities can have exponential effects toward long-term stewardship. Let's look deeper into this last point.

Seed Exchange and Distribution

We know that if nobody grows the seeds, they will die. Not only must we continue to grow them, we must get them out into the world where others will grow them too. To this end, most seed savers participate in some form of exchange, from independent mail-order seed companies to Internet lists.

The most dynamic type of seed exchange is the community seed swap. A seed swap is something like a gardeners' flea market with an emphasis on seeds, plants, and propagative material. At my first swap people brought vegetable and herb seeds, strawberry plants, and several varieties of home-brewed beer. Only a few people came, but we had a great time drinking the beer and carrying on about plants and politics.

The next year almost a hundred people showed up, bringing a large diversity of seeds, plants, fruits, vegetables, herbal remedies, handcrafts, and more. Although it seemed like everyone left with as much as they had brought, we still had a large, diverse cache of seeds left over—enough for twenty gardens. It was like magic beans or stone soup—it seemed the more we gave away, the more we had to share. Later I recognized varieties from the seed swap in the gardens of my neighbors. I also recognized more of the neighbors themselves and saw that our annual seed exchange had become an essential component to building our ecological community (see the sidebar on page 158).

Growing and sharing seeds builds community and promotes diversity on all levels. In a way, mixing plants, seeds, cultures, and individuals is a form of inter-*kin*dom procreation. And like other forms of procreation, seed swapping is another way to simultaneously ensure the survival of our species and have a great time! Anyone can organize a seed swap with some simple resources and just a few hours. I will get deeper into the details of organizing community events in the next few chapters, but here's a quick lesson on seed swaps.

First, decide whether to work alone or in a group. Two or three people is plenty. For a single person the process takes about twenty hours, stretched out over several months. Take a minute to jot down goals. This may include short-term incentives like "Get free seed for my garden" or long-term goals such as "Increase the food security and genetic diversity of my bioregion."

Now find out whether anyone else around you is doing similar work. A local university is a good place to start. Make a list of contacts. Visit garden centers. Look online and ask around for local seed savers. There may already be seed exchanges going on nearby.

Establish a date and place for the event several months in advance. Possible sites include schools, churches, bookstores, parks, community centers, and private homes. Most places will donate the space for free, and many will provide tables, chairs, and even audiovisual equipment.

Make a list of what you will need for the event, such as tables, outdoor shelter, transportation, photocopies, volunteers to help set up, and telephone and Internet access for promoting the event. If you circulate this list with a flyer for the event, you will probably be able to get many things donated. You may need to make a nominal investment for photocopying and extra seed envelopes; this money can be recovered later by putting out a donation jar at the seed swap. At past events our donation jar has yielded anywhere from forty-five to three hundred dollars.

Look for local scholars and professionals to invite to the seed swap as guest speakers or workshop instructors. These might be university students or professors, landscape designers, farmers, authors, or a vaudeville troupe doing puppet shows about seed saving. At a seed swap people are often preoccupied with the seeds themselves, but a short workshop or demonstration goes over well and adds another dimension to the gathering. Also invite activist groups or garden clubs to set up information tables.

Many people will bring seeds to the swap, but others will come empty-handed. Sequester seed donations from local growers and seed companies in advance so there is surplus at the event. See the section on seed storage, and stash the donations accordingly until the day of the swap.

Make a flyer and post it around town about three weeks before the event. To reach a wider variety of people, send a press release to local media sources, and follow up with phone calls a few days before the event. Bring tables and chairs, set up an hour or two early, and display the seeds so they are easily accessible.

It helps to make small signs to help organize seeds by plant family, so people know where to look and where to put the seeds they bring. Provide empty envelopes for people to stash small quantities of seeds. Recycled junk-mail/business-reply envelopes work great—seal them, cut them in half, and you have two little envelopes that can be labeled, filled with seeds, and folded shut.

As people arrive the seed swap will probably take one of two shapes. Sometimes participants set up personal displays of their seeds and other goods. This is the "marketplace" version of seed swapping, where people negotiate individual exchanges with one another. I prefer the

Seed Swaps for Cultural Evolution
by Nick Routledge

The Sages insist there is a fundamental unity through all diversity. So where's the evidence? One of the most potent examples may well be manifested in the palpable reality of the humble seed swap. Think about it. Take two ostensibly separate worlds, those of humans and of plants, and imagine any singular occasion that better affords the opportunity to both witness and nurture the "energetics of togetherness" between them.

At a seed swap, is it the people who are collectively engendering deeper and stronger interrelationships in the green world, or vice versa, and then some? Where are the boundaries between the dynamic interplays of these two cultures? Look with eyes that see. They don't exist. They're an illusion. And seed swaps don't simply serve to drop the veil of separateness, they're also fundamentally about catalyzing the birth of profound collective synergies and strengths that each realm, plant and human, brings to the other. You'll be hard-pressed to find a higher expression of the gift of life to itself, anywhere.

Which is, of course, why seed swaps are where the sharing and creation of real power is grounded, not the rootless and utterly temporary illusion that passes for social physicianship we see in capitols and elsewhere. Deep gardeners know that you can walk out of a seed swap with a form of authentic power in your pocket, with the literal potential to transform the politics of an entire bioregion. And of course the cosmic irony is that this form of power transcends all political differences.

As the Sages say, conscious evolution is not about gaining power, but about becoming power. Perhaps that's why our experience around seed swaps consistently demonstrates that they don't just attract the finest seeds in any locale, but some of the finest people too. Local seed swaps are where the deepest indigenous wisdom of land and people becomes most potentized, shared, and enlivened; they stand at the arrowpoint of the evolutionary impulse in any bioregion.

other version, the potluck-style seed swap, where people add their seed to what is out on the tables, perhaps with a note about the variety and growing procedures. Donate any surplus at the end of the event to a local seed bank or garden project, or store it until the next seed swap.

Start the event with a circle of all people who come. Have everyone introduce themselves and identify what types of seeds or goods they brought. This is also a great time to announce workshops or guest speakers, pass around a mailing list, and point out the donation jar. Then everyone just goes for it. The only rule is: Don't take more than half of anything.

In the past seven years I have traded seed for homemade lotions, teas, baskets, gourds, jewelry, vegetables, lodging, herbal medicines, and counseling. Through face-to-face exchange I have shared seeds with more than two thousand people, and those seeds have surely been passed on again. This simple act builds regional food security and stew-

ards global genetic diversity. In addition, you'll save money, meet interesting people, make good use of surplus resources, and have heaps of
good organic fun!

Now that we've explored some of the elements of an ecological
garden, how can we bring it all together into a functional whole? The
next chapter will outline a design formula that will help you integrate
these elements, along with the other aspects of your home and lifestyle,
into a holistic ecological system.

**Organize a local seed swap and watch as your community
grows stronger, lusher, and more diverse.**

7. Ecological Design

In many ways, the environmental crisis is a design crisis. It is a consequence of how things are made, buildings are constructed, and landscapes are used. Design manifests culture, and culture rests firmly on the foundation of what we believe to be true about the world. . . . It is clear that we have not given design a rich enough context. We have used design cleverly in the service of narrowly defined human interests, but have neglected its relationship with our fellow creatures. Such myopic design cannot fail to degrade the living world, and, by extension, our own health.

—**Sim Van Der Ryn and Stuart Cowan**[1]

Through design we have the opportunity to participate in this relationship with nature by applying the ethics we hold toward the earth as a whole, or macrocosm, to our given site, or microcosm. When these ethics are applied correctly, the design, once realized, is synaesthetic, eliciting a sensory response from its human occupants. Nature responds to the human input by taking on certain forms (growth). Humans respond to nature's input by experiencing joy and a heightened awareness (growth). When this level of interaction with nature is achieved, human intervention is not so apparent, and appears to be "naturally" occurring. Examples of this are visible in the habitats of many indigenous peoples who are truly "one" with their environment. The degree of beauty inherent in functional design is evidence of how closely connected the designer is with nature.

—**Patty Ceglia**[2]

Bringing It All Together

Now that we have seen how to improve the ecological integrity of the elements in our garden, the next step is to assemble those elements into a functional whole. The ecological gardener assumes that every garden is linked with the larger community, which includes not just the natural setting but also the social and economic cycles within.

We develop this link through developing a proactive natural design that emphasizes the creation of functional and ecologically harmonious relationships, starting with the garden and spiraling outward.

Thus the water cycle connects with the plants, waste in the house becomes compost, surplus food, energy, and information recycle into the community, and so on. The success (or failure) of these relationships depends upon the lasting integrity of the overall design, which evolves and adapts alongside the elements within. Whatever types of project you choose, whether a home garden, a large-scale community program, or anything in between, design is the process by which your vision becomes reality.

Whether we realize it or not, all of us are ecological designers; for good or ill, much of what we do is design work. When we forge a path, plant a garden, or put things away in the kitchen, we are designing. When we make a list of things to do, we are designing. Anytime we interact with people and objects, we are designing a system, and if that design becomes intentional then we gain access to the full potential of that system.

Defined as the "shaping of matter, energy, and process . . . a hinge that connects culture and nature through exchanges of materials, flows of energy, and choices of land use,"[3] design is all around us. From the shape of our shoes to the layout of our cities, someone designed every human-made thing we see. And all design is ecological design in that it either hurts or helps nature, whether it was intended to or not.

By developing an ecological design we can unite our ideas with nature's resources and create truly thriving homes, gardens, and communities. As ecological designers, our goal is to become central participants in a self-reliant, diverse, and productive ecosystem that includes not only our own homestead but also the whole community in which it resides. This includes biological and ecological contexts as well as social, economic, and other human concerns. And because this is such a lofty goal, it is essential that we develop a cohesive yet adaptable plan of action.

The design process clarifies our goals and ideas, gets them on paper, and provides a road map for implementation. A carefully thought-out written design saves time and money, prevents mistakes, and helps communicate ideas to others. It is much easier

to correct mistakes on paper than on land. Of course, your long-term needs and goals will change, and a good design leaves plenty of room for those changes.

This is not to say that we should attempt to redesign every inch of the earth; wilderness areas should be left as such, and even the most meticulous design is not complete without a little room for the inevitable and ubiquitous chaos of nature. However, we should, indeed we must, reevaluate the function of our current human settlements and develop detailed plans to implement options that are more ecological.

We must go beyond human sustainability to embrace a vision of humanity that is not just surviving but able and willing to truly thrive, in perpetuity, while actually regenerating and contributing to the natural environment. In this way we replace unconscious evolution with conscious natural selection and rejoin the whole as willing stewards of the earth.

The Spiral Design Wheel

If we are to live in harmony with nature, it needs to feel natural. We have to integrate the notion of ecological design *into* our regular lives and make it easy and fun for our friends and neighbors to follow suit.

Over the last several years, I have become increasingly fascinated with ecological design theory. I have studied several different approaches, including permaculture, biodynamics, natural farming, and ornamental landscaping and have pulled my favorite parts together to build a simple and practical formula that can be used by anyone on a variety of projects, regardless of academic or practical training. I call this the "spiral design wheel" and have used it to design a variety of projects, including some of those described in this book.

I will explain each phase of the wheel in an order that makes sense to me, but it doesn't matter whether you jump around a little. Ecological living is not a linear process any more than we live in a linear world. There is no starting or stopping point—the whole design evolves simultaneously, and parts of it change and grow depending on what you're working on at the time.

To develop a basic plan of action, I recommend a process called

Gobradime, which is an acronym for Goals–Observation–Boundaries–Resources–Analysis–Design–Implementation–Maintenance–Evaluation.[4]

Now is the time to get out your garden journal and review the observations, resource lists, plant lists, and other design notes that you have accumulated so far. Through the following process, you will use these notes to develop a whole-system design and a timeline for implementation. If you haven't been making lists and keeping notes yet, don't despair—start now.

Above all remember that your project, if it involves people and especially if it involves plants, is an organism rather than a mechanism. This wheel, just like any system, is most effective when coupled with a good degree of common sense and natural intuition. Trust your instincts and use the formula to help you refine them. Be careful not to become obsessed with controlling every aspect of the design.

If we are to live in harmony with nature, it needs to feel natural.

The process of moving through each little step can seem a bit tedious, so don't try to do it all at once. Do take the time to work through the entire process on paper before making any changes in the garden, at least as a loose brainstorm—trust me, you will thank yourself later.

Look Deep

Remember that bit about observation and record keeping, about microcosms and macrocosms, in the beginning of chapter 2? Go back and reread it. Prolonged and thoughtful observation is better than protracted and thoughtless action. Looking deep is our best strategy for solving problems, from choosing what to grow to learning how best to contribute to the community. Learn to read the land. Become a good listener. Attune yourself to the cycles of nature.

Observation is at the very heart of ecological living and is the key to finding and cooperating with nature's patterns and cycles. Lie down on the ground and look at the world around you. What do you see? How do you want to change it? What is the most effective and most ecological way to proceed? Take your time, make educated choices, and try to avoid irreparable errors.

We find the words LOOK DEEP at the center of the wheel, to remind us to return to our observations again and again, through every step of our

Spiral design wheel

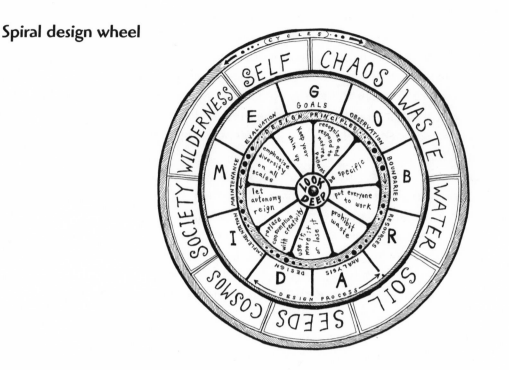

work, using all of our senses to determine what steps to take—or not to take—next.

Gobradime: The Design Process

Gobradime is a formula for the design, development, implementation, and perpetual maintenance of any project, small or large. Whether you use it exactly as is or sculpt it to fit your needs, this systematic process helps you cover all the bases and stay organized while putting your dreams into action. It works at any scale, for organizing a closet, installing a small garden, developing a whole site, or organizing a bioregional resource alliance.

Use it to design your home garden, in each layer of the design, and again for the whole. Just as you will apply multiple patterns of nature, you will also apply multiple layers of design. Try it, and you will be amazed at how easily it all comes together.

Step One: Goals

The first step in any design is to identify personal and collective goals. What do you need? What do you want to accomplish and why? What will be the outcomes of your work, and how do these reflect your ethical ideals and practical limitations? Remember, it is much easier to redesign on paper than after the project is half built.

Documenting the design process on paper creates a means for communicating ideas with others, provides a realistic plan for successful implementation, and, later, gives you something to refer back to when evaluating the effectiveness of your work. Write down a list of goals and prioritize them by going down the list and rating each goal on a scale of 1 to 5, with 1 representing the highest priority. Then sort the list so that the things you want to accomplish first are at the top. This will help you develop a timeline later on.

Refer back to these lists often, to keep yourself on track and get ideas for future projects, but don't get bogged down in the idea of accomplishing something that doesn't continue to inspire you. Goals are like flowers—some of them come back every year, and others last only a season. Our goals should change as we do, and any good design allows for this perpetual change.

Step Two: Observation (and Objectives)

Though looking deep is an important part of every step of the design process, here is the point when we use our powers of observation to make sense of our individual goals. Remember that this is not a linear process—you should spiral around to every step again and again, over many years, as you hone and perfect your design.

With every goal comes a family of objectives, which make up the strategy for achieving the goal. For example, the goal of building garden soil that is ecologically sound will include objectives such as building compost, finding good sources of mulch, and planting cover crops. Thorough observation is the key to developing realistic objectives that will bring you quickly and efficiently closer to your goals.

Go through your list of goals and compare it with the observations you have made so far. Go back out and look deeper, with each goal in mind, to determine which objectives will help you meet that goal. Write it all down, listing basic observations such as "Northwest corner is very shady" and noting ideas for potential action, such as "Plant shade lovers in northwest corner."

Also look for the social and ethical components of your project. For example, is there a gathering place? Do you need one? How do all of the elements affect one another, and how will people and other inhabitants benefit from a new design? Where are the problems, what are the challenges, and how will changes improve the ethical standpoint of the site?

This process also works quite well for designing community projects, such as skill-sharing events, seed swaps, collective gardens, and more. In community work, observation means looking for other activists, finding out what they are doing, and determining ways to integrate your collective vision. Can you plug in with them, or is your idea a new one to the area? What are the obvious and demonstrable needs for your project? Is it worth doing? Carefully examine each of these questions against your ideas and goals, and choose a project that will be simultaneously fulfilling for you and effective for the community.

Step Three: Boundaries

Now is the time to find and establish boundaries. This means everything from physical boundaries such as property lines and flows of energy to personal boundaries like how much time you want to spend in the garden and how hard you want to work.

For a site design this step will include drawing up a base map of the site. Pace or measure each distance on the ground and do your best to develop a map that is to scale. Note the following things on the map: lot boundaries, buildings, doors, decks, patios, driveways, fences, hedges, trees, gardens, and any other physical objects on the site. Add in permanent and temporary paths, and make note of any objects that may be temporarily missing, such as parked cars or seasonal motor-home storage.

Now document the flows of water and of human and animal traffic through the site, using dashed lines and arrows. This will establish the main paths through your design. Moving a well-trodden path is rarely a good idea; it is much easier to adapt the design to behavior patterns, rather than the opposite, so go with the flow.

This map will provide the basis for your design—make multiple copies or use transparent tissue paper to overlay new ideas and to develop a multiphase implementation plan. If you are developing a community project, the map might be more of a brain map or timeline for the project, with the varied commitments of participating individuals noted along the sides.

Other types of boundaries will include legal, political, or social issues such as land-use laws or potential issues with the surrounding community. You should also consider the boundaries of what you call your community, but I'll get into this in the next few chapters. For now just try to foresee any barriers to your projects and note them for later analysis.

Finally, define and document your own personal boundaries. Where and when will you work? Where and when will you rest? Whom will you work with and how? How long do you want to be involved with the project? Should you develop it in a way that others will be able to take over when you move on? How much money do you want to spend? Start small and accept help.

It is virtually impossible for one family on a small urban lot to be totally self-sufficient. If we can work together as a neighborhood, however, we can easily create self-reliant bioregional communities that meet their own needs while stewarding the natural ecology.

Set clear, realistic boundaries.

Each single being has potential to make exponential effects on the whole, and it is up to you to determine which of these butterfly effects you choose to initiate. Meanwhile, set clear, realistic boundaries and communicate them to yourself and the group you work with. This will help you avoid burnout and frustration later on. Take your time, do the best you can, and see stewardship not as work but as life, now and forever.

Step Four: Resources

Now you start assessing and assembling the varied resources you will need to put these big dreams into action. Go back through your observations and start making lists of the resources available on-site. List existing biological resources, waste materials, and potential sources for more. Make an overlay or copy of your base map and note every potential resource, such as water, sun, compost, manure, wood piles, and neighbors who might like to volunteer.

Ask yourself: *What's there? What can we do without? What do we need? Where can we get it for free, or with the minimum output?* Types of resources include money, labor, garden supplies, building materials, access to facilities, and information from experts.

If you can't find what you need for free, try to innovate something that will fulfill the same function. Often a customized, handmade solution is the most effective. Our most powerful tool for building an ecological culture is our own creativity. Use it. Your imagination is renewable, easy to find, and free, limited only by your own mind. (See the sidebar on page 182 for ways to get creative.)

Also, tap into the information resources available through local libraries and bookstores, and learn as much as you can from that ever-expanding space-age miracle, the Internet. Do some research and see whether anyone else has solved the same problem or shared the same goals. You should never copy anything exactly, because every design should be site-specific, but usually another person's solution is easily adapted to a similar problem. If it still seems impossible, try reassessing your goals—just a little—to make room for an alternative plan that makes good use of the resources and ideas you have now. Again, refer to the sidebar on page 182 for help in getting creative.

As you assemble lists of what you have and what you need, it will become apparent that you don't need everything all at once. Rather, there will be a flow of resources in and out of the project, the nature of which will change and evolve over time. Try to envision this flow, organize your lists in chronological order, and layer them into your timeline and phase plans.

Step Five: Analysis

Analysis helps define weaknesses and ways to overcome them and brings random ideas together to form a cohesive plan. Through this process you will determine how you can use the resources available to you to achieve the goals you have set for yourself, with the greatest amount of harmony with what is already happening and in line with your ethical and practical limitations.

Now you can bring together the stacks of notes you've assembled so far and synthesize them toward a tangible design. These notes, though always expanding, should include at least the following information:

1. Observations from around your yard and neighborhood, made over a few days or a few seasons.
2. Goals and proposed objectives, sorted by priority.

3. Catalog of local and surplus resources, including organic food, land, water, tools, mulch, plants, seeds, and building materials. You will add to this list with almost every new observation. Date each entry and note locations where possible.

4. Base map.

5. Notes about personal, ecological, and other boundaries.

6. The water cycle: maps of land contours, drawings of rain catchment and graywater ideas, and brainstormed lists of tasks and project ideas.

7. The soil conditions: existing weeds, moisture content, structure and depth of topsoil, and types of insects and worms.

8. Ideas for bed designs and notes about existing microclimates and plans of action.

9. Plant lists: what you like to eat, what you want to grow, companion plants and polyculture ideas, sketches of multidimensional plantings, species lists for what you have and want to get, and potential sources for propagative material.

10. Seed lists: again, what you have, what you want, and where to get it. Also note present and future selection criteria and breeding ideas.

There are several good ways to analyze your notes and get them ready to plug into your design. First just reread all of your notes and brainstorm a list of tasks and project ideas. This pushes the analysis away from theoretical ideas and toward concrete action, which is what you want.

Next, try the zone and sector analysis method described in the sidebar on page 174. This will help you place elements in locations relative to their needs and outputs, and it is the first step toward bringing your assorted home and garden projects into a strategic whole. Take a copy of your base map, go through your list of tasks, and place each activity into the proper zone. Also do this with each element, such as the herb garden, the tool shed, the pond, the slime monster, the chicken coop, and so forth. Make little notecards and move them around on the map to consider the effects of varied combinations. This will show you what work needs to be done where and what your options are for the specific placement of each item.

Another helpful tool for analyzing needs against resources is called

Use an overlay system to design the many layers and phases of your project.

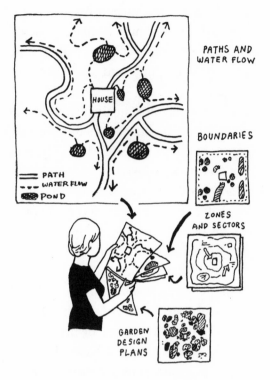

input–output analysis. Choose any element of the design, whether the whole garden or a single plant. On one side of a piece of paper list all the contributions that element makes to the whole. On the other side list the needs of that element and the resources it requires to function. Do this with several connected elements, and look for ways to overlap needs with resources and surplus with shortages.

Throughout your analysis, ask questions such as:

- What are the economic and ecological costs to implement and maintain the design?
- What are the yields and how can they be improved?
- Where are the imbalances and how can they be corrected?
- What work can we avoid doing?
- What are the best and worst places for each element?
- How is everything affecting everything else?
- How can we use what is available now to turn problems into solutions?

- If nothing was here, what would we bring in?
- How can I best adhere to my ethics and principles, with the least amount of input and the greatest benefit to myself and the earth?

Develop your own lists of questions and criteria, based on your specific circumstances, and use them to evaluate each new opportunity. Find the connections between elements, think about the relationships and how you want to change them, and start choosing where and when to implement each change.

This is also an excellent time to review the ecological design principles described later in this chapter and to measure the ecological integrity of each part of your home and garden. But remember, do not get bogged down in linear analysis or you'll bury yourself in the paper trail before you ever get a chance to get dirty in the garden.

Finally, don't overlook the value of intuition, aesthetics, and random assembly as design tools. Sometimes just putting a plant or other element where you think it looks nice, or where you happened to set it down first, works better than anything else. If you get stuck, try using a process of elimination: Ask yourself *Where shouldn't this go?* and see where that takes you.

Step Six: Design

Now you are ready to develop a multiple-phase design and plan for implementation. Go back again to your notes, starting with the ten

INPUT

FOOD
WATER
SHELTER
SPACE

OUTPUT

FEATHERS
MANURE
BABY GEESE
EGGS

An example of using input–output analysis to determine the needs and resources of an element in your design

items listed above, and choose a plan of action according to your analysis of the information you have available. Go through everything again and write a list of actions that will bring your visions into reality. Continue to prioritize these actions by sorting them according to which goal they help to meet and how important that goal is to you.

Make several copies of your base map and begin placing your tasks and elements in location relative to their needs and outputs. Think well in advance, and develop several phases to complete over the next several years. For each phase develop a different map and write a loose budget to accommodate that phase. Write down how many labor-hours you estimate for each step and determine ways to find the help and the funds that you need.

If you follow these steps, you will end up with a handful of maps and lists, sorted into chronological order according to priority, all laid out according to where each action will occur. Now you just have to start going down the list and getting the work done.

Step Seven: Implementation

Hang up the maps, notes, and design plans on a central bulletin board where everyone can see them. This is the time to stop writing and start actually moving stuff around. Do take time to jot down notes as you develop new ideas or make changes to the original design—this will save time later when you evaluate your work. Also, be sure to take plenty of time to step back, rest, and reflect on your progress.

It is easy to become consumed with the first phase of implementation, but pace yourself so you stay sane and are able to follow through with the rest of the plan. Don't burn yourself out. Take your time and focus on doing less right, rather than more wrong.

Remember to feed and hydrate yourself and other volunteers, and try to work things out if people become agitated or have trouble working together. See chapter 11 for tips on working with groups. In general, be compassionate and true to your goals and ethical commitments, and have fun putting peace into action!

Step Eight: Maintenance (and Monitoring)

As implementation progresses you will need to monitor and maintain existing systems. Some people develop detailed forms to document the data generated by their projects, such as growth rates, yields and potential yields, and climatic patterns. The point is to find and record successes and problems (including potential problems) with the design, so you can either repeat patterns or go back and rework them to improve the whole.

Ideally, in a home system you will be living in and interacting with the design as it comes about. Pay attention to the ways in which your life improves or becomes more difficult through these changes, and adjust your design patterns to best embrace the personal patterns of yourself and the other people involved.

Step Nine: Evaluation

As each phase is completed, get together with your working group and evaluate your progress. Identify strengths, weaknesses, opportunities, and challenges, and compare notes about what should change or what is working well.

This step is often overlooked by tired and overwhelmed activists who just want to move right on to the next phase of the project. However, evaluation is the key to a sustainable and realistically evolving plan, and it is of the utmost importance that we each set aside enough time to effectively and productively evaluate our work against our original goals and against the ethics and ideals we have chosen.

Write down your evaluations and attach them to the maps and notes from the appropriate phase. As you evaluate, you will discover new goals, new ideas, and new ways to improve the efficiency and ecological integrity of your design. When you are ready, start again with the *G* and continue to spiral through the process. And, of course, don't forget to evaluate your actions and ideas against the next ring of the design wheel: the ecological design principles.

Proverbs for a Peaceful Evolution: Ecological Design Principles

In every book or course on permaculture or ecological design you will find a set of design principles: short phrases meant to guide the designer toward results that harmonize with nature. When researching

Zones and Sectors

Many ecological designers use permaculture's zone and sector analysis system. Zones represent patterns of human use, while sectors are the natural influences on the project. Make an overlay for each on your base map and use the descriptions below to determine how to place the elements in your garden and home system in a way that makes practical and ecological sense.

Sectors

Sectors are the wild and/or uncontrollable influences over the site. The primary sectors in most gardens are sun, shade, wind, frost, wildlife, fire hazards, and varying levels of moisture and soil fertility. On an urban site other uncontrollable influences might include car noise, the neighbor's cats, or that ugly billboard that you can see across the alley. Be sure to consider "Sector C," or the influence of children on your site. See chapter 12 for more on this topic.

Make note of as many sectors as you can find, and design your garden to accommodate or overcome the opportunities and obstacles they present.

Zones

Zones represent patterns of human use, and placing elements into the appropriate zone will save heaps of time and money. Some items, such as water collection, composting, wildlife forage, and sacred spaces, will be woven into several zones.

The junctions between zones, between sectors, and between zones and sectors will yield edge effects like increased diversity and specialized microclimates. Look for and note these opportunities, and compare them with your needs and resources. Try to develop a concrete vision of how people, energy, and materials flow through the project, and draw these patterns on the map.

Zone 0: Yourself, your personal cycles, your relationships, and your behavior.

Zone 1: Most intensively used, closest to home. Includes house, greenhouse, workshop, kitchen gardens, compost, chickens, and anything else that needs daily care.

Zone 2: Intensively used, very near home. Includes secondary greenhouses, larger gardens and composting areas, water catchment, solar shower, sauna.

Zone 3: Regular use. Includes some external structures, field crops, larger water storages, orchards, and recreational elements.

Zone 4: Minimal use. Includes timber, more field crops and fruit trees, forage pasture, mushroom cultivation, and more large water storage.

Zone 5: Unmanaged. Used for minimal foraging and recreation; left as a wild area for nonhuman species to inhabit.

Zone and sector analysis is an excellent way to begin placing elements onto a site. Most urban homes have only the first two or three zones, and a whole-system design must contain all of them. In the country zones 3 and 4 would include field crops, fruit trees, and a woodlot. In the city these zones might extend into a local park, a neighbor's house, or a dumpster, where you grow or acquire more food, building materials, and fuel. Zone 5 becomes your effort toward the restoration of local wild areas.

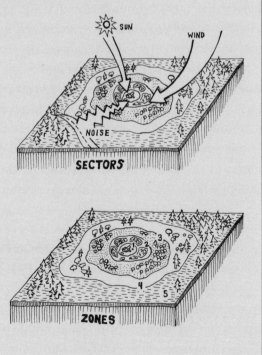

this book, I came across no fewer than 50 different principles, each with their own piece of wisdom for the would-be earth steward. Based on research, natural law, and experiential knowledge, these principles came from some of the greatest minds of our time—Jude Hobbs, Tom Ward, Toby Hemenway, Rosalind Creasy, Graham Bell, Bill Mollison, Sim Van Der Ryn, Stuart Cowan, John Todd—ecologists and educators who grow diverse organic gardens and whose ideas have changed the way millions of people treat the Earth.

I thought about listing all 50 principles, but instead decided to synthesize them into my own set—short, sweet, and easy to remember. I humbly offer you the results below and hope they will help and inspire you to solve design problems throughout every aspect of your life.

I will explain each principle, then list a few sample strategies that you can use in your garden. You will remember some of these ideas from the previous chapters—indeed, we have seen examples of each principle in every element of the paradise garden. Now we bring them together.

1. Emphasize Diversity on All Scales

Again we find diversity at the top of the list. Nature is not single-minded, and neither are we. This variety is our number one resource and, thus, our first priority. This includes using a diversity of resources and strategies, as well as holding diverse views and having diverse goals.

Work toward a diverse community, human and otherwise. Remember that diversity is alive, and that to conserve it, we must grow and interact with it. Simply, if you devote your landscape to growing as much diversity as possible, you will not fail in your quest for paradise.

Sample Strategies
- Build compost from many different ingredients to encourage diverse soil communities that will support healthy plants.
- Grow food in many locations in case one spot fails to yield.
- Establish multiple pathways.
- Eat many different types of food to encourage a healthy body.
- Work with different kinds of people to increase your understanding of other cultures.

- Create edges around the garden to enhance the diversity of species.
- Catch water at several points and direct it into different parts of the garden.
- Grow seeds of different varieties each year and save seeds for many reasons.
- Look for unusual ways to solve problems and look past the first or most obvious answer.
- Leave parts of your landscape wild to encourage nonhuman benefits.
- Never pull a plant you don't recognize—make weeding an educational and intentional experience.
- Let every species in your garden go to seed at least once every few years.
- Grow things that yield in the winter or off-season to ensure a year-round food supply.
- Always look for new information and don't get set in your ways.
- Meet needs with multiple resources, such as collecting mulch materials from several places.
- Make each resource meet multiple needs, such as using a greenhouse to grow plants, heat water, and store tools.

2. Recognize and Respond to Natural Patterns

The power of nature is far greater than the strength of any structure, so why not tap into some of that power and make things easier on yourself? Nature (including you and your garden) is not just a bank of resources; she is an ideal model of evolving ecological systems, and we can look to her for guidance at any phase of our planning. Inspired by nature, we offer our ideas and she provides the ways and means to vitalize them.

Many of the best examples from nature manifest themselves through specific, repeated patterns. We need only look at a leaf, a trickle of water, or our own fingertips to recognize the familiar branching, swirling, or webbing pattern, each only one layer in the complex matrix of flows, links, and connections that unite us together with all nature's mystery. For centuries people have used natural patterns to design gardens and communities, and through understanding these patterns we can use them to solve design problems.

For an excellent overview of nature's most common patterns, see Peter Stevens's book *Patterns in Nature*. Also be sure to check out Toby Hemenway's website, www.patternliteracy.com.

Much of what we do every day works against nature, and changing the dominant paradigm does not happen overnight. However, we can move in leaps and bounds if we make every effort to go with the flow. If we emphasize cooperation over competition and treat our garden as an organism rather than a mechanism, then we harness the power of nature's plan without needing to overanalyze it.

Sample Strategies
- Take a break in the winter.
- Build an herb spiral.
- Use branching patterns for garden paths.
- Mulch every autumn.
- Use gravity to direct water.
- Let plants go to seed.
- Harvest what already grows there.
- Recognize microclimates and use them.

3. Be Specific

Many varying factors, including climate, topography, social and cultural paradigms, and of course the needs and desires of the designer, require that each design be site-specific. Deeper, each detail of that design, from the shape of the kitchen garden to the species of thyme, should be chosen through a new and careful process, rather than by imitating a book or other example.

Architectural designer Patty Ceglia writes, "The design process should generate its own solutions, structure, technologies, connections, and aesthetics. Don't automatically copy someone else. Never apply [an idea] just because you've seen it before."[5]

An ecological life has no template—we must adapt and evolve with the ecology around us. Every design should be ultraspecific and should embrace both the strengths and the weaknesses of that site. Start with the needs and functions and break down design components to accommodate those needs. Determine which questions to ask based on the specific circumstances, then find specific answers for those questions. Make small, slow changes that relate to the exact influences and needs of your site.

Thus, rather than designing a "garden," with whatever generic elements this seems to entail, we design a place to grow food, to read in the shade, to play with children, and to learn about nature. Each layer adapts to the specific purpose for the individuals involved, and each solution has specific details that are unique to the problem at hand.

An ecological life has no template.

Sample Strategies
- Observe sites where similar problems exist, and adapt solutions to accommodate your own needs.
- Choose specific plants ("wild marjoram (*Origanum vulgare*) and lemon thyme (*Thymus serpyllum*)") for each function, rather than general categories ("herbs").
- Brainstorm a list of needs and functions, and fill each with a specific resource.
- Look for details out of place, and adjust them as needed.
- Choose each variety of fruit and vegetable based on local reputation. Don't settle for just any lettuce when you could have one that will do especially well in your bioregion.
- Learn about all the insects and birds in your garden, and plant what they specifically like to eat.

4. Put Everyone to Work
Take action toward facilitating the flow of resources into working niches, and cover your bases from as many angles as possible. This includes techniques such as multitasking, plant stacking, time stacking, and recruiting volunteers.

You should get something from your work. As they say, you cannot work on an empty stomach, and unless your project provides some sort of physical or emotional return you will lose interest quickly. This interaction with, and enjoyment of, the fruits of your labor validates your ideas and keeps you motivated. By making every detail work to our advantage we increase the sum of yields and get more for our work.

To increase the sum of yields means to diversify and multiply the types of yields we get. For example, a vegetable garden provides vegetables, but it could also provide flowers, compost materials, and educational opportunities. So for the same amount of space, we can get five times as much reward just by planning carefully.

Remember that yield is not the gross harvest—it is the difference between what you put in and what you end up with. Never take the whole yield. Try to get as much as you can from each stage of each element in your system without degrading the ethics of that project. In this way every need is met by multiple resources, and every resource fills multiple needs.

Sample Strategies
- Choose plants that you can use for at least two different purposes.
- Let insects and birds pollinate your seed crops.
- Make use of every niche and every microclimate.
- Host hands-on workshops and direct the energy toward projects in your garden and community.
- Meet needs with multiple resources, such as when catching water from multiple sources.
- Value all roles in nature, even those you cannot define.

5. Prohibit Waste

The seven R's of cycling are: Rethink, Redesign, Reduce, Reuse, Repair, Refuse, Recycle. Put every element, every yield, and every potential waste through these steps and see if you can close the loop. Go back to the section on cyclic opportunity, in chapter 3, and make sure you are tapping the flow wherever possible.

Each time a resource is lost it must be replaced or the system will falter and change. Conversely, unused surplus can become pollution. Some designers view pollution as evidence of an incomplete design. By replacing used resources and finding uses for our surplus, we strengthen and create more yields for the whole system and improve the overall integrity of our design.

This principle also calls for the recirculation of knowledge: I teach ten people, they each teach ten more, and so on. In this way we can exponentially share useful skills and information and incite new projects everywhere we go. Exponential learning makes it possible to share large amounts of knowledge in a short period of time. By empowering others through communication and setting examples, we can spread stories of peace in action and connect needs with resources across the globe.

Sample Strategies
- Use found items such as cardboard, wood, metal, and plants to build perennial gardens.
- Compost everything you can, from garden and kitchen debris to paper, human wastes, and old clothes.
- Find or create outlets for your surplus: Start with Internet lists, free boxes, and food banks.
- Buy nothing new, and start at the waste stream when looking for resources.
- Let your mistakes be tools for learning, and keep meticulous notes to help avoid larger mistakes later.
- Replace used resources in nature by planting trees and participating in restoration work.
- Work through the cyclic considerations discussed later in this chapter and close the loop wherever you can.

6. Use It, Move It, or Lose It

Place each element in your design in a location relative to its function. If you spend an extra fifteen minutes every day going out of your way to look for something, you waste almost four days a year that you could use for a vacation or creative project instead. Like putting the soap near the sink, so too can we place every useful item just where we need it.

If you can't find a place for something, maybe it doesn't belong on-site at all. No matter how useful an item may seem, if you don't use it, consider letting it go. Open space provides room for new ideas, and someone else may need just that item for a special project. Sometimes surplus stuff represents things you think you want to do with your life but haven't made the time for. Perhaps it's time to admit to yourself that you may never actually restore that old Chevy truck, and maybe you'd rather have the driveway for a greenhouse instead.

Sample Strategies

- Build compost in the garden, rather than in a bin off to the side.
- Store water barrels wherever you need water, such as near the shower, doghouse, chicken yard, and garden.
- Store different types of tools in the areas where you need them, rather than keeping them in a central tool shed.
- Eliminate dead space by moving out unused items or taking down walls and fences to open the flow.
- Notice microclimates and grow in each what will do well there.
- Get rid of anything that hasn't been used for three years or more. Life is too short to keep the same stuff the whole time.
- Rearrange your house and yard to reflect what you do there, not what the rooms are called.
- Cook on the patio, do art in the kitchen, sleep in the garden, and turn the bedroom into a dance studio. Literally, don't just think but eat, sleep, and live outside the box!

7. Replace Consumption with Creativity

Start small and work outward. It is better to have a small, functional system than a large, dysfunctional one. Rather than planting a huge, intricate garden across every inch of your yard and then attempting to maintain it while conducting the rest of your life, create an integrated system of spaces that encompasses what you want to eat, what you want to do, and how you want to live.

Localize your needs, simplify your desires, and look for the solution that will require the least amount of energy. Each choice carries a certain degree of ecological accountability, and the more you can avoid deep embedded energies in items such as fossil fuels, fresh lumber, plastics, and disposable goods, the closer you can come to ecological harmony. Remember, you can't buy your way to an ecological life—you have to create it.

This principle teaches us to make the least change for the greatest effect. Sometimes an aspect of a design needs only a small adjustment to produce a large improvement. Rather than changing everything around or starting from scratch, we can save time and money when we make what is already happening work to our advantage and generate new ideas in the process. To this end, find solutions in the form of

Our Most Powerful Tool

In his book *A Whack on the Side of the Head*, Dr. Roger von Oech writes that "the real key in being creative lies in what you do with your knowledge."[6] Von Oech presents an array of tips and exercises for spurring creative thought. This excellent book, combined with my own experience with bending the rules, inspired the following set of mental tools to help you flush out your brain and let the ideas flow. If you get stuck, use these exercises to help get the ideas flowing.

Seventeen Ways to Get Creative

1. Take risks. Do not fear failure—it is just another opportunity.
2. Look deep. Look past the proverbial trees and into the subtle details of the forest.
3. Ask *What if?* Speculate, and options will arise.
4. Go to new places. Refresh your mind, your settings, and your relationships.
5. Go to old places and expand. Return to old ideas, inspirations, and colleagues.
6. Be willing to relearn. Question old habits and be willing to unlearn what is no longer useful.
7. Change the rules. Evaluate assumptions, question convention, and change often.
8. Switch roles. Put on a different hat and swap tasks with others.
9. Make work fun. Laugh or quit. Life is too short to waste on suffering, especially if you have a choice.
10. Rock the boat. It's fun, as long as it doesn't tip over in shark-infested waters.
11. Look for more than one right answer. There is usually another solution.
12. Spend time thinking. Not working, writing, talking, or meditating—just thinking.
13. Spend time not thinking. Let preconceived ideas go, and allow for spontaneity.
14. Ask dumb, repetitious, and impractical questions. Ignorance is a blank canvas.
15. Write everything down. Carry a small notebook and use it every day.
16. Write everything down. Review your notes and file them for future reference.
17. Write everything down. Keeping records prevents mistakes and leaves a legacy.

subtle changes rather than added inputs. Instead of looking for what you need to do to improve your garden, look for what you can *stop* doing that will make it more beautiful, more ecological, easier to maintain, and more likely to meet your goals.

In industrial society we often rate our success according to how much we produce, and how quickly and how large. In an ecological design we evaluate success in terms of how well we conserve and perpetuate diversity, how creatively we use available resources, and how little work is needed to maintain a lush, abundant garden. This principle reminds us that less is more, and that thoughtful contemplation is the first and most important task of every project.

Creativity is our most valuable and versatile design tool.

Sample Strategies

- Glean produce from local farms rather than growing a surplus of the same things.
- Match technology to need—don't use a tractor to do a shovel's work.
- Store resources high on-site and let gravity help direct them into the garden.
- Mulch instead of tilling.
- Reproduce local plants from free seeds and cuttings, rather than buying starts.
- Practice voluntary simplicity (see chapter 8).
- Spend a few days resting in the garden, rather than working in it.
- Make hay while the sun shines.
- Use cardboard instead of landscape cloth under garden beds.
- Make compost tea instead of buying fertilizer.
- Replace industry with information by doing the appropriate research and thinking things through.

8. Let Autonomy Reign

Nature provides many patterns and models for systems that perpetuate themselves without destroying their resource base, and most of these systems self-perpetuate without the need for maintenance or interference by humans. If we can learn to trust nature, we can let her do most of the work in our home gardens as well.

Our best allies in these efforts are the organisms already living around us. We can see that even the smallest insect has an essential job to perform in the system. All creatures work, all plants have a purpose, and beneath every city there are hundreds of tons of bacteria, working all through the year to create and repair life. If we pay attention to the tiny details, they will provide opportunities for exponential improvements.

On the other hand, if we overlook the negative impact of a particular element, then it may inhibit or damage the whole. If we can recognize the function and worth of as many details as possible and increase our awareness of the intrinsic interconnectedness of all things, then we can match needs with resources and initiate new, self-sustaining cycles.

This principle teaches us to look for autonomous yield, and to try to mimic the conditions that created it. Encourage volunteer plants and make things easy on yourself. Let leaves fall where they may and do what *feels* right in the garden, rather than what garden magazines say you should do. Work toward low-maintenance, abundant systems that will outlive you.

Autonomy and personal responsibility are the tenets of a free society. The more we practice our understanding of them in the garden, the easier it will be to practice them with one another. To do this we must first recognize and value functional interdependence in the garden and in our communities. Only then can we rejoin the whole without losing the integrity of any individual part.

Sample Strategies

- Use prolific weeds for food, fiber, and mulch rather than eradicating them.
- Let tomatoes and cucumbers sprawl on the ground instead of trellising them.
- Harvest and eat wild foods such as blackberries and maple syrup.
- Make paths where people will walk instead of trying to get people to walk on a new path.
- Use biological resources that will self-perpetuate to solve problems, such as living machines that cleanse wastewater.
- Establish living fences with plants such as filbert, willow, apple, and hawthorn.
- Encourage diverse insect and wildlife populations, and observe rather than interfere with their cycles.
- Ask not what the garden can do for you, but what you can do for the garden.

9. Keep Your Chin Up

This final principle is easily the most useful, and the most important to uphold. Attitude is everything, and in our tolerance and flexibility lie the keys to a long and happy life. If you don't have fun while gardening, you probably won't spend much time doing it. Make choices that will make you happy, and that will result in the ongoing enjoyment of your garden space and your life. The garden should be your sanctuary, not just another obligation. Do what comes naturally to you, and create a space that encourages you to be yourself.

Traditional permaculture teaches us several attitudinal principles, such as "Mistakes are tools for learning," "Problems are solutions," and "The designer limits the yield." These ring true throughout every phase of life. If we are not consistently open to change, challenges, and new ideas, we will severely limit the success of our work and waste time trying to keep things the same. Nature never stops evolving, and neither can we. By remaining flexible and receptive to feedback, we become adaptable lifelong learners, so that no matter how impossible the situation might seem, if we keep a good attitude, open our minds, and think creatively, the solution will come.

This principle of flexibility also applies to your body. You can't work on an empty stomach, and you can't build a bridge with a bad back. The following strategies include some of the most important things we can do for our bodies and, by extension, the gardens they tend.

Sample Strategies
- Keep a journal of frustrating moments, and refer to it later to avoid repeated mistakes.
- Be kind and willing to negotiate problems with fellow workers.
- Identify your behavioral weak spots and abuse issues, and work through them with a counselor.
- Spend a few minutes resting each day—show me a workaholic and I'll show you a shortcut to total burnout. Love your hammock as you do your pitchfork: as an essential tool.
- Listen to the birds, smell the flowers, and take time to enjoy the fruits of your labor.
- Eat well, drink plenty of water, and stretch daily.

**Take time each day to relax in the garden and
enjoy the fruits of your labors.**

- Stand up straight. Take a few dance classes and learn how to
  hold your spine correctly.
- Have a dance party in the garden.
- Sleep in the garden.
- Make love in the garden.
- Be proud of your work, share it with others, and welcome
  their positive and negative feedback.

Cyclic Considerations

The next ring in the design wheel asks us to consider nine natural
cycles. Each of these cycles has a profoundly significant influence on
our work, and by working with rather than against them we avoid mistakes and bring our garden into an easier harmony with nature.

We've looked at how cycles present opportunities, and how we can
interact with a cycle and divert its flow into our projects. Within each
of the cycles below there are countless opportunities, between the
source and the sink, to increase yield and efficiency. Learning to recog-

nize cycles deepens our understanding of nature and helps us place our ecological selves in context with our natural surroundings.

Through each step of the design process, look at the way your plans might influence each cycle. Also look for opportunities to make your work easier by tapping into what's already flowing. Several of the nine cycles I emphasize here have been covered in previous chapters, so I will just run through them briefly:

1. *Waste.* Again, I cannot overstate the importance of recycling waste toward our goals. Remember to look first to the waste cycle for resources, and to avoid sending resources to the sink. See chapter 2 for details.
2. *Water.* See chapter 3.
3. *Soil.* See chapter 4.
4. *Seeds.* See chapters 5 and 6.
5. *Cosmos.* All gardeners must consider the patterns of the sun, but what about the rest of the cosmos? I strongly recommend also noting the patterns of the moon and other planets through each phase of the design process. They will affect you, your plants, soil communities, and many other aspects of your work.
6. *Society.* This includes asking yourself what your community needs and what it can provide. Consider the social impacts of your work and look for ways to make it more powerful and more beneficial.
7. *Wilderness.* Always leave a little bit of your garden wild, and always direct some of your energy toward preserving and perpetuating wild places nearby. When the wilderness goes, we go, so take the time to consider it.
8. *Self.* Your own cycles are just as important as the rest. How do you feel? What do you need? There will be times when you are deeply inspired to turn your whole town into a paradise garden, and times when you couldn't care less. Note these patterns and compare them with the other cycles so that you can see when to tap the flow of your own positive energy.
9. *Chaos.* In the words of John Briggs, "The scientistic culture that has increasingly surrounded us—and some would say imprisoned us—for the last 100 years sees the world in terms

of analysis, quantification, symmetry, and mechanism. Chaos helps free us from these confines. By appreciating chaos, we begin to envision the world as a flux of patterns enlivened with sudden turns, strange mirrors, subtle and surprising relationships, and the continual fascination with the unknown."[7]

Always keep in mind that the natural cycles have their own agenda. Try your best to integrate rather than interfere with them. The more you keep track of your options, the more educated your garden choices will become.

This spiral design process, while it may seem laborious or complicated, will help you bring your garden closer to paradise. These principles and techniques also apply to designing other layers of our lives, such as how we live at home and how we interact with the community. The next few chapters will take us beyond the garden to examine the other pieces of the puzzle, such as consumer choices, community involvement, group process, and working with younger generations to ensure the paradise gardens of the future. We'll start at home and spiral outward.

8. Beyond the Garden

Slowly, even among the squarest of citizens, the suspicion is growing that it is the very nature of our vastly developed industrial system to produce an environment which is poisonous to our bodies and toxic to our minds. Perhaps the making and buying of goods is *not* the main goal of a sane society. Perhaps a bigger Gross National Product is not a god worth sacrificing our lives to. Perhaps we must question the whole orientation of American values. The early labor-union leader Sam Gompers once summed up the aims of the labor movement as "More!" But maybe now we need less.

—**Ernest Callenbach**[1]

We must be the change we wish to see in the world.

—**M. K. Gandhi**[2]

Everything needful to be completely human is available to us in the environment—the garden and neighborhood. We can rely on this truth because "humanness" is a creation of the environment, the most recent manifestation of a coevolution between our genes and all the other genes out there that has been going on since the beginning of life on earth. Much chancier is the possibility that everything we need to be completely human is available to us in the city, or through money.

—**Joe Hollis**[3]

Stepping Lightly on the Earth

So far most of this book has been about gardening. Not just any gardening, but the type that results in low-maintenance perennial edible ecosystems that lend themselves to the long-term ecological health of a bioregion. This is a lifetime's pursuit, and one that can be deeply fulfilling for the people who do it.

Unfortunately just growing gardens will not convert this wasteful, polluting society into a fruitful and healthy one. Our gardens must not only produce food for ourselves and other living beings, but also create a backdrop for whole communities of people working together to reduce their personal and collective impact on the natural world. Our gardens provide the bounty and the inspiration, but it is us, the gardeners, who must provide the real change.

This change comes in many colors. At the top of the list is consumer choices. From what we put on and into our bodies, where we sleep, and how we get around to how we make money and educate children, every choice we make has deep ecological implications. Every time we spend money, there is an ecological choice to make: *To harm or to help the earth?* And while it may not seem like one family's changes could affect a whole world, the vast environmental destruction we see today is a direct result of irresponsible, irreverent consumption.

> *Every time we spend money, there is an ecological choice to make.*

Our consumer choices reflect our lifestyles, and it is these lifestyles that we can and must change to develop and promote more ecological ways. Our individual lifestyles bleed into our families' lifestyles and into the neighborhoods around us. And as we change as individuals, our communities change with us. Like a butterfly effect, our evolution toward ecological harmony is exponential.

As I said in the beginning of this book, if we insist that our human communities not only provide for their own needs but also contribute to and improve the natural environment, we will move toward a healthy, thriving human ecology. The garden is an excellent place to start, but we must go beyond it to incorporate ecological ethics into every aspect of our daily lives.

Fortunately the design principles I discussed in chapter 7 not only work well in the garden but also apply to the rest of our world. We can improve the ecological integrity of our lifestyles through applying these principles wherever possible. By using the spiral design concept to evaluate our homes, jobs, and communities, we can identify opportunities for sharing space, recycling waste, and eating and growing organic food. I touched on some of these ideas in the first two chapters of this book. Now I'll go deeper, into an assortment of options and practical strategies.

Some of these options may seem radical, unrealistic, impractical, or somehow intimidating when compared with what is currently familiar. Still, remember that electricity, bleach, petrochemicals, and many of the other things that help maintain this superclean, paranoid culture are all inventions of the past few centuries, and humans have been thriving on Earth for millions of years. Could our recent, rapid decline toward extinction be due to these modern "conveniences"? Could they in fact be harming rather than helping us?

A thorough treatise on the art of ecological living could fill a hundred volumes, but the main point is this: As individuals, neighborhoods, and communities begin to fulfill their needs on a local, more simplified basis, the extent to which they degrade the natural environment decreases. By consuming less, learning to make the most out of what we have, and sharing surplus, we can slow the destruction caused by our culture and improve our personal and community environments.

Get Over It

This chapter is a plea to examine your comfort level and determine whether the things you think you need are enriching or just sugarcoating your life. Do you really need all those cars, appliances, chemicals, subscriptions, new clothes, plastic toys, and airplane vacations? Does anyone really want to keep up with the Joneses?

When I tell people I live on about six thousand dollars a year, that I don't have a refrigerator or hot water in my kitchen, and that I compost my own manure, they think I'm crazy. They say in disgust, "How can you *live* like that?" Yet this is how the vast majority of people in the world live. Sure, many of those people do not have a choice. They struggle every day to feed their children, stay healthy, and survive in bleak or hopeless poverty—much of which is caused by the exploitation of land, labor, and natural resources by wealthier cultures (like ours).

Yet millions of families around the world find joy in a voluntary simplicity. They grow much of their own food, make the best out of available resources, and enjoy the natural luxury of a simple, frugal life. They go dancing instead of shopping and watch birds instead of television. This way of living increases our connection to the earth, enriches our character, and usually improves our physical health.

Your ecological footprint is the number of acres required to support your lifestyle.

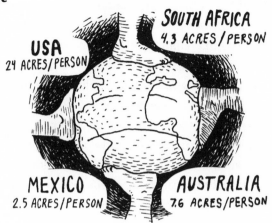

Much of the harmful consumption in the United States and other Western cultures is a result of paranoia about germs and disease. We are terrified of bacteria, yet our biology depends on them to survive. Show me a house full of cleaning supplies and I will show you a medicine cabinet full of pharmaceutical drugs.

Vinegar, natural soap, baking soda, a good scrub brush, and some thick cotton rags are all anyone needs to clean a house. The chlorine-based chemicals that sterilize our homes pollute natural waterways and cause cancer and ozone depletion. I never use chlorine, yet I rarely get sick, never go to the doctor or take medications, and am physically stronger at age thirty-four than I was at twenty. Without digressing too much, I will just say that you will be doing yourself, your family, and the earth a favor if you never use another chlorine-based chemical again.

Everyone has their own comfort level, and it is important to feel safe in our work and living environments; still, it is surprisingly empowering to challenge yourself to let go of what you think you need to make room for the life you really want. Again, this is not a demand that everyone get rid of everything they own and move to a commune in Tennessee; rather, this is a gentle encouragement toward a rational assessment of our addiction to consumerism, and toward taking control of our lives.

It is up to each of us to examine where we are now against where we would like to be and to formulate a plan of action. In general, look at what it takes to furnish what you eat and use, and wherever possible

Embedded Energy and Your Ecological Footprint

Everything we use has deep ecological implications. It is easy to overlook the damage our everyday lives do to the natural environment, but we can gain a more tangible understanding of the embedded energy in our lifestyles by determining our "ecological footprint."

The international Earth Day Network offers an ecological footprint analysis.[4] Through an online questionnaire, you can estimate how many acres of land, in your own country and elsewhere, it takes to produce what you consume. According to this group, the average person in the United States requires twenty-four acres, yet worldwide there exist only four and a half biologically productive acres per person.

This means that if everyone lived like the average American, we would need five more Earths just to sustain the current population. In Sweden the average citizen has a footprint of about twelve acres, while Mexico is setting examples at two and a half acres per person.

I took the quiz and found out that, even though I am a vegetarian and have a relatively ecofriendly lifestyle, I still require eight acres' worth of natural resources to support myself. If everyone lived like me, we would still need twice as much Earth than exists to sustain the current population. If I cut out dairy products, my ecological footprint drops by two acres, and if I stop using airplanes I'm down to just four acres total, which is, theoretically, a sustainable lifestyle for this planet. These changes are possible for me, and necessary if I want to walk my talk. And you?

minimize the energy required to support your lifestyle. This is not about being perfect, but about striving for balance. It is about acknowledging responsibility, getting creative, and challenging ourselves to improve. The best we can do is work toward an awareness that will allow us to live comfortably and creatively, and without harming others or the environment.

That being said, here are some options. As you read through, think back to the design principles in the preceding chapter. Many of them will recur here, as we see how lessons learned in the garden apply throughout our lives.

Eat Good Food

If you change only one thing about your lifestyle, this should be it. An organic diet of fresh, local foods leads to a sound mind, a sound body, and a sound ecology. In a way, organic food is a gateway drug to an ecological consciousness. When you eat organically, your body chemistry changes and you become more attuned to the subtle harmonies of nature.

I know I sound a little far out here, but millions of people are victims of the self-imposed physical and emotional malnutrition that results from a lifetime of gastronomic complacency—and look at the sick, unsustainable culture they live in. I am here to tell you: The food is the key. This is biologically, spiritually, socially, and simply, true.

Many common diseases can be largely avoided through dietary means, including cancer, heart disease, diabetes, and of course emphysema, alcoholism, and obesity. Other afflictions, such as asthma, fatigue, chronic pain, and most skin problems, can be traced back to food allergies, most commonly to industrial foods such as wheat, soy, and meat.

An ecological lifestyle depends upon responsible and ethical food choices. It is extremely difficult to become a creative, self-actualized individual in a healthy, ecological culture when all you've had to eat is Twinkies and Taco Bell. Arguably much of the violence and stupidity in the world today could be avoided if people were better nourished and thus better able to make rational choices. When was the last time you behaved poorly because you were not feeding yourself properly?

One of the biggest barriers to eating a 100 percent local and organic diet is availability. Especially in urban areas, even if you grow a big

You are what you eat.

garden at home, you will probably have to supplement your diet with food from off site, but shrink-wrapped organic mangoes from five thousand miles away are not the solution. Look for supplies as close to home as possible, and try to avoid trucked-in and/or packaged goods. The average piece of produce consumed in the United States travels around fifteen hundred miles from farm to table, almost as far as Sacagawea traveled with Lewis and Clark, and three times farther than a healthy American walks in a whole year. Consider the embedded energies in everything you consume and make choices accordingly.

Consuming local, unpackaged, organically grown food reduces pollution and builds stronger communities. Especially in the United States, where the prevalence of consumerism has pulled us out of our gardens and into the mall, it is essential that we seek out and support producers and distributors of healthy, live food. This way we nurture local food security and ourselves at once. If you must import goods from afar, however, order in bulk from a local natural food store or online. If you don't have a good local distributor, consider starting an organic food cooperative in your town or neighborhood.

When making consumer choices, beware of toxics wrapped in a green shroud—many companies label products as natural and even organic when the ingredients are barely edible, let alone good for you. Educate yourself about where your food comes from and make wise choices.

You might notice that I am avoiding a debate about animal products. This is such a multilayered issue that I will say only that whether you choose to be omnivorous, vegetarian, vegan, or opportunivore, let those choices come from a deep commitment to living in peaceful harmony with all species.

If you can't find any organic farms or food sources locally, ask your current grocer to start stocking organic foods. Look online for organic garden clubs, food buyers' co-ops, and regional farm associations. You might find a whole new community of people to share your time and interests with!

Going organic isn't just about organic food or organic gardening: It's a way of life. It's not about certification or shopping at the most politically correct supermarket. Going organic is about taking control of your food supply and, thus, your life.

Share the Wealth

I cannot overstate the importance of sharing food, seeds, information, and other surpluses with your immediate community. Sharing reduces waste, encourages participation, and strengthens connections among people. As we recycle resources, promote biodiversity, and encourage relationships, we not only improve our own lives but also increase the integrity and liveability of the whole community.

Because it is impossible to create a self-reliant human settlement on one urban lot, these interactions are essential. We cannot conserve diversity, regenerate the natural world, and save the human race all by ourselves. We must work together in well-organized yet autonomous networks to develop alternatives and bring about long-term, localized change.

When I worked for Greenpeace I spent four nights a week for three years walking through all sorts of neighborhoods, knocking on doors and introducing myself to people. I found common ground with many people, and we talked about a wide range of issues, from toxics and pollution to cancer, education, and child care. Year after year I returned to the same houses, and people again welcomed me inside, gave me tea and cookies, and shared their latest concerns and successes.

An interesting thing about this work was the fact that many of the people whom I spoke with shared the interests and concerns of their

Liberate resources from the waste stream to help liberate your community from unsustainable consumer cycles.

neighbors, yet they did not know one another. For example, three houses on the same street all had organic vegetable gardens, yet the people had never met. Another house had a pile of unwanted wood out back while the neighbors bought firewood from the store.

Everywhere I went people who lived on the same city block had much in common yet were totally unaware of the close proximity of their like-minded neighbors. If just one person had initiated a project or event in such a neighborhood, these people would have been able to connect, share resources, and organize toward a better community together.

Sharing improves our collective situation in several ways. First, we meet new people and learn about their interests. Through these connections, we make new friends, find new jobs, share new experiences, and discover new opportunities.

Next, we gain better access to food, land, education, health care, child care, and professional services. In the event of natural or political disaster, local support networks will be better equipped to survive than most isolated individuals could ever hope to be.

Third, we improve the environmental health of our bioregions when communities work together to provide food, shelter, and other resources to one another, and when they form coalitions to conserve water, restore wilderness, and steward organic farmland.

Sharing, the act of giving away what we have, challenges social and economic barriers by giving underprivileged people better access to resources and information. This helps establish a truer equality among community members and creates a healthy climate for a mutual and ecological evolution. We are already a part of the ecological community that biologically supports us, and becoming intentional participants in the human community within that ecology opens up unlimited possibilities for peace and abundance.

In short, sharing helps give our lives more meaning and helps others find meaning through us. By letting go of our individualistic aspirations and embracing the needs of the whole, we and our communities become simultaneously stronger, more essential, and more successful. We'll jump deeper into strategies for building community in the next chapter. But first, let's try on some personal choices that can set an example for our communities while enriching our own lives now.

Close the Loop

The seven R's of cycling

The seven R's of cycling

Here again we find the basic ecological principle of turning waste into resources. Remember the seven R's of cyclic opportunity: Rethink, Redesign, Reduce, Reuse, Repair, Refuse, Recycle. Move through your home and workplace and see how many ways you can close the loop between what you use, what you produce, what you share, and what you can do without.

Most households these days recycle glass, cans, and paper, but recycling goes far beyond these consumer items. We can recycle clothes, dishes, toys, tools, plants, food, knowledge, wood, metal, bikes, and much more. It is not enough just to send the trash to the recycling center—we must also consume recycled materials and limit what we consume as much as possible. We should look for and prefer recycled resources to new ones, and we must follow our surplus through its complete life cycle to ensure its efficient use.

Think about the heaps of useful building materials collecting dust in every alley in the United States. In Eugene an organization called Bring Recycling collects and recycles these valuable resources. The group operates a used building-materials warehouse where people can buy recycled lumber, metal, hardware, insulation, plumbing, doors, windows, and more for a fraction of what it would cost new. In 2001 Bring recycled more than two hundred thousand tons of landfill-bound materials back into the community for reuse.[5]

These materials are often of a very high quality. For example, an old deck that was built with old-growth redwood but later torn down would make an excellent guest cottage or sauna. You can't get wood like that anymore—those trees are either gone or protected now, and imagine that valuable wood going into the landfill! Why are we still logging old-growth forests when most landfills are 60 percent wood?[6]

We built our entire chicken coop out of materials we found in the orchard or tangled in the grass around the farm. By capturing waste, we generated a resource, created a larger space for the chickens, increased our egg production, cleaned up some of the junk around the farm, became better builders, and didn't spend a dime.

Ride a Bike

How we get around has a tremendous effect on the environment, our personal health, and how we treat other cultures. Automobile accidents are one of the leading causes of death, and road building destroys native ecosystems around the world daily. Cars kill people, animals, and insects and perpetuate the illusion that we can sustain an isolated, temperature-controlled, Mach-speed culture.

We know that cars are horrible, airplanes worse, and trains and buses still pretty bad for the environment. But everyone wants to get from point A to point B sometimes, and we owe it to ourselves and our planet to use the most appropriate, energy-efficient means possible, even if it means we have to give up a little privacy or convenience to do it.

The first and most obvious solution is to ditch that stinky old car and get on your bike. I grew up in the suburbs of Los Angeles, and while I spent plenty of time on a bike as a teenager, when I got my driver's license at sixteen it was all over. I didn't get on a bike again for almost ten years. When I finally did, I fell totally in love. Cars are prisons. Bikes are freedom. Why sit in traffic when you could be cruising happily along the river, singing with the birds and getting in shape?

In many places bikes are most people's primary form of transportation. This is usually an economic choice, but you will find that people in these places are generally healthier, and that the air and water quality is much better in areas with fewer cars than in big, car-ridden

Ride a bike instead of driving to improve your own health and that of the environment.

cities such as Los Angeles or New York. Still, even these metropolitan areas have well-developed bike paths that lead all around the city. Maps are often available at local bike shops. Many city buses will allow you to bring a bike on board or have a rack mounted on the front of the bus for times when you need to get somewhere farther or faster.

Sure, you might get wet when it rains or be a little sore the first few weeks, but life is short—why not experience it firsthand rather than from inside a rolling metal box? I don't know how to convince you that the joys of choosing a bike as your main means of transportation far outweigh the inconveniences. I can only say, get a decent bike that fits your body (very important), put on a helmet to protect your brilliant mind, and give it a chance. Once you spend a few weeks cruising around, getting used to the new experience and increased exercise, you will surely agree that riding a bike to work, school, and everywhere else is easy and empowering.

If riding a bike instead of driving just doesn't work for you—for physical, climatic, or other reasons—then here are a few other suggestions that will help you reduce your impact:

Ride the Bus. Public transportation, whether bus, train, or rickshaw, isn't just for people who are too young, too old, or too poor to drive. It's for everyone, and if you pay taxes then you're paying for it anyway, so why not ride? Riding the bus gives you time to read and interact with a diverse cross section of your community. With just a little planning and commitment, you can probably replace most of your driving with public transportation.

Share a Car. In many countries private vehicles don't go anywhere unless they are full of people pitching in for gas money. We can also make this choice because we care about the environment. In South and Central America drivers pull up to busy intersections and call out for people who need rides around town. In the States car sharing usually happens in organized collectives, where people share insurance costs and coordinate rides and driving privileges through a website or central bulletin board.

Go Biodiesel or SVO. Biodiesel is diesel fuel made from vegetable sources, most often soybeans, and it will power most diesel engines without any mechanical alterations. While the viability of such a fuel is entirely dependent on the integrity of the agriculture that produces it, it is a decidedly more feasible and less polluting option than the continued dependence on rapidly dwindling fossil fuel supplies.

Another, even more innovative solution is the use of *recycled* vegetable oil, also known as SVO, to run a diesel engine. The SVO approach does require a significant mechanical adjustment to your diesel engine. Kits and information can be found online; also look in the resources section for some good places to start.[7] Still, SVO is not perfect. You have to consider the embedded energy in the car itself (metal, plastic, labor, textiles), as well as in the fryer grease. Then there are the emissions caused by the burning oil, which, though less than with petrochemicals, still pollute. There are also several other alternative fuels being developed and used around the world, but none of them could be considered ecologically sustainable. Most of these seem "better" in some way than petrofuels, but generally, with cars, airplanes, and other gas hogs, the bad outweighs the good when you consider the long term. Here's another option:

Stay Home. In his treatise on paradise gardening Joe Hollis expounds the virtues of staying home. He writes, "The solution is not gasohol but reducing the reason for traveling (usually the getting and spending of money). Why not spend less time going away to make money to buy food and more time growing it?" This brings us to another crucial and related point.

Unplug Your Life

If you haven't killed your television already, the time is now. You will never regret it. If you are used to spending a lot of time channel-surfing, it might be hard to imagine what else to do, but once you get started you will never run out of ideas.

The amount of electricity you use is directly proportionate to the long-term damage your lifestyle inflicts upon your ecology. If you want to live with nature, you have to go outside. Turn everything off, leave the stereo headphones behind, and cultivate an outdoor life, rich in experience rather than gadgetry. Go outside and garden. Go for a walk. Stretch. Sing. Play an instrument. Write poetry. Tell jokes. Talk to your neighbors. Daydream. Hang out with dogs and cats. Watch birds. Go swimming. Take a nap. Cook. Read. Play with children. Dance. Make love.

Once you're free from the TV, take a look around at the rest of the machines in your life. Why not eliminate the microwave, the coffee-maker, the leaf blower, the alarm clock, and the bug zapper, and open up all that space for creative projects? Wasteful energy sinks like these are unnecessary trinkets at best. Even mainstream essentials such as stoves, refrigerators, and water heaters can become more efficient or be eliminated altogether, depending on your diet, climate, and comfort level.

We'll start with the small stuff. First, replace the microwave with better planning; fewer leftovers means less need for reheating. It doesn't really take that much longer to cook food on a regular stove anyway. Next, drink organic tea from local herbs instead of coffee, or at least use a French press instead of an electric brewer. Leaf blowers and bug zappers are just absurd—lose them immediately if you are at all serious about ecological living. Other appliances? Dry clothes outside or over a woodstove. Wash dishes by hand. Shave with a straight razor. Most electric gadgets are just wasting precious energy as well as your time and your money.

The stove, fridge, and water heater are a little more difficult to let go of for some people. Let's look at each of these briefly.

Energy-Efficient Cooking and Heating

There are several excellent ways to conserve energy while cooking food, heating water, and heating your house. You can use recycled materials to build solar ovens, solar water heaters, fuel-efficient stoves, and heat

Build a simple yet highly efficient rocket stove out of recycled tin cans.

Cook with a Blanket Box

One way to reduce energy consumption in the kitchen is to use a blanket box for cooking. A blanket box insulates the pot so you can take it off the stove but keep cooking whatever is inside. The box should be big enough to hold a soup pan or stew pot. An insulated picnic cooler, found used at a thrift store, works very well, or just build a simple box out of recycled plywood scraps. Choose a pot with a tight-fitting lid—I prefer stainless steel, with good handles. Now all you need is a small wool blanket.

The blanket box works great for steaming rice or vegetables, cooking beans or grains, and keeping food warm for hours. Just bring the food to a rolling boil on the stove, simmer for a few minutes, put on the lid, turn off the stove, and place the pot in the box. Wrap the blanket carefully around the pot, so you don't upset the seal on the lid but do com-pletely surround the pot with wool. Now go do something else for a while and come back when you're hungry! Blanket boxes work so well, and save so much energy, they should come standard in every house, right beside the stove.

A blanket box uses the insulating power of wool to conserve fuel.

exchangers, as well as to insulate existing stoves, water tanks, and buildings. I don't have room in this book to go into much detail about these effective and highly valuable options, but I can provide a brief overview and direct you to the resources section for a list of excellent references.

We'll start with cooking. Most people in the States use either an electric stove—the least efficient use of energy—or a gas stove, which is better, but still very consumptive and wasteful. But around the world the most common way to cook food is on a wood-burning stove. Aprovecho Research Center in Cottage Grove, Oregon, has a team of stove builders who travel around the world building fuel-efficient wood-burning stoves. Many of their designs are easy to construct with recycled resources and use less fuel and cause less pollution than any other type of cooking. They also offer some excellent designs for solar ovens that bake bread (and cookies!) using just the sun.

Whatever type of stove you use, you can save fuel by building a small shield that fits around the flame and your pot, keeping the heat focused on cooking your food rather than letting it dissipate outward. You can also use a blanket box (see the sidebar above), which uses insulation to finish cooking the food after you remove it from the stove.

When using a woodstove to heat a building, consider building a heat exchanger. This is a double-walled metal cylinder that wraps around your

This solar shower uses a flat plate collector to heat water and a recycled tank to store it.

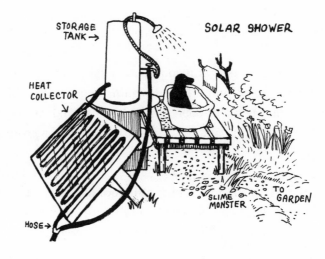

stovepipe, much like the little cooking shield above wraps around a warm pot. The heat exchanger increases the surface area of the stovepipe and keeps significantly more of the heat from the stove in the room. Heat exchangers have been shown to cut fuel needs in half or better.

Similar technologies can be used to build an assortment of water heaters. Some of these use glass to magnify the sun's rays and heat the water. Others involve running water pipes through or around stovepipes, using surplus heat from the stove. Some of these gadgets use gravity or convection to direct the water, while others require a pressurized water source. I have seen dozens of good examples of ecofriendly water heating, all of which could have been built by almost anyone in her own backyard. Again, I regret that there is no room here to discuss specific designs, but the resources section will point you in the right direction.

Eschew Freon

This includes the refrigerator and most air conditioners. You don't have to give up on keeping you or your food cool; there are excellent alternatives, such as draft boxes, root cellars, solar fans, and design strategies.

The last refrigerator I lived with was like a fourth housemate in a small house with an adjacent living room/kitchen layout. We had no choice. We didn't want the fridge in our faces all day, every day, so we set him up out in the carport and put a nice comfy chair in his place in the kitchen. We ran an extension cord out to him, but once he was out of sight, we found we never really wanted that ugly old fridge at our parties anyway. We kept our food in the cabinets, in bread boxes and jars, and started using the fridge only for luxury items like cheese and ice cream.

One day the neglected old fridge died. He took one final ticking-and-groaning heave and just shut down. We called the landlord and asked him to send a hearse. He asked if we wanted a replacement and we told him no thanks. That was four years ago, and though I have been known to stash a tub of ice cream in the neighbor's fridge, I haven't lived with one since.

Of all the consumer objects found in the average American home, the refrigerator is the most hideous, the most horrible. It's huge. It hums all night. It leaks. It's toxic, from start to finish. And it's ugly. Even the most elegant designer refrigerator is a homely behemoth at best. Yet for many of us it hums happily through our relationship with food, every day, every hour of our lives. The fridge is where it all comes from and where it all goes to die. Later, we argue over who gets to scrape the green fur and pink goo out from under the drawers where we keep our "fresh" foods.

Refrigeration deteriorates nutritional value and kills the flavor in many fresh fruits and vegetables. You may have experienced a garden-fresh tomato that tasted like hell after just a few hours in the fridge. Most of what people refrigerate will keep just fine on a shady shelf,

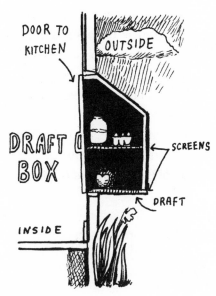

A draft box filters cool air through stored food to preserve it.

unrefrigerated. Fresh eggs will keep for months; bread, fruits, and vegetables will last a week; most condiments have vinegar, which is an excellent natural preservative, and will keep for years.

Getting rid of your refrigerator is a great way to open up space in the kitchen, reduce unpleasant cleaning chores, and cut a big chunk out of your energy consumption at home. People lived without refrigerators for millennia, and billions still do. Mainstream society as a whole is extremely paranoid about bacteria, but as long as we wash our hands often and don't eat anything that smells rotten, there isn't much to fear. Buying local food helps; it's fresher and will last much longer unrefrigerated.

Try building a draft box and/or a root cellar to store perishables. A draft box is a simple wooden cabinet with screened shelves, mounted onto a shady side of the house. One side opens into the kitchen, like any other cabinet. The back of the box is screened but open to the outside. The draft box uses convection to bring cool air up through the stored food.

There are also several types of root cellars, from a small pit with a picnic cooler in it to an actual structure built into the side of a hill. See the resources section for a list of excellent books on storing and preserving food. The point here is that your fridge is unnecessary and it might be time to let it go.

As for the air conditioners, try opening windows across the car or room from each other to get a cross-ventilation going. Invest in a solar-powered fan. Or try hanging damp cotton sheets in a breezy spot near the house and setting up an outdoor room there. They will create a cool microclimate that you can work, eat, or sleep in.

In short, as we lessen our dependence upon electricity, petrochemicals, and manufactured gadgets, we come closer to a more natural lifestyle. Plus we save money on electric bills and gadget purchase and repair costs.

Buy Less and Buy Local

So far we've looked at a wide array of consumer choices, from making dietary changes to using appropriate transportation and getting rid of unnecessary gadgets. When you simplify your life in these ways, you will quickly find that you need to go shopping much less, and that you

Build a stronger local economy by keeping your money in your community as long as possible.

need to buy less stuff to sustain your lifestyle. Still, until these ideas take deeper root in our culture, you will need to buy some things to support yourself and your family. Here are some pointers to help make those purchases as ecological as possible.

First, remember the design principle from the last chapter: "Replace consumption with creativity." Every time you think you need to buy something, ask yourself how you can avoid buying it, what you can use instead, or whether you can innovate something out of recycled materials. A home full of handcrafted dishes and restored furniture is far more ecological—and in my opinion much more interesting—than a house full of prefab junk from Wal-Mart.

When you decide that you must have something, and that the only way to get it is by buying it, look for a source as close to you as possible. Choose a geographic area that makes sense for you, and buy only goods from that region. Some people buy only stuff made in America; others insist that everything they consume be produced within a five-hundred-mile radius of their home. The closer you come to home, the less likely your purchases are to support the use of fossil fuels, excessive packaging and pollution, and questionable to horrid labor circumstances. Even Fair Trade goods are transported using diesel or jet fuel, and just because workers are being paid more than at other factories near them doesn't mean they are making a living wage, or that they have access to any of the privileges the American distributors have. I suggest avoiding international goods whenever you can and looking for local alternatives to luxury items such as coffee, sugar, silk, petrochemicals, and—sadly—chocolate.

Beyond supporting local and organic economies, buying less and buying local means stepping away from the consumer culture and getting out from under the burden of so much stuff. Not only do you save money from buying less stuff (and selling what you have), but you also gain time by saving work hours to pay for stuff and spending less time moving all that stuff around (imagine never having to clean out the garage again). You create open space for new projects and change the aesthetics of your home by eliminating so much clutter and plastic.

Make Time

One of the most common excuses I hear for why people don't garden and do the other things in this book is "I don't have time." Another is "I don't have any money." We've looked at many ways to be frugal with money by making good use of available resources, but what about time? I know of several excellent strategies for bringing more free time into a busy life, but before we get into the details, let's make an important foray into the ways we as a culture perceive and document time.

The ancient Mayan calendar followed the cycles of Venus, the first and brightest star in the sky. Our modern clock and calendar system is based on the movements of Earth and her moon. However, these heavenly bodies never return to the exact same place twice. They rotate, they orbit, they speed up and slow down, but they do not do these things the same way every time. Because of this, the tools we use to document the passage of time must fudge the truth into predictable, repeating cycles, which are programmed into machines and printed out years ahead.

Eliminate your television and see how much more time you have for learning and leisure.

Billions of people organize their lives around this little ruse, convinced that the passage of time is a straight line from birth to death. Any little quiver, any bump on this long and narrow road, is seen as a perversion, an unlikely superstition best reserved for mad scientists and acidheads. But nothing in nature moves in a straight line, and time is no exception.

Time is not linear; it's a cycle. It curls, spills, flows around obstacles, pools, flashes with light and darkness. It can be swallowed, absorbed, filtered, lost, and found. Time is not static; like every other element in a design, its form and value are relative to scale and placement within the system. A weekend for us is a lifetime to a butterfly. She will emerge, learn to survive, explore, and procreate, and then grow old and find a place to die, all in the time it takes us to mow the lawn, watch a few football games, and eat nine meals.

In reality, what we know about time is just a twinkle in the eye of the all-encompassing face of what we don't understand, scientifically or otherwise. So why then do we need clocks, calendars, and computers to keep track of how long we've been alive, awake, asleep, at work, or on vacation? Some would say mainly for commerce. Businessmen in early urban cultures invented machines that would document time to assist them in collecting debts and managing investments.[8] Since then time has become synonymous with money, and around the world people sell their personal time to make money to survive.

Like money, time can be spent or saved, wasted and lost, and we never seem to have enough of it. But this commodified attitude about time does not take into account the many layers of experience that each moment contains. Unlike money, time is something of nature, something that exists all around us, whether we see it as valid or not. Money is about stuff, power, ownership; time is about life, experience, and freedom. To break out of this bewitching but utterly false marriage between money and time, we must return to the understanding of time as a pattern in living nature and find ways to integrate that pattern into our gardens and other projects.

Our perception of time has a great influence over the way we live. Just as the past and future exist in our minds, memories, records, and designs, so does the present exist in many layers at once. Like a paradise garden, our experience grows in exponential directions at once. Consider a time when you were traveling and every day became a significant and memorable series of events. Or a moment when you were passionately in love, or deeply involved in a project, and the whole day went by in what seemed like two hours. Was it like dreamtime, where lifetimes can go by in the twitch of an eye? How are these experiences of time different from when you are driving to work, watching television, or shopping?

Woody Guthrie once said, "You can't kill time without injuring eternity." So how can we make best use of the now while planning for the future, learning from the past, and being completely present? Here are some ideas.

Get Rid of Clocks, Calendars, and Mirrors

Try spending a week without any clocks, calendars, or mirrors. More consumer gadgets, these objects document and reflect the passage of time and keep us pretending that everything is linear, predictable, and altogether unnatural. Not to say you should never use one again, but consider letting go of your dependence on manufactured timekeeping objects. You will be amazed at the results. I could write a whole book on just this concept. Imagine waking up when you feel rested, eating when you are hungry, celebrating holidays on whatever day you want, and basing your self-image on how you feel rather than how you look.

I haven't used an alarm clock for ten years, because I just can't take the intrusion. Waking up like that can't be good for mental health. I am a true believer in every person's right to sleep as much as she needs to, but even when you have to get up early there are other ways to rouse yourself. Many people claim to have an excellent internal clock, and they tell stories of waking up right before the alarm goes off. You can probably do this too. If you tend to sleep very heavily and feel dependent on an alarm clock, try taking afternoon naps, cutting back on caffeine and sugar, and scheduling appointments for later in the day.

By removing the clock we place trust in ourselves to know when it is the right time to do something, such as wake up, eat, go to work, go to bed, and so forth. This might seem impractical for some people, but just try it for a few weeks. If you enjoy being free of the alarm but need to get up early every single morning, get a rooster or move your bed so that the morning sun shines on your face through the window. Or ask a neighbor who is a naturally early riser to wake you up for morning yoga, and you'll stack function, friendship, and exercise.

Get Organized

Go through your house, garden, workplace, and anywhere else you spend time and organize it. Get rid of useless junk. Label drawers and cupboards if you need to. Make sure that everything is organized in such a way that you waste no time finding what you need.

If you spend five minutes every day looking for your keys, that's thirty hours each year. If you spend a few minutes creating a convenient place to keep your keys and train yourself to put them there, you can use the saved time for something you enjoy. Similarly, if you spend an extra two minutes every time you walk out of the way to a toolshed, and you go there four times a week, you can save yourself seven hours a year by moving the toolshed closer to the path. Use this principle of relative location to establish easy, efficient patterns of use, and you will open up blocks of time in your life.

Stack Functions

Another way to bend time is to stack functions, or multitask, all day, every day. In this way we can get large amounts of work done with minimal time and effort. At home I am never empty-handed. I am always getting something, putting something away, moving something to a more relative location. If I am walking from one end of the house or the other, I always try to bring something with me that needs to go where I am going. It is possible, however, to overdo it, so be sure to give your mind and body a break whenever it seems appropriate. Don't be a workaholic, and remember to look before you leap. This brings us to the next point.

Think Things Through

A stitch in time saves nine, right? Just because you are making best use of your time doesn't mean you need to be in a hurry. Haste makes waste, for real. Keep your wits about you, and take a minute to evaluate the effectiveness of each action. This sort of temperance could save years of time spent correcting mistakes. Use your observation skills to identify good opportunities, and make prudent choices that reflect your ecological ethic.

Quit Your Job

Now you think I'm crazy for sure, but you can certainly live on much less money, work less at unwanted jobs, and actually live a higher-quality life because of the freedom and creativity that comes with simplifying your life. It may be hard to imagine being able to pay the bills, but you'll be surprised at how much money you save when you stop buying things new, limit purchases to those items you absolutely need, use alternative transportation, and cut back on the less essential things like cable TV and junk food. You can probably live a healthy, natural life on half as much money as you currently spend, and be at least as content as you are now, but doing less harm to the earth.

If you aren't ready for an early retirement, consider evaluating the ecological integrity of your livelihood. Does the job you do cause more harm to the environment than you can correct by your own efforts? If so, how do you feel about it? Can you find a way to make ends meet that is more true to your ethics? This issue of "right livelihood" can be a sensitive one, but as we work to better our gardens and communities we must ask ourselves whether our worktime is as well spent as the boss might have us believe.

Take a moment to ask yourself—even write it down—*What would I do with my time if I could retire today and not have to worry about money?* Be realistic: Not everyone can live like a millionaire, and in fact no one should if we are to create an ecological, sane, healthy culture.

Again, once you make some changes in your lifestyle you may not need that job as much as you once did. Many jobs are just self-perpetuating time sinks; we have to dress nicely for work so we pay for expensive, uncomfortable clothes; we have to drive there so we buy cars and gas; we spend more money at the bar after work, and on therapy, shopping sprees, and expensive vacations, just to recover from the drudgery of it all. Then we spend more money trying to prove to ourselves that we don't spend all our money making money: We buy Jet Skis, dune buggies, computer games, DVD players. Yet these are the products of a consumer society desperate for some tangible validation of its success, and quite obviously part of the problem, not the solution. Not only do these "toys" damage the environment from start to finish, they also rob us of our last hours of free time.

When expounding the virtues of ecological living, I am not just talking about the small but significant patches of forest saved by using recycled paper, or the fraction of a reduction in the local landfill because you sent less trash there. The best things about ecological living are the indirect effects in ourselves as we become more ecological individuals, and how that transformation manifests itself through every aspect of our lives.

We must return to the understanding of time as a pattern in living nature.

9. Into the Community

To maintain a healthy community, all of the links must be present, regardless of whether they seem immediately favorable or unfavorable to [humanity's] aims. . . . As the intricacies of the community are investigated ever more deeply, it soon becomes obvious that it is impossible to distinguish friend from foe, a beneficial animal from an injurious one. . . . Most communities are in a constant state of change, their make-up varying not only from season to season, but also from day to day, even from minute to minute.

—Peter Farb[1]

What Is Community?

One of the fastest and most rewarding ways to improve the ecological health of your community is by organizing projects that share resources and spread information about organic food, paradise gardening, and ecological design. So far I've defined most of these ideas, but what do I mean by *community*?

The definitions and boundaries of community can be based on geography, politics, creative interests, gender, or culture, and they are as numerous and varied as individuals on the planet. People who live in the same neighborhood may consider themselves a community; others who participate in an Internet mailing list feel part of a community, while still others restrict their definition to include only the most intentional groups within which they choose to work or socialize.

In the science of ecology, the localized combinations of plants, animals, insects, and other living things are called biotic communities. In biotic communities the interactions of climate, shelter, food, competition, and unique habitat help define the characteristics of each species, and of the niche that each species fills in the community. Throughout every community the presence or absence of life in certain niches will determine the success or failure of the functions related to that niche. The whole system is in a constant state of change, from season to season and minute to minute, as niches in time and space are filled and refilled.

As we relate these ecological ideas to human communities, we see that our lives are also involved in a complex web of action and reaction, and no matter what we do we affect the whole. A healthy community depends upon healthy relationships, whether between the lettuce and the broccoli, the gardener and the garden, or the individuals and the whole. There is no hierarchical "food chain." Rather, all organisms interact through a complex, ever-changing web of life and death.

Beyond food, shelter, and the survival of our species, we also look to our community for the emotional bonds and shared sense of belonging that are such innate characteristics of our humanity. To humans, community means love, learning, empowerment, and ultimately survival.

Each of us already lives in a community—an overlapping biological, ecological, social, and ethereal community. It is up to us to choose what to contribute, what niches to fill, and what actions to take. Like the garden, the community outlives us, and each action has a butterfly effect for many generations. If we seek opportunities to enhance the ecological whole, now and in perpetuity, we can easily find ourselves doing projects that will enable the human community to live more naturally.

This chapter contains an overview of the types of projects I have seen and worked with over the past fifteen years. Whether gardens, workshops, events, installations, or direct action, these projects build and beautify community. Whether food, information, creative expression, or concerns about a local issue, these projects match needs with resources and spur new and independent projects and networks, with exponential success. Mimic or model after them as you will, but remember to be specific, and to look deep into your own community for its unique potential. Use the spiral design techniques discussed in chapter 7 and the skills you learned in the garden to develop projects that harmonize with the natural ecology (see the sidebar on page 218). Remember, the medium is the message, so focus on creating opportunities for individuals, rather than on dictating dogma to the masses.

Garden Projects

In every city there are thousands of acres of unused space. A twenty-five-square-foot area

Ecological design combines biological communities with urban needs to create a balanced blend of nature and technology.

has the potential to grow more than a hundred pounds of vegetables per year. If we can transform these spaces into fertile food gardens and shady fruit groves, we will directly increase the quantity of local organic food that is available. As whole families and communities eat more organic food, their health will improve and their relationships with one another and the earth will improve.

From planting a tree in the park to starting a school garden, growing food in public spaces is one of the best ways to create educational opportunities and generate lots of good organic food. Communities benefit from garden projects through cleaner air, improved personal health, and increased food security; you benefit from the food and exercise; and the land benefits from the new infusion of life.

Demonstration Garden

Even a tiny plot can become a demonstration garden, showing visitors how to sheet-mulch, build compost, save seeds, or any number of other useful activities. Most demonstration gardens offer examples of a range of techniques so visitors can compare and contrast. Some places will also offer a simple map and/or brochure with a self-guided tour.

Often demonstration gardens are on public land and are maintained by a collective of people, but you can turn your front yard into a demonstration garden by making signs, visible from the street, that tell visitors about the demonstrations and where they can learn more.

A working demonstration garden generates food while sharing useful information.

Food Bank Garden

Eugene's largest food bank, Food for Lane County, organizes several community gardens. Some of these gardens offer volunteer programs and educational internships to the general public, while others work with disadvantaged youth or local high schools, teaching organic gardening and growing food for distribution through the food bank. A food bank garden can be a large project such as these, or just a small section of your garden dedicated to growing food to give away.

School Garden Project

Any of these projects could and should include children of all ages. See chapter 12 for an assortment of ideas for school gardens and working with children.

Community-Supported Agriculture

Community-supported agriculture, or CSA, is an innovative and effective type of food-sharing project. Farmers sell shares of the harvest in advance, and customers receive weekly deliveries throughout the year.

This model works well on a small to medium scale and is an excellent way to share a garden space without being overrun with people or

Using Gobradime to Build Community

Using ecological design processes to organize community projects brings the ecological ethics we embrace in ourselves through to the rest of the community. Just as in the garden, developing a detailed plan of action helps ensure smooth and effective implementation. Try using Gobradime and the rest of the spiral design wheel to develop and implement projects like the ones in this chapter. Move through each step, asking slightly different questions than you did in the garden, as relates to the project at hand. Here are some examples of these new and rephrased questions:

Goals: What do you want to achieve and why? In what ways will you as an individual, and the community as a whole, benefit from this project? Write it all down . . .

Observation: Who's already organizing similar projects? Can you plug in, or is your idea a new one to the area you're working in? What are the obvious and demonstrable needs for your project?

Boundaries: How big a project do you want to do, and how much time do you want to spend? Whom will you work with, in what neighborhoods, for how long?

Resources: What are your resources? What do you need? Who has what you need and how can you collaborate with them? Raise money, make contacts, find volunteers, and so on.

Analysis: Is your project worth doing? Will it have the desired effect? How will you bring needs and resources together to achieve your goals?

Design: Develop a timeline, establish an infrastructure, find volunteer coordinators, define roles, delineate and delegate tasks, and get ready for action. Write down details for the project and communicate with your group to figure out how it's going to work. Develop a multiple-phase plan if necessary, then get down to business.

Implementation: Make it real. Do your best and your projects will succeed. Start small and take plenty of time for rest and reflection.

Maintenance/monitoring: Is it a onetime event or an ongoing program? Do you need more funding? Are you going to organize another event? Check in with your group process and volunteer satisfaction level and make sure everyone is still having fun.

Evaluation: Talk with others. Review your notes through the process. Some organizers (like me) pass out evaluation forms and invite participants to comment and critique the project. What worked? What didn't? Write it all down while the experience is fresh, then put your notes, receipts, photos, the mailing list, and copies of the flyer and press releases in a file. Use these notes to help organize similar projects in the future, or pass them on to a fellow activist.

overwhelmed with work. Growers receive compensation for their produce, and they know in advance how much to grow; customers receive fresh, local food from a source they can feel good about supporting. Many CSAs also offer a work-trade option in which people can volunteer in the garden for a discount on their share.

Giveaway Gardens

Someone once donated a truckload of organic fruit trees to Food Not Lawns, so we organized a free workshop about tree planting and spent an afternoon planting trees around the neighborhood. Today those trees provide hundreds of pounds of food every year. For the people who live in the houses that received trees it was a beautiful and multifunctional addition to their landscape; for us it was a learning experience; and for the trees it was a new home.

There is a group called People's Earth Action (PEA), in California, that starts gardens for elderly and handicapped people who can care for a garden but do not have the physical ability to get it started. Volunteering to install a garden for someone sends the message of shared resources and mutual aid and inspires others who see the results to help their neighbors as well.

Community Greenhouse/Nursery

You can build a greenhouse big enough for a whole neighborhood's vegetable starts with just one pickup load of recycled materials. Divide up the space among the people who helped build the greenhouse, or just volunteer some time to fill the space with seeded flats and give the starts away to whoever can use them. Here's what we did:

A supportive neighbor had a driveway but no car, and since she was renting she didn't want to tear up the driveway to put in a garden. Instead she donated the space to a community greenhouse project. A local awning company donated a six- by twenty-foot aluminum frame; we built supports out of recycled pallet wood and covered the structure with a piece of surplus plastic from a local farm.

Over the next two years we grew and gave away more than a thousand vegetable starts, grown from donated seed, in donated pots—all for free, all organic. Local garden centers donated the seeds and potting soil, and people took turns watering the starts until they were ready to put out on the street to give away. When the renter moved we transferred the small greenhouse to our farm, and we still grow seeds and food in it today.

Events

A small event can be organized in just a few hours. Larger events take months of planning, but the potential for building community through shared interaction is so great that it is well worth the effort. If you have never organized an event, start with something small and work up to the weeklong conference after you gain some experience.

Many places, such as bookstores, churches, schools, or public parks, will happily host a small event. Ask around for a free space with good lighting that can hold the number of people you expect. In the absence of a public space, many events go over just fine in someone's house or backyard. The following are examples of fun, easy-to-organize events.

Resource Exchange

I discussed the seed swap in chapter 6 as an easy way to exchange seeds and plants. This model also works well for many other types of resources, such as books, tools, clothes, food, bike parts, art supplies, and information. The University of Oregon hosts an annual "Gear Swap" where people meet in an unused classroom for an evening and swap surplus athletic gear. Unless you want to go for the flea-market feel, it makes sense to define what type of resources you would like to exchange at your event.

Sometimes a resource exchange goes over so well that people decide to organize a permanent space to cache and distribute surplus resources. MECCA, the Materials Exchange Center for the Creative Arts in Eugene, Oregon, started when a local activist realized that literally tons of useful art supplies were going into the landfill every year. She diverted the flow of these materials to MECCA, where people can now find all sorts of paper, paints, and an assortment of useful recycled materials for art projects of many kinds.

That's My Farmer

John Pitney of the First United Methodist Church in Eugene organizes an annual event called That's My Farmer. He was the first in his church to get a CSA membership for his family and has now organized a collaboration among several local churches that includes more than 180 families doing CSA.

At the event representatives from local farms set up tables with educational information about their practices and what types of produce and programs they offer. The event is widely publicized and open to the public, and hundreds of people come together each year to match needs with resources.

Very simple to organize, this event is a great way to build food security and the local economy. According to Pitney, the best organizing tool is the event itself, so pass around a volunteer sign-up sheet and network farmers and other participants for future events.

Starving Artist Convention

I once organized a hodgepodge group of local artists to bring together all of our piled-up artwork for a cheap art convention—a one-night-only showcase of original local art. Nothing was priced at more than a hundred dollars, and most pieces were less than twenty. The bookstore hosting the event took a nominal cut of the sales, and most of the artists went home with a pocket full of cash and a sense of satisfaction about distributing original artwork to the low-income community. A similar type of event could be set up in which artists would be asked to donate artwork to sell for a common cause, such as a community garden or communal art studio space.

Community Vaudeville Show

People love to laugh, and getting them laughing is a sure way to encourage them to share and change. I have had tremendous success organizing local performers into community variety shows to raise money for local projects. The low-tech nature of traditional variety or vaudeville-type performance arts (including dance, singing, skits, jokes, and acoustic music) makes them the perfect medium for communicating ecological ethics and ideals. Sets and costumes can be made with recycled materials, and songs and skits can communicate ecological themes.

Here is a basic how-to for organizing such a show:

First, set a date and find a venue. A place for all ages is best, but bars or clubs work well too. Ask for the booking agent and talk to her about what you want to do. She will most likely give you the space for free or ask for a percentage of the door.

Next, contact local performers. Approach people whom you've seen perform around your community, and put an ad in the paper advertising for volunteer performers. You can host an audition or just ask people about what they want to do. You don't want to censor people, but it is a good idea to choose a variety of acts rather than booking a whole show of jugglers or solo folk guitar players. Encourage performers to deviate from their set into material they wouldn't normally perform. Because each person gets only a few minutes, folks have an opportunity to try something new. Push for this—it makes for a fresher and more diverse show. When you have a list of interesting acts, choose someone to emcee. This should be someone who is at least vaguely familiar with the other performers and isn't afraid to be funny and engage with the audience.

Also be sure to book a house band for the evening. It will fill in the spaces when people are arriving, during intermission, and when an act needs musical backup, as many dancers and jugglers do. The individual performers will usually volunteer their short act for the cause, but because the house band makes a huge difference in how well a show comes off, choose a good one and be willing to pay it a little. I usually offer the house band about 25 percent of the door after a show—anywhere from $125 to $500. It's not much, but while most of the performers at an event like this are on stage for only ten minutes or so, the house band is working all night.

Once you know who will perform, put everyone's name on a poster and start spreading the word. Do plenty of publicity to make sure people come. Your volunteer performers will be much happier if the show is a success and then will be fired up to do it again. See the next chapter for a plethora of ideas about outreach and publicity. You will inevitably run into some people who passionately want to help with the show but don't want to perform. Plug them into spots like set building, flyering, or stage managing. You will need the extra help.

I recommend hosting a rehearsal potluck to bring the performers and other volunteers together before the show. This will give them a chance to coordinate with one another and will strengthen newfound community ties. Host a thank-you dinner after the show to bring everyone together again to exchange feedback and make links for the future.

Superhero Bike Rides

A group of bike geeks I know likes to get together with their bikes and dress up like superheroes with names like the Dynamic Accumulator and Flaming Echidna. They ride around different parts of the country, camping with their bikes and performing random acts of kindness. Whenever they see someone working, they get off their bikes and help. As you can imagine, this is a fabulous way to meet people, get exercise, and challenge the dominant capitalist paradigm in this country.

Volunteer projects like superhero bike rides blur the lines between work and play.

Street Theater

Street theater continues to be one of the best ways to draw attention to important issues. There are many forms of street theater, from puppet shows and elaborately planned skits to improvisational performances and audience-participation shows. I have seen people on stilts passing out flyers, fire dancers chanting mantras about local issues, and puppet shows educating coffeehouse crowds about the dangers of genetic engineering.

Under the guise of entertainment, these shows can educate, inspire, and incite all types of audiences, from environmental activists to elementary schoolchildren. Generally street theater occurs in public, free of charge, but feel free to pass the proverbial hat to raise funds for costumes, travel, and other expenses.

The Bread and Puppet Theater in Vermont has a long and illustrious history of pageants, parades, and theater pieces whose style harks back to old-time vaudeville days. Out of earthen materials they make magnificent giant puppets, telling childlike but profound stories of every-person's plight, from surviving the war culture and dreaming of being a better person to struggling with the inevitable death. Another troupe, Art and Revolution, specializes in political messages, from ancient forest issues to genetic engineering, and incorporates choreographed dance pieces into shows.

Street theater comes in many flavors, with options such as improvisational and planned skits, choral performances, puppet shows, stilts walkers, dancers, musicians, and marching bands. There are countless examples—try an Internet search under "street theater," "radical theater," "giant puppets," "activist theater," and so forth. Also be sure to check out some of the stuff about "invisible theater," where troupes go into the mall or a restaurant and stage a scene meant to bring attention to a pertinent issue, without giving away the fact that they are actors.

Whatever form of street theater you choose, remember that the medium is the message: If you are promoting nonviolence, don't use guns in your skit. If you are teaching about ecology, don't make the sets out of toxic materials. If you are trying to recruit volunteers for a garden project, make a show about plants, seeds, or food-related issues. Connect with local drama classes and theater troupes and embrace your inner clown!

Installations

Public art installations, including murals, sculptures, and sidewalk mosaics, can renew an ugly area, provide a focal point and conversation piece for locals, and convey the long-term vision of the artist to the community. MECCA, the same group I mentioned above, also organized a program in which at-risk youth worked together to design and install a mosaic sculpture in Eugene out of recycled materials. The youths had something fun to do for the summer, and the neighborhood received an interesting historical sculpture to view for years to come.

Kari Johnson, a low-income artist-activist in Eugene, acquired a city grant to do a mural on a local bicycle co-op building and another grant to do paintings with youth downtown. You could paint an educational mural depicting local plants and animals, with their common and scientific names, and perhaps a bit of folklore and practical use information.

Lending Library

Just as a regular library has books and other media to lend, so too can we create and participate in libraries of tools, musical instruments, computer software, costumes, art and photo supplies, transportation, and much more. Often a local church, school, or community center will donate a small space for the lending library, and members will each throw in a few tools or a few dollars to buy the shared materials. Or you can create a Web-based library by posting available loans on an Internet list.

Playgrounds and Dog Parks

Many cities include in their budgets money for new playgrounds and dog parks and will accept a proposal from a group of neighbors who want to install one. Alternatively, raise the money among neighbors or use free materials and volunteer labor to build simple, natural play areas for children and dogs to run free. You will create a natural focal point for your neighborhood where people can gather, communicate, and have fun. You may, however, run into some weird insurance issues, so do some research and find out what needs to happen.

Intersection Repair

The City Repair Project, a group in Portland, Oregon, organizes an annual Village Building Convergence to bring neighbors together toward a shared vision of ecological community living. This event always includes "intersection repair" actions that create four-corner free spaces to encourage community interaction. City Repair founder Mark Lakeman says that there are inherent problems with the grid system of

Build a mobile tool library onto a sturdy bike cart and share it around the community.

organizing cities, in that a grid is more conducive to commerce and competition than to community sharing and mutual aid. He feels that "place making" projects like intersection repair help unify neighborhoods around shared resources, increase the quality of life for the neighbors, and develop lasting, more ecological systems.[2]

The intersection repair projects consist of getting together a group of volunteers to build varied attractions at corners where four blocks meet. One such attraction was a small community library; another was a teahouse where the neighbors took turns putting out hot water and tea bags every morning. Other options might include free boxes, play structures, covered benches, water fountains, or a little shack with a desk and some art supplies. Get creative and make good use of what you have available.

If you can get away with it, either by getting a permit or by choosing the right time and place, paint a round mural in the street amid the four corners. This completely changes the feel of the space and encourages a plaza effect. One such mural in Portland was a sunflower, and another a Celtic knot design. Once the intersection has been properly "repaired," throw a big block party so everyone who lives nearby can get acquainted with one another and their new community resources.

Education Projects

All projects have the potential to educate us and others, especially if we take the time to add an educational element, such as informative placards at a community garden or an article written about the superhero bike ride. However, there is a lot of potential for mutual empowerment and increased effectiveness when we take the time to research and create intentional learning situations. Here are a few examples, followed by a short section on amateur teaching skills.

Field Trips
A one-day trip to a local farm or restoration project is a great way to meet new people and gain exposure to new options. Often field trips involve bringing a volunteer work crew to a local project and helping for the day. This builds community and sometime results in paid work for volunteers later.

Study Groups

Remember study groups in school? Well, you don't have to be a high school or college student to be in a study group. One of the first projects I ever organized was a life drawing group. We got together once a week, took turns modeling, and practiced drawing and painting. We soon had a close-knit group of artists critiquing one another's work and brainstorming about other projects.

Later I helped organize a sustainable horticulture study group. We agreed on books to study, then met once a week to discuss what we had learned. This is a great format for learning things—the weekly connection builds continuity and gives people an impetus to find and share new information.

Workshops and Skill Sharing

Just about everyone has some skill that they could teach during a short workshop, and sharing information is a great way to solidify the knowledge in your own mind. Why not offer a free or low-cost workshop to your community? This will increase the local skill set and unite people of like interests. You may even learn a thing or two yourself.

Pick a date, time, and place (a quiet bookstore, an empty church, or a classroom at a university would be a good option), and advertise well in advance to bring in enough students for a dynamic experience. If it goes well, organize a longer course or a series of related workshops. If you don't feel confident enough to teach or facilitate a learning experience, find a local expert who is willing to volunteer a few hours to lead a workshop.

Food Not Lawns organized an education project in 2001 with a permaculture design course and several other related workshops. This project took place over a nine-month period, with classes happening all over the neighborhood. We put out a single schedule for all of the classes and hired local experts to teach. Sixteen low-income Whiteaker neighbors earned permaculture design certification, and the course triggered an explosion of related projects throughout the neighborhood, from rain catchments and small graywater ponds to total conversions of yard and home spaces.

Because payment for the teachers was subsidized by a grant from the city, which we applied for in advance, we were able to offer the classes free of tuition. If no funding is available, teachers would have to volunteer or students would have to pay. Even during a free workshop, it is still a good idea to pass the hat—this helps defray any costs to the teacher, such as mileage and photocopies for handouts.

I once attended a community skill-sharing event in Oakland, California. A wide array of community members had networked to develop a series of workshops in several locations around town, all occurring within a three-day period. Participants arrived at a central location and were given a map and schedule. Then we just biked around and learned stuff.

Because most of the workshops happened at the teachers' homes or workplaces, the cost of the event was nominal—just enough for photocopies for flyers and maps. In three days I gained hands-on experience in screen printing, home graywater systems, seed saving, sheet mulching, and bike repair. Sure, there wasn't enough time to master any of these skills, but I had a thorough introduction and gained better access to more information. Some skill shares have a central theme, such as environmental activism or food politics, while others are wide open, with participants posting topics on a central board as they arrive.

Free School

Once you start organizing study groups, workshops, and courses, it makes sense to publish a local free-school schedule. All it takes is one or two people to hunt around for free classes and compile them into a schedule, which is then photocopied and distributed around town. Here's the basic process:

1. Look around town for free learning opportunities. These could include classes, workshops, demonstrations, presentations, or even performances. Check the paper, at local universities, and in any alternative publications. Compile a list and organize it either chronologically or by subject.

2. Also ask within your direct community for people who are willing to teach classes. At this point there are a couple of options: Do you want to let teachers organize all aspects (time, place, dates) of their classes, or do you want to line up a venue that will be available at the same time each week to make it

easier for teachers and students to organize themselves? Keep it simple, but do what you can to make things happen.

3. Now create the schedule. You can do one every month, one a season, or even just one a year. List each learning opportunity with the time, date, location, a short description, and what if any materials to bring. Include contact information and a deadline for the next schedule, so people can call you to add events in the future.

4. Photocopy the schedule and post it around town, or just list everything on a website and advertise the address.

5. Keep a copy of every old schedule in a binder for future reference, and develop a file of contact information for teachers. I'm always asking people at parties and events if they'd like to teach anything—people tend to have a lot of hidden skills.

6. An occasional (or monthly) teacher potluck will build community, help keep the momentum going, and provide an opportunity to organize for a benefit show, exchange skills with one another, or raise a little money for photocopies.

School Presentations

Work through teachers or a local humanities council to get appointments to go into area schools and give presentations and lead discussions on relevant issues. Alternatively, be the convener and connect speakers with schools and teachers. In 1996 and 1997 I participated in the Cascadia Education Project, wherein a group of forest activists put together a slide show and other activities and presented them to elementary schools around Eugene. At one school we planted fruit trees; at another we passed out endangered-species coloring books and talked about genetic conservation.

The project was relatively simple: We called the schools and left messages with our contact information and what we had to offer. Our all-volunteer collective met once every few weeks to sign up for presentation dates and collectively wrote a proposal for and received a small grant to buy a slide projector and to pay for photocopies. We all gained valuable experience, and the students and teachers alike were excited about what we had to offer.

Internships and Mentorship Programs

Many education centers, organic farms, and community organizations offer internships and mentorship programs. Ask locally or visit some of the varied Internet resources (see the resources section) with links to these types of opportunities.

I once did an amazing apprenticeship with a ninety-year-old sculpture welder in Oakland, California. I heard about his artwork, got his phone number, called him up, and asked if he needed a volunteer. He invited me over, we hit it off, and I spent the next three months helping him sculpt and learning to weld. Neither of us paid a cent, and we both benefited from the experience.

If there is someone in your community whose work you admire, approach her and volunteer to help. We can learn much from allowing one another to lead projects, and through respecting and seeking out the wisdom of our elders. If you are a wise elder, consider looking for an apprentice (or many) to pass your skills on to.

Learn by Teaching

There is an ancient Chinese saying: "When I hear, I forget. When I see, I remember. When I do, I understand." You do not have to be an expert to teach a workshop on something; if you are willing to embrace a few simple leadership skills, you can bring together a group of people and facilitate a discussion or work party on any topic.

Often what I will do is gather materials such as books, examples, slides, or supplies to make something. For example, one of the first classes I taught was papier-mâché maskmaking. I got some recycled clay to make molds, which we sculpted and then covered with recycled tinfoil and papier-mâché to make strong, colorful Halloween masks. We all had a great time, and people made an array of beautiful masks: a crow, a bear, and a lion goddess with great antlers. All I did was show how I had done something in the past; I never told participants how to do anything in the future, and I think this is one key to the egalitarian sharing of information, especially with hands-on skills.

If you choose the role of facilitator rather than teacher, you become an equal participant in the collective learning process. The facilitator mediates the flow, helps resolve conflicts, encourages discussion, and makes everything easier but allows the group dynamic to dictate the

Tips for the Amateur Educator

The following was inspired by the *Tao of Teaching*,[3] with help from the *Permaculture Teachers Manual*[4] and my first permaculture teacher, Jude Hobbs.[5]

Silence is a virtue: The facilitator speaks the least. Be a good listener, never interrupt, guide the discussion when needed, then give it back over to the students and see where it flows.

Walk the talk: Teaching about ecology and voluntary simplicity creates a situation in which people expect you to be accountable for what you teach. It is important to embrace the ethics we share. People can be very critical, and this criticism can block their ability to learn. Look into every aspect of your work and show as much integrity as possible, always.

Be transparent: If you do not know the answer to something or have not tried it yourself, just tell people. They will respect your honesty.

Application breeds learning: Hands-on is key. Talk about it, then do it. Help people find a relevance between what they are learning and their daily lives, and show them how the new information will improve those lives.

Embrace diversity: Here it is again, diversity as our ally! Use different methods to cater to different learning styles, and reach out to students who are diverse in terms of skills, experience, ethnicity, and economic circumstances.

---

real learning experience. See the sidebar above for more tips for the amateur educator.

In this way I advocate learning by teaching, or strengthening your own knowledge of something by sharing that knowledge with others. Of course you may be an expert at something and happy to embrace the teacher role. This is also fine, but still consider some ways to more effectively ensure that your students will grasp and retain what you have to share. Meaningful experiences, led by a confident yet humble and open facilitator, will send the message of equality, not superiority, and encourage inspiration, interaction, and deep learning.

Here are some simple suggestions for things to do in class besides lecture and ways to integrate students and yourself into a shared learning experience.

Show and Tell. Just like grade school, and it still works! Invite students to bring their own slides, photos, or actual examples of their work and give a presentation to the class.

Name Games. Learning names is essential to building community, so set aside time at each and every workshop to make sure that people are comfortable addressing one another by name. Here's a simple game that works every time: Toss a hat around between people, saying the name of the person you are throwing the hat to until everyone feels they know one another's names—it usually takes only five minutes or so.

Resource Oval. This is an excellent activity that gets those endorphins flowing and inspires participants to get to know one another beyond the name level. Ask each person to write her name and three things she knows how to do or is a resource for on a small piece of paper. Have everyone tape the paper to their chests and stand in two lines, facing each other. If there is an odd number of people, don't worry—just place three people at one end and go with the flow.

Now ring a small bell, and have people engage in conversation with the person directly across from them (or with their group of three), using the words on the paper as conversation starters, until you ring the bell again, three to five minutes later. Each time the bell rings, everyone moves one position to the right and the whole oval shifts. People again jump into a short conversation with the person they are now facing, until the bell rings again. The whole thing goes on until everyone is back in their original position. Ring the bell one more time and ask people to just mingle around, talking to anyone they might have missed or really want to go back to. This game is a big rush for everyone, and a great way to build community quickly.

Brainstorming. Toss out a subject or several of them, and make lists or mind maps to bring together the thoughts and goals of the group. Brainstorming is a great way to come up with tasks to complete a project or break out of an idea flow that is stuck. I use it all the time, almost every day, to solve problems and share information.

Breakout Groups. Small-group discussions or work projects are a great way to change the energy in a room and bring people out of their shell. Groups of three to five usually work best—try to mix up people who don't know one another and break up cliques wherever possible.

Go-Arounds. Ask participants to each share something about themselves. It is a good idea to use a time limit, especially with a large group, because go-arounds can take hours if people are feeling talkative. Also try asking specific, less generic questions like *What was your first experience with plants?* that will engender a mix of responses, rather than *Why did you come here today?*—which is more likely to cause everyone to say pretty much the same thing.

Videos. There are many thousands of excellent educational videos available through interlibrary loan and your local public broadcasting station. Look for some that will help you get your point across, or schedule a whole event just to watch good videos.

Slide Shows. Slides provide an excellent backdrop for a lecture and add visual punctuation to what you say. In general, keep slide shows and videos short (thirty minutes or less) so people don't nod off in the dark. Remember sleeping through those interminable filmstrips in school?

Handouts. Type up your own ideas or photocopy books and articles to make an informative handout for people to follow in class and take home. Worksheets can be fun as well; I used to always make handouts, but now I just ask people to take notes. Handouts are especially good when teaching outdoors, where people may not have a surface to take notes on but would do well to have something in writing to refer to during the workshop.

Design Projects. Work in small groups or in pairs to practice designing an artistic piece, a garden, or a community project. Use overlays or other techniques, and encourage the group to follow through on a design that they will actually use rather than just making up pie-in-the-sky drawings.

Guest Teachers. Invite others to share information that you are not as confident with or to facilitate the group in a new style. This adds diversity and helps maintain students' interest in an ongoing course. Guest teachers can be found throughout the community, from the preschool to the university, and everywhere there are peers and elders who have information to share. Often a local expert will be too shy to teach her own workshop but can be convinced to make a presentation at one of yours.

Readings. Invite participants to bring in books or articles and share readings related to the area of study. Also try asking people to write things to read to the class. I once asked students in an urban ecological design class to write a journal entry reflecting on their personal ecological ethics and later invited them to share what they had written with the class. Some of the readings were brilliant and started the rest of the class on an amazing philosophical discussion.

Games. Cooperative games and movement exercises can break up the monotony of a sit-down class and get those creative juices flowing. These are especially helpful after lunch, when most people's natural rhythm is more suited to taking a nap than to learning something new.

Evaluations. The key to improving your teaching skills and interpersonal interactions, evaluations are the necessary end to every workshop. You can make an evaluation form and photocopy it or just ask people to write down what they liked the best and least, and how they suggest you change the workshop in the future.

Encourage inspiration, interaction, and deep learning.

Also be sure to bring some tools, such as chalkboard or newsprint to write on, an easel to hold it up, chalk or markers, evaluation sheets, a slide projector and slides, your camera (to document the workshop), handouts, a bell, and any related books and magazines to show students.

In *Teaching as a Subversive Activity*[6] radical education theorists Neil Postman and Charles Weingartner advocate educating with an attitude of inclusion and encouraging an inquiry-based method that gives students the power over what they learn. This process empowers students and teaches them how to educate themselves. When these ideas are combined with ecological design principles, the individual not only becomes a lifelong learner but also becomes a learner who can educate herself and others about ecological living and earth stewardship. Can you imagine a society full of self-empowered critical thinkers, taking care of the earth and sharing skills with one another?

Direct Action Gets the Goods

Practicing ecological living is a deeply subversive act.

Much of what we have been talking about in this book could be called direct action. In a culture that force-feeds our every fleeting whim through high-speed cable and drive-through windows, growing food and sharing surplus are radical actions. When you make the decision to do something out of the cultural norm, you change culture. Practicing ecological living is a deeply subversive act. If every community was self-reliant, interdependent, and socially functional, corporate control would be impossible.

Traditionally the term *direct action* refers to people going to the point of production or destruction and attempting to halt or change the destructive behavior. Sometimes the people involved in an action will risk arrest, and sometimes not. Sometimes those who do risk it will become incarcerated; often they are not.

Most direct actions are part of a larger campaign, and there are always plenty of places to plug in besides front and center, where you are sure to get arrested. For example, Greenpeace does a lot of actions in which people suspend themselves from skyscrapers or lock down to whaling ships. These people almost invariably face criminal charges, but the actions are each accompanied by a support group that conducts an extensive outreach and education campaign geared toward making real, lasting changes in the policy around the issue.

Some of these projects are of a reactive nature, meaning they are in response to something that is already happening, such as animal abuse or environmental destruction. Others lean more toward preventive measures like gardening and community building. The best actions are a blend of the proactive and reactive tactics, mixing politics and current events with infrastructure-building strategies and long-term vision.

Protests and Demonstrations

For many people the first thing that comes to mind when you say "direct action" is the classic nonviolent protest/march/demonstration event. Envision streets filled with crowds of people waving banners, giving speeches, singing songs, and perhaps being attacked and arrested by riot police, all in the name of free speech and the alleged right of citizens to be able to invoke change. Sometimes the demonstration will block entry to an international trade meeting; other times it will march into the executive offices of an earth-damaging corporation. At still other times a protest is simply a demonstration of solidarity, meant as an outreach tool rather than an intervention.

This traditional tactic is still very effective at bringing together communities of people and at drawing media attention to an issue. However, in these days of questionable civil rights, extended jail sentences, and politicians who blatantly disregard public opinion, the non-violent civil street protest is losing its flavor faster than ever before.

Despite these setbacks, a large demonstration still serves a primary purpose: to demonstrate. It is a lot easier to convince people that a bad thing is happening by giving them a chance to see it up close than by just telling them about it. When people experience something firsthand, they will remember and respond.

I have attended dozens, maybe a hundred, demonstrations and had a wide range of experiences from revelatory bliss to rained-on, tear-gassed hell. Few if any of these actions achieved the goal the crowd was chanting for, but all of them helped build community by alerting locals about pertinent issues and bringing them together to share ideas.

Sometimes even a small demonstration can quickly become violent, usually (in my experience) as a result of police overreaction to civil unrest. In just a few minutes things can get really crazy and a lot of people can get arrested, beaten, tear-gassed, and sometimes killed by police. This is not so rare as it may seem.

Fortunately there is usually an opportunity to avoid such harsh treatment by dispersing when things get ugly. But if you don't want to submit to the police state, if you feel the need to stand your ground to be heard as you voice your concerns, then you might have to risk arrest.

Risking Arrest

When something terrible is happening, you might decide that you have to break the law to stop it. Sometimes this action will help buy time, as when tree-sitters occupy a forest to stop a logging operation while an associated organization fights in court to have the timber sale repealed. Often an illegal action is the last resort when other avenues have failed, and many people believe that stopping crimes against nature is far more important than obeying judicial laws.

Protesters enjoyed a good fight from the 1960s through the 1990s, with mostly misdemeanor charges and a few bruises to tell about. However, a few of those activists did end up dead or in prison, and now antiterrorism laws are changing everything.

So if you do choose to break the law, take time beforehand to educate yourself about the real and long-term risks to yourself and your community. Consider whether your action will help in the big picture or whether you might be overwhelmed by your own small perspective and perhaps acting rashly. Know that you and your colleagues might get caught, even if you feel invincible at the moment. Read about the Earth Liberation Front and Operation Backfire if you don't believe me.

Call me a conspiracy theorist, but I have seen these things up close, and what I'm saying is very real. The FBI, ATF, etc., are made up of intelligent, extremely well-trained individuals with the full-time job of enforcing the law. So do your homework. The Internet is the most obvious resource, but also seek out people who have been arrested for activism and ask them what they experienced. Read about the federal grand jury and its history of pulling information from activist communities, causing people to lose trust, faith, and hope in a movement. And please, attend a nonviolence training session, where people discuss these issues and act out possible scenarios to practice remaining calm to help avoid police brutality and trumped-up charges. See the sidebar on page 238 for more on dealing with jail and arrest.

If you are very clever, and very careful, you won't get caught and you can pull off an innovative, effective action that will educate the public, help stop harmful practices, and bring you and your community into better harmony with each other and the Earth. People are making change through direct action all over the world, doing projects like those listed below.

See the sidebar on page 238

Remember, when you resist the dominant paradigm, it will find new ways to dominate you. There is a saying that I learned as a fledgling activist: "Tactics repeated are easily defeated." Consider these ideas as general options, but, just as in the garden, it is important to design each action to be specific to your issue and resources. Work with your community to define your own problems and solutions, then do what makes sense for you.

Throughout your action planning, always balance sharing information with a sincere attitude of careful discretion. Sometimes a public action can upset a more covert one, so try to develop a cohesive community effort, rather than tripping wires and causing conflict.

Which leads me to this very important point: Throughout the ecological movement you will find many kinds of people and many kinds of actions. Because of the very sensitive nature of these actions, in that we don't know how far "they" will go to stop us, I will give only very general descriptions, and no specific names, places, or contacts. When it comes to breaking the law, you must seek out your own compañeros and develop close-knit, trusted affinity groups for action. Even within those groups, share only what is absolutely necessary.

That being said, here are some types of projects to look for. Some are easy to organize; others require that you first seek out existing projects and gain access to more knowledge and resources. All of these actions are, in my opinion, effective means of promoting ecological ethics and sharing resources toward the goal of building healthy ecological communities.

It is increasingly important to educate yourself about your rights.

Training Camps

The action camp provides an entry point for future and fellow activists. Many action campaigns host training camps where new and experienced activists get together, swap skills and ideas, and develop a campaign.

Jail Support and Solidarity

When doing illegal action, it is helpful to have pre-arranged jail support, including but not limited to pro bono lawyers, central phone numbers for people to call when arrested, and funds for bail and fines. I feel that the huge amounts of money and energy spent on getting people out of jail and supporting them while they're locked up could be better spent provoking real change without sending people to jail in the first place.

This may sound cowardly or reformist, but this book is packed full of solution-oriented ideas, and I hope people will be able to find empowering alternatives to getting themselves locked up. It is getting harder and harder to get out of jail, especially for actions that challenge the capitalist paradigm, and I believe that most actions that will result in immediate arrest and long-term imprisonment are just not worth the sacrifice. You'll be much more valuable to your community from this side of the iron bars, and when you don't have fines, legal fees, and parole officers to answer to.

Still, if you think you might become incarcerated for even a short time, take the following precautions to help protect yourself from abuse:

Establish a support network: Choose a support person who will avoid her own arrest but try to witness yours. Make sure she has a phone number that accepts collect calls and memorize it so you can call her from jail after the cops have taken all your stuff. It also helps to establish legal support and funding for bail *before* the action, rather than after. Many lawyers will defend activists pro bono, which means they don't get paid unless you do. Otherwise you will need a legal fund or will have to accept the court-appointed defense attorney.

Know your rights: The cops won't tell you anything that you can trust. Their job is to bust you, not to maintain your civil rights. Educate yourself ahead of time about what you can and cannot get away with on the inside and don't talk to anyone about the action except your own lawyer and support people. Use your time in jail to talk with the other prisoners about organic food, sharing resources, and ecological community. But watch out for informants and undercover agents. Not only will they use what you say against you in court, but they'll also use it against your friends, and to infiltrate and undermine your community for many years to come.

Choose a tactic and stick to it: Will you walk, talk, eat, give your name, pay bail? There are many levels of cooperation and noncompliance with the system, and pros and cons to all of them. Again, talk with more experienced activists and develop a plan that you believe will work.

Later, the camps provide food, education, and support for covert actions and public demonstrations. However, training camps also provide a point of entry for infiltrators and law enforcement agencies, so ask a lot of questions, check references where possible, and take note when people behave suspiciously or inconsistently.

Most action camps occur in support of rural action campaigns that help halt logging, mining, nuclear testing, unsustainable development, or other harmful practices. These campaigns could include any assortment of tactics, from tree-sitting and road blockades in old-growth forests to deep-cover information gathering that will later be used in court against the perpetrator. I will go no further into detail about these types of actions, choosing instead to focus on urban strategies such as the ones described below.

Critical-Mass Bike Rides

In cities across the world, bicycle commuters organize large group rides by prearranging a time and place to meet up on bicycles, then taking over large sections of city streets in an impromptu parade of bicyclists. Some riders wear signs and wave banners about bicycle and pedestrian rights; others just cruise along enjoying the comfort of safety in numbers, often in stark contrast with their daily routine of dealing with inattentive and inconsiderate car drivers.

Some groups meet every morning before work and travel together across town. Others meet just once a month, as more of a demonstration. Sometimes there are large rides on major holidays or annual long-distance rides.

This is one of the easiest direct actions to organize because all you need is your bike and some flyers posted around town. If you plan a regular ride, such as the last Friday of the month, word will get out and more people will come every time. Don't get discouraged if no one shows up—attendance will ebb and flow with the seasons and as new people come and go.

Generally, the people on the ride will have a brief discussion at the outset to unify around a goal of educating rather than enraging the car drivers they see along the way. Sometimes critical-mass riders will be ticketed and arrested for blocking traffic or will be herded and corralled like so many head of cattle, so be careful and make good decisions about when enough is enough. You can usually get in a pretty wild ride, make a good statement, get silly on adrenaline, and disband before the riot cops can squeeze into their bike pants and cleats to come and stop you.

Food Not Bombs

I lived for several years in a shared community house in the low-income Whiteaker neighborhood of Eugene, Oregon. Every Sunday we cooked and served free hot meals in the park, waving a banner with the slogan FOOD NOT BOMBS. We fed ourselves and hundreds of others, and the servings were a hub of community activity.

We gleaned the ingredients for these meals from local merchants, either by donation or by getting into the trash around back. Once or twice a week I went around to local food stores, picking up donations: boxes of fresh avocados, trash bags full of bread, and five-gallon buckets filled with tofu and strawberries. All of this food was perfectly edible yet headed for the trash, and by salvaging it we fed the community, produced compost for local gardens, and changed a lot of people's attitudes about food, waste, sharing, and ecological living.

People love to eat, and the community that eats together stays together. Food Not Bombs is an international affiliation of mobile vegetarian soup kitchens that bring communities together with surplus local food for a daily, weekly, or monthly feast. These feasts are relatively easy to organize with a small group of people and yield exponential benefits that will ripple through your community for many years to come.

You can call your soup kitchen whatever you like, but there is a certain power found in uniting with an existing network. It helps to volunteer with an FNB chapter or other soup kitchen somewhere else before trying to start one yourself, but the process is not so difficult as it might seem. I highly recommend the book *Food Not Bombs* by C. T. Butler and Keith McHenry.[7] It is short and succinct and contains everything you need to know to start up a successful independent soup kitchen in your hometown, from gathering and cooking the food to dealing with the cops and health department if they try to shut you down.

Here are the basic steps to organizing a local Food Not Bombs:

1. Connect with local food banks and soup kitchens to determine what types of meals are already available. Chances are, there are no vegetarian meals being served for free with no religion and no bureaucratic paperwork required, but there's a chance you will find an existing group to work with and/or some potential sources of surplus food to use. Also connect with the national FNB through its website at www.foodnotbombs.org.

2. Next, host a meeting and gather together anyone who wants to participate. At the meeting work through the steps below to determine where, when, and with what food you will cook.

3. Choose a "cookhouse" where the meals will be prepared and assemble the equipment you will need to cook for large groups of people.

4. Choose a time, day, location, and dietary guidelines (vegetarian, vegan, organic, sugar-free, and so on), and put all this information on a flyer. If possible, provide a phone number

or website where people can contact you to donate food or volunteer.

5. Photocopy and distribute the flyer, and list meal times at local social service agencies. See the next chapter for much more on how to get the word out.

6. Take the flyers around to local food stores and gather donations. If possible, set up weekly pickups. Most stores throw away tons of good produce and will be happy to save it for you instead. Sometimes it takes a while to cultivate these relationships. Be patient and polite, and never be rude or pushy when asking for donations.

7. After you get the food, go through and organize it. Take out the rotten stuff and compost it at a local garden. Assess the rest for recipe ideas. Later, when you evaluate failures and successes like a huge pot of burned beans versus that dreamy onion soup, write down some stuff so you can remember the good recipes and avoid making mistakes twice. You may need to front a few bucks for spices and cooking oil, but this can be recovered by putting out a donation jar at the serving.

8. Now cook, serve, and clean up after the meal. Ask for volunteer dishwashers at the serving, and put out a sign-up sheet for people who want to get involved so you can call them about the next meeting or cook day. I recommend cooking within easy walking or biking distance to the public place where you will serve the food. It is much nicer and sends a stronger message to bring the meal on foot or by bike than to load the big sloshing mess into a vehicle and drive it across town. Think *neighborhood food network*, and don't forget to stock up your own pantry with the surplus produce and leftovers.

Guerrilla Gardening

Substitute the word *Lawns* for *Bombs*, pick up seeds and plants to give away instead of vegetables and tofu, and you've started a local chapter of Food Not Lawns! If you do this, be sure to send me your information and I'll put it up on our website.

A great way to distribute these surplus plants is by transplanting them into public spaces around your neighborhood. In the city and out

Guerrilla gardening is an excellent way to use direct action to increase your neighborhood's biodiversity.

of town there are many open spaces that are perfectly suitable for spreading seed balls, planting a tree, or growing a patch of vegetables. Neighbors may follow suit, and a tree you planted one year will have tulips and sunflowers coming up around it the next.

This practice, known fondly to some as guerrilla gardening, takes many forms across the globe and is a great way to both increase local food security and find good homes for otherwise wasted plants. You can go back and weed, prune, mulch, or water or just set up the gardens in a way that won't require future maintenance. Potential sites for guerrilla plantings include urban riverbanks, parks, highway beauty strips, residential side yards, alleyways, apartment-complex green areas, rest stops, traffic islands, parking lots, and friends' houses. I bet you can think of a few good places near your house right now.

Guerrilla gardens beautify the neighborhood, increase local diversity, and provide food for people, animals, and insects. You can add to existing gardens by planting bee-attracting plants to increase the pollination of a favorite cherry tree in a local park, or you can start a new garden where there was only a pile of leaves or dirt. Some people drop seeds of tenacious plants such as burdock and morning glory into cracks in the sidewalk, hoping to break it up and let nature through.

Here are some guidelines for successful guerrilla gardening:

First, scout the site. Does it have full sun or partial shade? Is it hot or cool, dry or moist? Is there room for a large shrub, a small perennial, a large tree, a whole garden, or just a few flowers or vegetables? Do people influence the site? Often a park or roadside is mowed or sprayed with toxins; consider these factors when choosing what and where to plant.

Next, make a simple design and choose plants that will grow well in the site. For instance, it doesn't make sense to plant lettuce in a parking lot that gets full sun and no water: Lettuce likes cool and moist conditions, and will either die in infancy or go to seed immediately in such a hot site. However, it does make sense to plant a fig tree on the edge of an irrigated river or parkside bike path, where it can grow to maturity and provide a nutritious snack for passing bikers.

When you are ready to plant, choose a time of the day that is not too conspicuous. Load up a wheelbarrow, bike cart, or truck with seeds and plants, a shovel, some rich compost, a bucket or three of water, and a bucket of mulch.

Because you may not be tending the garden as closely as a more legal one, use a dry-garden transplanting technique: Dig a hole twice as deep and twice as wide as the root-ball of the plant. If the plant is root-bound (the roots are wrapped around themselves in a tight ball), gently loosen the roots by pulling them apart with fingers or sharp clippers before planting. Put some compost or natural fertilizer in the bottom of the hole. Dunk the roots in a bucket of water or compost tea for a few minutes and place them in the hole. Hold the plant erect and fill the hole with fertile compost, being careful not to damage the roots or leave them exposed. Firm the soil around the plant so there is no wobble to the stem, and provide a trellis or support poles if needed. Dig a very shallow trench around the base of the plant to create a reservoir for

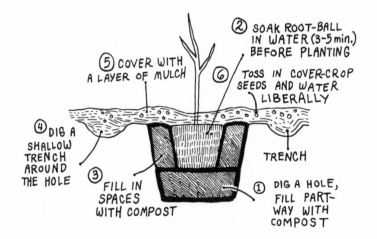

When planting trees, firm up the soil, water deeply, and finish with a thick mulch.

water and top it off with a thick layer of mulch. Water liberally: Use three times as much water as the volume of the pot the plant was in. Sow the seeds of some good companion plants and hope for the best.

Plants that will do particularly well in this situation include sunchoke, squash, berries, fruit trees (especially figs, plums, apples, and cherries), fennel, potatoes, radish, salsify, turnips, kale, filberts, passiflora, kiwi, tomatillo, bamboo, tomatoes, amaranth, garlic, rosemary, nettle, roses, and poppies, to name a few. Keep in mind that most plants, and especially fruit trees, will need more water the first year than after they are established, so try to include a few follow-up visits in your guerrilla plans.

Pirate Radio

Broadcast equipment is not overly complicated to build, and though it is still illegal to broadcast without an FCC license, many people believe it is within our free-speech rights to broadcast as we choose on the public airwaves. Most FCC regulations are allegedly there to protect us from vulgarity, violence, and the like—ironically, stuff most Americans readily pay for elsewhere. In reality these regulations serve to censor the voice of the common people, making access to the airwaves available only to those who conform.

Some pirate stations rotate locations and bandwidths to avoid getting busted. Most stations do eventually get shut down and their equipment confiscated, but no one has served more than a few weeks in prison yet, because of the solid First Amendment defense that inevitably comes up. A community needs a forum for independent voices to speak out and be heard, and if the legal media cannot provide it we must do it ourselves. I was once involved at a station where community members took turns hosting call-in talk shows on politics, environmental issues, and feminism and played independent music from all over the world. The station was eventually raided and all of our equipment stolen by the FCC, but we had a good run and learned a lot, and no one served any time.

A compromise to all-out pirate radio would be to start a low-powered FM microbroadcasting collective licensed by the FCC. Many communities boast excellent community stations, and while broadcasters must obey the rules or risk shutdown, they manage to provide a venue for a wide diversity of radical and progressive programming.

Art Crime

As I said before, our most valuable tool is our own creativity. This is also our best defense against the (often violent) negative reactions of the current regime to our proposed changes in the system. I use the term *art crime* to describe any direct action that uses colorful, hypercreative tactics.

For example, a conservative mayor was running for his third term, and as is so often the case in this bipartisan system, there was no suitable alternative candidate—the Democratic opponent was a waffler at best and bound to lose. Some local radicals wanted to expose the anti-environmental, anti-civil-rights attitude of the mayor in the hope of at least weakening his campaign. One of the activists bought a ridiculous suit from the thrift store and started campaigning for his own spot on the mayoral ballot. His speeches were funny and poignant, and his entourage included an assortment of giant singing puppets.

The media attention paid to this eccentric new candidate forced the incumbent mayor to address some of the very real issues he had previously avoided. In a political system as disempowering as ours, an action like this doesn't change much in the big picture, but it did give local activists a good boost in morale and helped educate the public about just how corrupt our mayor really was.

Throughout our work, whether planting a garden in the yard or blockading a shipment of genetically modified corn, it is imperative that we retain a healthy sense of humor. It is okay to feel angry about the injustices around you, but hatred will make you sick. Laughter makes people shine, no matter what side of the issue they stand on. Here is another example:

Some ecological activists had built a village of tree houses high up in an old-growth stand that was slated for clear-cutting. The tree-sitters wanted to bring people from the community out for a day in the forest to experience the diverse natural splendor they were trying to protect. They had organized several public hikes, with marginal success, but were struggling to gain the support they would need to stop the timber sale.

When they decided to put on a backwoods circus, people from town flooded out to the site for a day in the forest with dancing clowns, jugglers, and even an aerial trapeze show. This action gave a fresh face to the tree-sit, which local media had previously labeled as hostile, militant, and violent. People later talked about how the performance drew them out to the forest, but it was the trees that put on the real show.

This chapter has explored a wide range of community projects, from installing a small public garden that grows food for the neighborhood to launching a national ad campaign about a relevant social or ecological issue. As with anything, the best way to gain a better understanding of the value and meaning behind work like this is to do it.

Whatever types of projects you choose, their success will relate directly to how many people learn about and get involved in them. A well-organized, sincere outreach plan is the foundation of an exponential sharing of knowledge and resources, and this exponential effect will ensure the long-term benefits of your work. The next chapter will outline an assortment of strategies for finding and connecting with like-minded people in your neighborhood and beyond.

10. Reaching Out

Good things come to those who wait; everything comes to those who hustle while they wait.

—Anonymous

Making Connections

Ecology is about relationships, and the integrity of any ecological community depends upon the health and abundance of its diverse, interconnected relationships—from the smallest microorganisms to you and your neighbors. Making friends with the people who live nearby will improve your garden and community projects by expanding bioregional cash and resource networks and improving the scope and quality of local awareness. Knowing the neighbors increases economic and emotional support networks and decreases crime and violence.

Most of us know at least a few folks in the neighborhood. But think of the macrocosm that is the larger ecological niche you share with the other people in your town, in your bioregion. What percentage of those people can you call friends? How many of their names do you know? How many of them will be watching your back if and when disaster strikes? How many of them might be interested in doing projects with you but don't know you exist?

When you start organizing community projects like the ones in the preceding chapter, you will need to use a diversity of strategies for finding people who want and need to participate, and who have something to contribute. Whether it's a small garden or a large community event, the success of any project depends upon successful outreach and fund-raising efforts, and that's what this chapter is about.

Who to Connect With

Before you start doing outreach, think about the types of people you would like to work with. Remember to strive for diversity wherever

possible. This means reaching out to people from cultures other than your own, of diverse lifestyles and sexual preferences, from a wide age range, and from all economic situations. Offer flyers and brochures in multiple languages. Work in ethnic and low-income neighborhoods, and make your events physically and financially accessible for a broad range of people.

Try to think of as many diverse groups as you can, while considering what types of people might be interested in your work. For example, if you are doing garden projects, reach out to students, children, teachers, parents, environmental groups, outdoor education programs, basket weavers, other gardeners, and anyone else who likes and uses plants. If you're working in peace and politics, you might want to communicate with lawyers, lobbyists, journalists, gun control groups, and anti-military organizations. For wilderness restoration contact hikers, bird-watchers, native plant societies, botanists, geologists, cross-country skiers, and other outdoor enthusiasts. Look for people who love nature, such as hikers, fisherpeople, mountain bikers, pagans, tribal communities, and primitive-skills enthusiasts.

Brainstorm a list and write it down to use as a starting point on your outreach campaign. Then use the methods and materials in this chapter to launch a simple, low-cost publicity campaign that will help you find volunteers, publicize events, educate your community, and build support for your projects.

This campaign should include establishing a presence in the community, developing outreach materials, and putting out the word through a diversity of media strategies, from spoken word to print and broadcast media. We'll look at all of these in the next few pages.

Many of these strategies double as fund-raising schemes, and there is no harm in always keeping a donation jar handy. There are also several good ways to raise larger sums of money for community projects. You will find an overview of fund-raising at the end of this chapter.

Establishing a Presence in the Community

The first step to finding like-minded people in your community is to establish yourself and your project as a competent, beneficial force in

When reaching out to the community, start with your next-door neighbors and spiral outward.

the neighborhood. Set up a free box and give away quality surplus. Smile at the people you see on the street and introduce yourself. Talk about your gardens and other projects, and invite your new friends to share their passions too. Then, as you move into a more formal outreach phase to find volunteers and build support for a specific project, use the ideas below to help shape your approach.

Name Your Project and Write a Mission Statement

If you are starting an organization or ongoing project such as a community garden or tool library, you should give it a good name and write a short mission statement. Consider your goals and your purpose, and come up with a name and a sentence or two that tells people what you are doing and why.

Acronyms, puns, people's names, plants—there is no limit to the sources of inspiration when it comes to finding names for your projects. Be clever, but do not confuse people with a name that is too cryptic or militant. Choose a name that makes sense for you and stick with it. It takes time to build up name recognition for a project, and it can be confusing when the same people do a bunch of projects under several different names, so be clear and distinct.

Food Not Lawns was a name that started as a joke and just stuck. People loved the concept so we kept the name, but it was also a bit limiting—folks assumed that we were interested only in growing food, not other beneficial plants, or that our work was entirely focused on converting lawns to gardens. Some people even thought we were a lawn-mowing service! Still, for our purposes it made sense to keep the name and go with the momentum we had built.

Once you have a name, write your mission statement. This can be up to 150 words long, but it should be clear, succinct, and easy to understand. The mission statement, or a synopsis of it, will be on your business cards and brochures, in your press releases and funding proposals, and on the home page of your website. It is what you will use to communicate with new participants about what you are trying to accomplish.

When writing the mission statement, try to combine visionary ideas with realistic options. Find a balance between idealism and achievable, measurable goals, and write a statement that reflects both. Outline the problem and your proposed solution, and include a description of your activities. Have others look it over and edit it down to a tight, concise statement of purpose.

Talk about Your Project

Tap into the power of everyday conversation. As your project progresses, whether it is your own garden or a full-scale community project, you will undoubtedly have much to talk about. So talk about it. Tell your friends, neighbors, family, and coworkers what you are up to. Ask them what their interests are, and look for ways to connect.

Many people will want to know what you are doing, and you don't want to sound like a broken record, but you should develop a succinct, two-minute "rap" about your work. New people need to know what they are getting involved in, and you need to be able to tell them.

It helps to jot down a few paragraphs using a basic problem–solution scenario. Have fun with it, trying a few different versions to see what people understand the best. As you become more comfortable your rap will change and evolve, depending on whom you are talking with and the depth of the interaction.

Once you have a good rap you can expand it into a longer workshop or presentation and offer it to local schools and community groups. If you are nervous about talking to people, refer back to the section on amateur teaching in chapter 9, and see the sidebar below for tips on speaking in public.

If people are interested in your work, invite them to get involved and ask them to tell their friends, neighbors, family, and coworkers about it. This type of outreach has exponential benefits, and you will soon see the excellent results as new people volunteer and/or donate money and materials.

Better Public Speaking

Speaking in public is a major phobia for many millions of people, but it needn't be. If you have an opportunity to talk about your project and the issues around it, it is a waste to let a fear of speaking in front of others inhibit the opportunity for building support. The tips below will help you get a grip on your fear and share your ideas effectively and comfortably. Even if you are already a confident public speaker, you can always sharpen your skills. Use these concepts to develop your talk, and jot down some basic notes to bring along.

Know your purpose: Be clear about your goals, and make sure your talk reinforces those goals.

Know your audience: Do the necessary research and tailor what you say to the needs of your listeners. Relate your topic to their daily lives.

Establish credibility: Give a brief explanation of why you are qualified to talk on your subject and how you are involved in the project at hand.

Be deliberate: Speak slowly and enunciate carefully. Repeat key phrases. Repeat key phrases. This seems weird in a regular conversation but is very effective in a presentation.

Make your point: Choose up to three main points and use supporting arguments to make them. Keep your talk clear and succinct, but provide enough information to make a strong impression.

Stick to the facts: Opinions and emotions are good ways to punctuate a point, but be sure to provide plenty of tangible backup for what you want people to believe.

Ask for action: A presentation without a request for action is a lost opportunity. Tell listeners what they can do to help.

Use visual aids: Slides, photos, and/or charts make a more memorable presentation and can help make your point. Keep things relatively simple, however, so your visual aids don't upstage you.

Answer questions: This can be the most terrifying part, but it is always a good idea to leave room in your talk for questions. If you don't know the answer, say so; people will appreciate your honesty. Make a note of these things and find out before your next talk.

Finish with flair: Save the most shocking statistic or tantalizing tidbit for the very end. Leave them hungry to learn more, and tell them how they can do it.

Practice your talk in front of a mirror. This will help you relax and will show you your body language. When you give your talk, stand up straight, breathe deeply, and speak from the diaphragm.

Be sure to drink plenty of water beforehand—you don't want to have a coughing fit or a headache in the middle of a presentation. Smile, use eye contact, and maintain open body language. Have fun and good luck!

Choose a Spokesperson

If you are working with a group of people, consider choosing a spokesperson. Media, individuals, and other organizers want a main person to contact or refer to. If there is no one who can talk to them, you will lose prospective volunteers and miss out on valuable publicity opportunities.

If you do not choose a spokesperson, the media may just interview anyone standing around. Sometimes this can be fine, but you may end up with a quote about your project from someone who doesn't really know what you are trying to do or how you want to represent your work to the world.

The spokesperson does not have to be the leader of your group, just someone who is informed and articulate and who understands the goals and activities of the project. It makes sense to rotate spokespeople, in order to maintain a balance of power in the project. See the next chapter for more on shared leadership. In the meantime do what makes sense to you, but make sure at least one person is ready to talk to the media and field questions at all times.

Set Up a Mailing List

Bring a notebook to every meeting, event, and social function you attend and invite people to write down their name, phone number, and/or e-mail address. Later, you can call them about upcoming events or set up an Internet mailing list. Many websites offer mailing-list hosting for free—try tribe.net or mutualaid.org, or go through a local Internet provider.

You can also do it the old-fashioned way, using snail mail and sending postcards for each new project, but this can get very expensive and is much more time consuming than just setting up a simple e-mail list.

Keeping a record of contacts is essential to maintaining a good ongoing outreach campaign. Every person who attends a workshop or garden tour, or who calls or e-mails you asking about your project, should go on your list for future reference.

Throw a Party

Don't underestimate the power of an informal garden party to bring the community together. Invite the neighbors over for an afternoon of organic food and conversation. Ask a few local musicians to sit in and you've got yourself an excellent opportunity for community organizing. At the party conduct garden tours, display photos of projects, and invite local activist groups to set up tables. Pass around a guest book so you can invite participants to future events.

Plant Flowers

As you establish your project be sure to use the tried-and-true gap-bridging method of planting beautiful flowers along the border between your garden and the neighbor's land. The flowers will bear your good tidings and provide a conversation piece to help break the ice.

Developing Outreach Materials

The next step is to develop informative outreach materials. These range from business cards to periodical newsletters to books like this one. Get creative and try to create items with plenty of useful information—these will have a longer shelf life than a vague flyer that people will just throw away. Here are some examples.

Make a Business Card

This is so simple, yet many activists do not use business cards. A business card is very important. Not only does it save you from a lot of scribbling your number, e-mail, or website on scraps of paper whenever you meet a potential volunteer, but a business card is your own tiny billboard as well.

Business cards can be made out of recycled paper and printed either at home, with a personal computer, or through a professional service. (Vistaprint.com offers free business cards—you pay just for shipping.) A business card informs people about what you have to offer and what you need and presents your work in a way over which you have complete creative control.

Make a Scrapbook

Put together a big scrapbook from recycled art materials and paste in articles, flyers, brochures, photos, volunteer sign-up sheets, letters, and other keepsakes from your projects. Put this out whenever you set up an information table or have an event; people will love looking through and seeing exactly what you've been up to.

The Food Not Lawns scrapbook has become a living history of our personal transformations as well as our gardens; it is one of my most prized possessions. I only wish I had started it a decade earlier!

Make a Brochure, Fact Sheet, or Newsletter

These are three different forms of what could be generally termed a leaflet. Use recycled paper and keep it simple. There are many formats for brochures, fact sheets, and newsletters, and most word-processing programs have templates. Generally newsletters are more in-depth than fact sheets or brochures, and they usually include articles, photographs, and advertisements from members and project participants.

Go to the office of a local nonprofit and look at the literature it has available. Printing can be expensive, so consider your resources before getting too deep into a full-color brochure or thirty-page newsletter. But don't just duplicate what others do—create something unique.

An array of outreach methods will help you reach a diverse audience.

The goal should be to produce a basic document that explains the who, what, where, when, why, and how of your work in a format that is innovative and engaging. Do some research and include interesting graphics and statistics, alluring photos, and informative charts.

Tell people how they will benefit from getting involved, and give them some specific options for doing so. Include contact information and relevant websites, and tell people how to sign up on your mailing list.

Make a Flyer

What I am calling a flyer is different from a leaflet, in that a leaflet advertises an ongoing project or organization while a flyer informs people about a specific event or string of events. This information may also be included in a newsletter or brochure, but it is important to advertise individual events for a few weeks before they occur.

Flyers can be any size, from a large poster on a billboard to a small handbill passed out to a large crowd of people. A good flyer is like a display ad: It has the name of your project; tells people what they will gain from being involved; and gives the date, place, and cost of the event.

Pay careful attention to the wording in your flyers, brochures, press releases, and especially your mission statement, and make sure that language does not reflect any unconscious racism, sexism, ageism, classism, or other prejudices. Ask feminists, alter-abled people, and people of color to help you create materials that are welcoming, inclusive, and culturally sensitive.

I always try to include fun graphics to catch people's eye and communicate my project's emphasis on beauty and creativity—a picture speaks a thousand words, right? For posting on bulletin boards, it is usually wise to make flyers eight and a half by eleven inches or larger. Put the upcoming event on the front and a general message about your project on the back, to lengthen the shelf life of flyers.

Sometimes I will make posters that are five and a half by seventeen inches by cutting an eleven-by-seventeen sheet lengthwise. This is a less common shape on bulletin boards and lends itself to an eclectic, old-fashioned style. Try different shapes, colors, and graphics. I prefer typed text on flyers, while others like to handwrite theirs. Have fun with it, and always save one of each flyer for your scrapbook. See the sidebar on page 256 for tips on distributing flyers.

Distributing Flyers

Many businesses have bulletin boards for people to post announcements and advertisements. Spend a day on a bicycle riding around your town and stopping at every coffee shop, grocery and health food store, patisserie, deli, school, church, and garden center, and ask if they have a place to post flyers for local projects. Make a list, in geographic order, of all of the places that allow flyers. Make copies of this list and you will then have a flyer route that is easy for you or another volunteer to follow or share.

Another great way to get out the word is to pass out handbills (small flyers—say, five and a half inches by four and a quarter inches) to large crowds of people coming out of a concert, museum, garden show, or other community event.

Come up with a five-word "sound bite" about the project to tell people as you hand them the flyer—this will help them to determine whether or not they want the information, and you will find fewer of your expensive flyers on the ground after the crowd has cleared.

This works especially well within twenty-four hours of the event. Once, for a benefit show, we dressed up like clowns and went to a big art opening downtown that was happening just two hours before our show was scheduled to start. We passed out two hundred flyers and had a fantastic time clowning around. We packed the house later that night, and I saw dozens of the same faces from the art opening; our show was just the thing they were looking for to top off their night.

Make a Banner

Make a large fabric banner—like a flag—with the name of your project, a graphic, and a short slogan. This is especially helpful at indoor events to hang outside for passersby. Many people will see the banner and stop to find out what is going on. Others who are looking for your event will be glad for the extra information, directing them in.

If you don't have time to sew something together, just paint a nice sign on a piece of plywood. We have a two-and-a-half by five-foot plywood sign like this that shows a big head of garlic behind the words FOOD NOT LAWNS EVENT TODAY. We've used it for years and have met hundreds of new people thanks to the extra effort.

Bumper Stickers

Bumper stickers are a mixed blessing. The materials used to make them can be quite toxic, from the plasticized paper to the glue that makes them stick. Still, there are recycled-paper options available, and stickers are an inexpensive and excellent way to spread the word (widely) about your work. Come up with a catchy slogan, put it and your project name on a batch of stickers, and give them away. Now watch as the name recognition for your project skyrockets.

Stickers are cheap to have printed at any screen printing shop. Or you can make your own: Silk screening is relatively easy, and perhaps a local student can help you. Linoleum block prints make great stickers—

just remember to carve the words in backward, and print on sticker paper. Once you have a master, you can photocopy as many stickers as you want on sticker paper, available at any stationery store.

Putting the Word Out

Once you've assembled some basic outreach materials you are ready for the fun part—getting out into the community and promoting your project. Use as many methods as possible, from word-of-mouth techniques such as canvassing and tabling to do-it-yourself media tactics like writing articles, putting out press releases, and giving radio interviews. I'll cover several good options below.

Alert the Media

Sometimes local media will catch wind of an interesting project and come sniffing around for the scoop. This is a mixed blessing, because while news stories can bring in tons of new support, the mainstream media often discolors projects and presents them in ways that we might not like or want. The media can be your enemy or your best friend, and your interactions with the media will be much more likely to succeed if you engage its representatives directly, proactively, rather than

Public art and performances are excellent ways to bring ecological ideals to large, diverse audiences.

waiting for a surprise visit from a reporter. To this end I encourage everyone to learn the fine art of the press release.

Use a press release to alert media—radio, print, TV, and online—of your upcoming events and to offer interviews and expert opinions. Write your press releases well and you will soon have a host of allies in both mainstream and alternative media.

Before I get into the art of writing a press release, let's look at the reality of the mainstream media. In 1977 more than fifty corporations composed the bulk of the international media. In 1999 fewer than twelve companies owned every major television and radio station in the world.[1] What's more, the boards of directors for these twelve corporations contained a grand total of only 155 individuals, including many who sat on boards for several media corporations. All these people also own large shares of other corporate and political organizations, from weapons contractors to pesticide companies.[2]

In short, the mainstream media is controlled by a handful of people who represent the politically conservative, privately educated, and economically privileged power elite. No wonder it is so difficult to get good media coverage of grassroots topics such as food security, ecological sustainability, and mutual aid.

Most editors are looking for conflict, freshness, relevance, and timeliness.

But do not get discouraged. There are hundreds of independent media organizations making their own alternative news opportunities and telling the other side of the story. You can find independent and alternative media through the Internet, cable access programs, and university radio stations and newspapers. Start with indymedia.org, ask other gardeners and activists, and look at local newsstands for independent and progressive publications.

Identify an assortment of media targets and send a compact, two- or three-page media kit. This should include the press release plus a few photographs, and perhaps a copy of your brochure or fact sheet. A press release is a business letter with specific information geared toward the needs of the media. There are several key points you need to cover in every press release. First, provide a succinct who, what, where, when, why, and how of your event, but more importantly give them a good hook to hang the story on.

What most editors are looking for is conflict, freshness, relevance, and timeliness.[3] Provide a clear picture as to why the topic is news now, and why their readers/viewers/listeners will want to know about it. Tie in your work to a local environmental dilemma or social issue and define how you are finding solutions. Be imaginative and provide quotes, testimonials, and/or interesting statistics to back up your opinions. This is the heart of your press release.

Be sure to mention any photo or interview opportunities that will be available at the event, and provide the name of your spokesperson and how and when she can be contacted. If you are charging admission to your event, include two or three free passes with each media kit in case a reporter and photographer want to cover the event. Your spelling and grammar throughout should be immaculate.

Send the concise, easy-to-understand packet to the city editor, assistant editor, or department editor—not to the executive editor, because it may be tossed out. Call ahead and ask to whom to address the packet.

Lay It All on the Table

Sometimes performers will allow local groups to set up an informational table at their show. Check with local venues as well as bookstores, grocery stores, schools, malls—anywhere that you can find a good flow of people. Farmer's markets are another great place to do outreach.

Set up a small table—anything from a TV tray to a card table or a whole booth, depending upon the circumstances with the host. Put out your scrapbook, newsletters, and any other outreach materials, with extra copies of some things for people to take, and offer a volunteer sign-up sheet or a mailing list.

Most places will also allow you to put out a jar for cash donations—we've raised up to five hundred dollars in a few hours this way. Always set up a table like this at your own events and staff it with a knowledgeable volunteer so people can sign up, ask questions, and give donations.

Organize an Info-Share

Host an evening of info swapping, with presentations, games, and/or workshops. Some groups have an annual or biannual event in which members invite new people to come and see members give a talk or show slides about their projects.

Alternatively, invite a guest speaker. Many large cities sponsor humanitarian organizations. These organizations often keep lists of

Set up information tables at local stores, schools, and events.

scholars in the area who offer presentations. You can ask a local writer, college professor, designer, school garden coordinator, or political activist. Well-known speakers will bring in more people and generate press for your project. Some guest speakers will offer a lecture or do hands-on activities, while others will show slides or a film and discuss their work.

Host the event at a local home or campus and advertise well in advance. At the info-share set up a table with information about your project and upcoming events, and invite people to sign up to be on your mailing list.

Canvassing

Door-to-door canvassing is still a reliable method of getting out the word about a local project. From vacuum cleaner salespeople to Jehovah's Witnesses to Greenpeace environmentalists, canvassers have been knocking on doors to gain support for their work for centuries. Most often used as a form of sales or fund-raising, canvassing is a great way to generate small amounts of money for a project.

However, it can be exhausting and disenchanting, as many people these days do not appreciate folks on their doorstep asking for money, even for a cause they believe in. Some people are very receptive, while others are downright abusive. Still, I see canvassing as perhaps the best way to connect with a group of people in a specific geographic area and inform them about a project or event nearby.

Most cities offer tax lot maps to the public, either free of charge or for a nominal fee. You can use these maps to keep track of where you have been and go back to see people who were not home the first time around. Give them contact information and a small flyer, and bring a clipboard to sign people up for your mailing list. If you are not trying to raise money, tell people right when they open the door that you are not fund-raising. Use your rap to inform them and determine their interest level, then invite them to get involved.

Don't take it personally if some people are rude. Just move on. Chances are, the next person will be friendlier. An evening of canvassing can result in as many as fifty new contacts, and a week of work can inform an entire neighborhood.

Sound terrifying? It can be. Canvassing is not for everyone, but it boosts confidence and spreads the word—and you might surprise yourself with your newfound skill at fund-raising!

Use the Internet

I've already discussed Internet mailing lists, but there are several other ways to use the Internet to promote your projects. The first is to set up your own website, either with your own domain or through a public host. Most Internet providers offer a small amount of free web space with your subscription, and there are dozens if not hundreds of resources online for public hosting space. Try tribe.net, myspace.com, friendster.com, and craigslist.org for starters.

Building the page can be relatively simple if you just want to post some basic information and a few photos. Most of the free online hosting services offer templates that you can just plug your photos and information into. If you want a more extensive site, however, with lots of links, articles, and contact forms, then you will need to put in a more significant effort. Try sitebuildernow.net for an inexpensive, easy-to-use tool, or find a local computer geek to help you.

Aside from having your own website, you can also post your events to the calendar and announcement pages of other organizations' pages.

A list of websites with calendars of ecological-design-oriented events can be found in the resources section. Most of these need your information several months in advance to give them time to get it up and published on the web, so plan ahead.

You can also post announcements to one or several of the literally thousands of public bulletin boards and mailing lists on the web. Most have an open membership. There are groups on every subject from astrophysics to zoology. Once you are a member you can post articles, calendar events, and whatever else anytime.

Write an Article

While you're using the Internet look for good places to publish articles. Writing articles about your work and related topics is a great way to build credibility and share information. With a little research and some good photos, you can create an article for a local publication that both educates the public and provides free advertising for your project.

Check around for local magazines and newspapers that run articles by freelance writers. Most publications have writer's guidelines that you will need to follow, but the average article is usually around fifteen hundred words long, or about six pages, double-spaced.

Be sure to include information about how readers can get involved. Some publications will even pay for your article and photos, adding funds to your project and experience to your résumé!

Publish a 'Zine

I used to produce a 'zine called *Weed Lover: A Sustainable Horticulture Reader*. The first issue was just twenty pages and offered a basic introduction to seed saving, ecological living, and biodynamic agriculture. I ran a first printing of a hundred stapled photocopies and sold them at conferences and workshops. Over the next two years I published five more issues, with a wide array of garden tips, plant lists, artwork, resources, and references for grassroots gardeners. I always sold as many copies as I made and years later am still meeting avid readers of the *Weed Lover*.

Some 'zines are periodicals, others onetime publications. You can write the articles yourself, get submissions from others, or photocopy interesting tidbits out of other publications and compile a verbal mosaic of ideas and sources. In all cases be sure to note your sources well, giving credit where credit is due. Print them yourself with a basic computer setup and a photocopier, or find a responsible press to publish your 'zine for you.

Give an Interview or Host a Radio Show

If there is a community radio station or local news show that broadcasts from your area, offer to give an interview. Or see what it takes to become a volunteer host. Many stations provide training and airtime in exchange for volunteer work. Most universities and some city colleges also have a radio station that allows the public to broadcast live and pre-recorded shows.

Make a Video or Television Show

Just as with radio, sometimes you can find training and access to equipment through a local college or television station, many of which offer free or low-cost classes. Some stations will also broadcast your films, either through an established program or by giving you your own slot on the schedule. Take a field trip to the local stations and see what type of resources they offer.

An educational video is a great way to share and distribute information to large and diverse groups of people. Videos can be distributed to schools, libraries, community centers, activist groups, and independent media networks. I have seen excellent amateur and independent films about bicycle transportation, homeless garden projects, ancient-forest defense, and so much more.

Place a Classified Ad

Line advertising is inexpensive and can be quite effective. Many publications have sections for advertising workshops and classes, and some offer free or discounted rates for nonprofit events.

The personals are another great place to advertise, and personal ads are usually free. For example, if you have organized a seed swap and want to get the word out, you could place something like "Avid organic gardener seeks kindred spirit. Meet me at the Seed Swap, City Park, next Saturday at noon."

Making Ends Meet

I've talked at length about making the best use of available resources, but as you organize and publicize your projects, you will inevitably need to come up with some cash. Here are a few strategies to help meet needs with resources.

The Magic Hat

Make a brief announcement and pass around an interesting-looking hat during or after a workshop or event. Borrow the hat from a workshop participant or just put a donation jar out in an obvious spot with a little sign noting what the money is for. A variation on this strategy includes putting multiple jars at locations around town at local businesses that support your work.

Benefit Shows and Special Events

Often a local band or two will play for free to raise money for a project. Depending on the popularity of the band (and the project), these shows can raise anything from two hundred to twenty thousand dollars, or even more. I have organized house parties, movie screenings, puppet shows, dinner theater, and forty-performer community variety shows to raise money.

Here's a good one: Some local forest activists organize an annual Trek for the Trees in which activists ride bikes out to a forest action camp and supporters pledge anywhere from one to twenty dollars per mile. The ride lasts two days and ends with a big party where riders and supporters can meet, mingle, and collect pledges.

Don't forget to pass the magic hat at all of your events to generate some extra cash flow.

Retail and Wholesale Sales

Make or grow stuff to sell at local farmer's markets or to stores and restaurants. Seeds can be sold to seed companies, herbs to herb distributors, and so on. Or host a sale of your own in a yard or parking lot. Ask people to donate things to sell or auction off, make refreshments, and perhaps get some musicians to provide ambience. Don't forget to set up an information table with materials that explain where the money is going.

Memberships and Pledge Drives

Some programs, such as community radio, host regular pledge drives where they put extra effort into asking for donations from individuals and businesses who support the programming. Many projects and organizations have paying members—people who regularly fund and participate in the project. Some membership organizations have a 501(c)3 federal nonprofit infrastructure (see the sidebar above); others operate below government radar. Look to organizations near you for a wide variety of models.

Grant Writing

Though most large grants require the above-mentioned nonprofit infrastructure, it is sometimes possible to get small grants for grassroots work. A list of some good opportunities can be found in the resources section. Alternatively, some nonprofits are willing to offer smaller local groups "umbrella" status, where the small group channels funding through the nonprofit. Ask around locally if you need umbrella status—find an organization that does similar work and write a succinct, well-organized proposal asking the group for fiscal support in the form of tax-deductible status.

When writing a grant proposal, read the application very carefully, and follow the directions to the letter. Use a basic problem–solution proposal, with measurable goals and explicit objectives. Be clear, brief, and specific as to the guidelines outlined by the funder. You will probably need to attach a realistic, detailed budget and a timeline and include a little (but not too much) supporting data, media clips, and brochures.

Most funders will be very specific about what they want you to provide, and many require a short letter of inquiry before they will accept a full application. The letter of inquiry should be flawlessly written, with a succinct overview of your goals, objectives, plan of action, and expected outcomes. Note how much funding you want, what you will spend it on, and why this group should be the one to pay for it.

Grant writing is a learned skill, and a bigger topic than I have room for here. Most community colleges offer short grant-writing seminars, and there are several free and inexpensive ones online—if you want to write grant proposals, take one of these workshops. It's fun and empowering to gain access to the millions of dollars out there for projects like yours. Or bite the bullet and hire a qualified professional grant writer. This might sound like a risky investment, but a good grant writer will generate funds to pay for herself and much more, while you are free to focus on the work you enjoy.

Donations

Individuals, businesses, and other organizations often have surplus goods that they are happy to donate to a community project. I have received donations of food, seeds, plants, soil, tools, paper, furniture, greenhouse materials, and much more over the years. Just start asking around and see what comes up.

I covered donations in chapter 2, when discussing urban waste resources and how to get them. Here are some more tips for getting local businesses and individuals to direct surplus goods and cash toward your project.

It helps to have a well-written request to give to potential donors so they can show it to the necessary decision makers and keep your contact information on file. Then send it or take it around to the businesses that seem like they would have access to what you need.

For example, if you want organic seeds, make a list of as many organic seed companies as you can find and send the letter to all of them. Include a brochure, a newspaper clipping, or some photos about your work, and follow up a few weeks later with a phone call or short e-mail.

Places to look for donations include nurseries and garden centers, schools and universities, bookstores, food stores, other stores, and restaurants. Most independently owned local businesses will be willing to either give a material donation or offer a discount. Larger chain establishments usually yield less favorable results but are still worth a try. In general, the more people you ask, the more support you will get.

Other organizations and community projects often have surplus from donations they have gathered. To make best use of the community surplus as a whole, tap into the work of fellow activists, coordinate fund-raising and donation efforts, and let resources flow among related projects.

Be careful not to spend so much time fund-raising and dealing with organizational logistics that you are too burned out to do the fun stuff— the projects that the funds support. Creating more corporate nonprofit office jobs will not save the world. A well-planned project should be able to work with minimal funding. Take pride in your frugality and innovations rather than your ability to raise and spend large amounts of money.

As your projects begin to succeed you will soon find yourself surrounded by groups of people who want to work with you. Interacting with these people, educating them, and directing their energy toward autonomous, integrated ecological community is no small task. You will need to hone your communication and conflict resolution skills and may need to unlearn some bad habits. The next chapters will explore the ways and means of making these interactions as functional, productive, and mutually beneficial as possible.

This classic hobo symbol represents people coming together to share ideas and then going apart to spread them further.

11. Working Together

I don't know the key to success, but the key to failure is trying to please everybody.

—Bill Cosby[1]

Wherever you go, there you are.

—Anonymous

Our deepest fear is not that we are inadequate. Our deepest fear is that we are powerful beyond measure. It is our light, not our darkness, that most frightens us. We ask ourselves, "Who am I to be brilliant, gorgeous, talented, and fabulous?" Actually, who are we not to be? . . . Your playing small doesn't serve the world. There's nothing enlightened about shrinking so that other people won't feel insecure around you. We were born to make manifest the glory . . . that is within us. It is not just in some of us; it's in everyone. And as we let our own light shine, we unconsciously give other people permission to do the same. As we are liberated from our own fear, our presence automatically liberates others.

—Nelson Mandela[2]

The Group Mind

Because it is impossible to build community all by yourself, learning and embracing a functional group process becomes as important a skill as building good compost. If you find yourself organizing community projects, you must learn to facilitate good communication and effective working relationships if you want those projects to succeed.

Community groups share workloads, resources, and information with one another and with other communities. Living and working together in community is a natural instinct of humans and many other animals—just look at wolves, chickens, and elk. Most people love spending time with their friends and families; in fact, community and companionship are essential to our mental health.

Some people prefer to work alone, and I fully encourage an individual's right to be empowered by her own ideas. However, I also believe that a brilliant idea comes with the responsibility to share it. Take credit for your ideas, but make them real or let them go like any other surplus. Even if you are allergic to meetings, you can't work in groups, or you do your most effective work by yourself, you owe it to your community and your planet to find a way to share your work.

Especially in urban environments, where we have the potential to interact with dozens and sometimes hundreds of people a day, it is essential to our ecological health that we learn to communicate and get along with others. Luckily this can be an immensely fun and rewarding experience. Like any system, a good working group is greater than the sum of its parts. You can achieve much more together than as individuals and can set an example of cooperation and peaceful interaction.

It can also be a very painful and frustrating experience, depending on how well the group is able to get along. In some groups the members seem to have a mystical connection with one another, agreeing on every step of the process. In my experience this is extremely rare. Other groups are just the wrong mix of personalities; these groups quickly erupt into dysfunctional chaos, and nothing ever gets accomplished. This is also relatively rare. Most groups are somewhere in between, and the faster those groups can find a functional process for sharing ideas, making decisions, taking action, and solving problems, the better equipped they will be to realize their collective goals.

Interacting with other people is one primary way in which we get to know one another and ourselves, and the best way to build healthy communities. Yet effective human interaction is a skill rarely taught in conventional settings. In this chapter I will outline some of the more effective methods for developing and maintaining a functional group process and will examine some solutions to the inevitable problems that occur.

Making Decisions

When you start sharing ideas and developing projects with a group, you will eventually have to arrive at some decisions together. What will

you do as a group? Where is your basis of unity? What actions will you take and why? How will you go about your work, and what problem-solving tools will you use?

In mainstream Western culture, and especially in the United States, most people seem to support some form of voting-based decision making. Even many radical activists speak often of voting and constitutional rights. These people eschew dictatorships, theocracy, communism, and other forms of government for being authoritarian, patriarchical, and oppressive.

Yet most examples of voting-based processes today are merely some form of authoritarianism in disguise. We vote, we watch the news, and the rich white men in power continue to bomb a new country every year. When we go out in the streets and exercise the meager "constitutional rights" afforded us, we go to jail and get shot by the police whose salaries we are forced to pay. This is not my idea of a free country, nor do I feel included in the decision-making process.

Voting-based systems rely on a majority rule, by which any leader or decision that receives the most votes wins. But what about the minority voters? Often those who are consistently outvoted feel powerless and disenfranchised. Sometimes these people will just leave the group, taking their ideas and resources with them.

Other times people will continue to work with the group but will be bitter and less invested in the outcome. A few will even take action in an effort to be heard and represented and may even sabotage a project. This occurs on some scale in every democracy, as is evident in the constant civil unrest in this country and most of the world. Not that other forms of rule don't provoke unrest, dissatisfaction, and often revolution. Quite the contrary, which is why we need to make finding ways to cooperate with one another a top priority.

A functional working group can accomplish far more than the sum of its individuals.

Without getting so deep into political analysis that I can't dig myself out before garden season, I will just say that I much prefer, and highly recommend, an egalitarian decision-making process, such as consensus, for collective projects.

Consensus and Shared Leadership

Consensus-based groups make an agreement to reach agreement on every decision. Any single person can block any decision if she feels it will inhibit or detract from the goals or integrity of the group, and the concerns of even a small minority are given equal weight as those of the majority. This is the most egalitarian form of group process, as it embraces the needs and ideas of every individual. When people share decision-making power, they also share responsibility for the impact of those decisions. They become invested in the project and devoted to the collective outcome.

Consensus embraces the principle of cooperation.

Consensus is not voting, nor is it compromise. Consensus is synergy; it is the symbiotic will of the group, expressed through finding a unified goal and sharing responsibility for achieving it. In many ways just participating in a consensus process empowers the community more than the resulting projects. The empowerment—and the learning—comes through the process as much as the product. The medium is still the message.

Consensus embraces the principle of cooperation, meaning tolerance of others' mistakes and willingness to learn from our own. None of this means there is no leadership; in fact, all members of the group should be encouraged to use their leadership skills to help ensure the fairness and effectiveness of each decision. The key to functional equality is not in denying power but in learning to share and respect it as a valuable and malleable resource. Like fire, water, work, and sex, power in many forms flows through all elements in our gardens and communities, and the more comfortable we can become with it, the better.

The Collective Process

Often consensus-based groups call themselves collectives. Most collectives come together via one or several group meetings. I have attended many different kinds of meetings. Some of them felt like a psychospiritual rejuvenation—a divine merging of the group mind, focused together toward a common, perfect goal. Other meetings felt like an eternity in the lowest circle of hell, with every interpersonal drama ever known to humankind dragged through the same communal pit at once. The primary difference between these meetings was the ability of the participants to conduct calm, mature relationships and to define and stick to clear, mutual boundaries.

The process described below deviates from traditional consensus formats that are based largely on parliamentary-style meetings, where everyone is forced to listen to the tireless rantings of the few and the call for consensus feels eerily like voting. I find such meetings long and frustrating, and rarely do they result in much action. Nothing breaks a project down faster than when the participants stop communicating, and nothing makes them stop communicating faster than when the communication process (usually meetings) becomes boring, hostile, or tedious.

Luckily long, boring meetings are not the only way to achieve powerful, consensus-based results. The process I prefer relies heavily on ecological design theory, using a systematic approach to finding and expressing the group will. Thus meetings become more like workshops, with an emphasis on action rather than rhetoric, and on building community through cultivating a powerful group dynamic rather than watching it deteriorate into dysfunctional, hypothetical chatter. But the collective process doesn't stop at the meeting. The meeting is only the launching pad for the action to follow. In the next few pages we'll work through a functional collective process, from the first meeting to the realization of unified goals.

A Semiformal Sharing of Ideas

Meetings should be short, informative, and fun, though sometimes with moments of tension and sincere seriousness. Use your meeting time to get the job done: Identify goals, objectives, and resources; delegate tasks; and share information about finished work and upcoming opportunities. I recommend not scheduling regular meetings (such as every Tuesday at five) but rather encouraging everyone in the collective to call a meeting whenever they feel they need to talk with more than a few people at a time about a project. This will help you avoid pointless meetings and will encourage shared leadership.

Schedule meetings for a specific time, say from 6 to 8 PM on a week-night, at a public place that closes early. This will help avoid long, dragged-out sessions that leave people feeling burned out and ready to skip the next meeting.

The convener—the person who called the meeting—arrives first and greets everyone as they come in. When everyone has arrived, they sit in a circle and a few people agree to take on a rotating leadership role for the meeting. Lasting for the duration of the meeting, the roles help the process move quickly yet comprehensively toward a common goal and plan for action. These roles vary from group to group but generally include a note keeper, a public scribe, a timekeeper, a "vibeswatcher," and a facilitator or two.

The note keeper keeps a detailed log of everything that is said and by whom and makes these notes available later, as needed. The note keeper also keeps track of important points and agreements made by the group, and the public scribe uses a chalkboard or large piece of paper to post these pertinent points during the meeting for all to see and relate to. The timekeeper offers friendly reminders when one person is talking for too long or the group becomes caught on a topic for longer than agreed. The vibeswatcher helps keep the conversation from becoming abusive and speaks up when mediation is needed or when the whole group needs to take a break.

Finally, the role of facilitator is to encourage egalitarian participation, prevent interruptions, and try to keep the group on topic. The facilitator is the anchor of the meeting. She keeps the meeting on track, moving the flow of conversation toward a solution and, ultimately, an action. She does not direct the meeting toward her own agenda but rather seeks opportunities to help bring the group toward a harmonized synthesis of collective will.

The role of facilitator, while not necessarily the most important, is often the most active and vocal and tends to fall into the hands of the most vocal, most leadership-inclined person in the group. If you want to effectively balance the flow of power, however, it is essential to rotate this and the other roles from meeting to meeting. (See the sidebar on page 275 for more ways to share power and leadership in a group.)

Once people have chosen roles for the meeting (this shouldn't take more than five minutes), the real fun begins. Here you have as many options as ways you can think of to communicate. The classic format involves taking turns speaking, moving through a list of agenda items, and working toward agreement. But sometimes it is more effective to have a "mingling meeting" in which participants group together at will, discussing topics that need to be discussed among the people who need to discuss them. The facilitator, note keeper, and vibeswatcher are still working; they are mingling too.

Sometimes the facilitator starts a go-around in which each person gives her name and a very brief introduction. Introductions can be a statement of purpose (*What do I want to get out of this project?*) or the answer to an ice-breaker question (*Who has inspired me the most and why?*). Some groups will also do a regular check-in where participants say how they are feeling personally, physically, and emotionally. These go-arounds can eat up the entire meeting time, so especially in a working group, where the same people meet often, consider skipping this step and getting right to work. You can always solve personal problems and get to know one another in a separate meeting, with a format focused on those things.

After introductions the collective either picks up unfinished business from a previous meeting or launches into a fresh brainstorming session about the topics the group wants to focus on. What are the relevant problems that you share? What do you collectively want to do about those problems? Cultivate your collective passion and develop some compelling ideas for action.

Sometimes it helps to brainstorm a list of agenda items first, and even to assign time limits to each item. Then work through the list and hash out each item in turn. Other times it is better to just let the group free-flow through an assortment of ideas, then come to a shared vision through a more organic process. Similarly, some collectives are comfortable with a raucous everyone-talks-at-once process, while others need a more orderly atmosphere. Check in with one another and be sure you're not oppressing yourselves.

Again, none of these activities needs to be done in a parliamentary, raise-your-hand-and-don't-speak-out-of-turn fashion. Some people have a hard time being comfortable in a group where everyone is talking at once, approaching the people they need to connect with, and writing tasks on a central board. Yet this same format, while chaotic to some, is highly effective for others. And just as it is crucial for the more bois-

Seven Ways to Share Power

It is a sociological fact that in every group, a leader or set of leaders will emerge. There is no reason to fear this power. Instead we must learn to embrace and mediate it for the good of the whole. Here are seven strategies to help you along:

1. **Talk less, listen more:** Check yourself when you are interrupting or responding to every comment. Encourage quiet people to speak and be heard.
2. **Let someone else run with your idea:** Toss your ideas into the group and let others morph and embrace them. Let go of your ego in the interests of effective group synergy.
3. **Share access to resources:** Let other people pick up donations and contact key people. Don't hoard valuable resources. Trust your collective as you trust yourself.
4. **Say no to new responsibilities:** Trying to do everything yourself is the direct road to total burnout. Learn when to say no, and how much you can realistically handle on your own.
5. **Let others make mistakes, offering advice only if they ask:** Don't micromanage your collective. If you aren't doing the work yourself, let those who are make the final call.
6. **Delegate responsibilities responsibly:** Don't assign difficult tasks to people who can't handle them. Believe in your group, but if you are in a position to delegate tasks, choose carefully, in a way that empowers collective members rather than setting them up for failure.
7. **Trust the people and the process:** If you don't believe in the people you work with, stop working with them. Remember that we are all working hard to learn how to live peacefully together. Trust your comrades and yourself to do the best you can. Similarly, if you don't trust the process, you owe it to yourself and your comrades to find a new one that really works.

terous members of a group to make room for quiet people, it is equally important for those timid folks to find the courage to speak up, assert themselves, and be heard.

In my opinion the most effective meetings are a blend of the above strategies, with time for getting to know one another, time for mingling, and time for carefully facilitated planning. Remember that a group process is like a garden design: You can get a plethora of ideas from books and examples, but you will ultimately need to develop a process that responds to the specific needs and desires of your unique situation. Talk with your group about the process, and find something that feels good to everyone.

Following Through

After a good brainstorming session, some interesting proposals should begin to take shape. Or perhaps someone has arrived at the meeting with a specific plan that she wants the group to follow. Either way, options should be moving away from the theoretical and toward the specific things you can do together to achieve a common goal.

Have a working meeting in the garden to avoid some of the stagnation that can occur in boardroom-style settings.

At this point the most common scenario is for a couple of proposals to form and for the group to either vote or argue over which one to choose. In an egalitarian group process, however, it often proves much more effective to turn to a design process like Gobradime (see chapter 7) to develop a specific set of actions in response to your specific collective theory. Have everyone in the group define their personal goals, observations, boundaries, and so on. Find threads of commonality and weave them into a synergistic plan of action. You can also have each person take a step back and brainstorm about it, then come back together and synthesize your ideas.

Throughout this process, consistently test for consensus. This means asking whether anyone in the group has concerns, questions, or problems with either the process or the potential products of your collective work. Consensus does not mean that everyone thinks the decision is the best one possible, or that they are sure it will work. It does mean that everyone feels included in the decision, that no person has decision-making power over any other, and that no one feels alienated by the process. For this to work everyone in the group must trust and respect one another and must be honest about their needs and resources.

Don't waste your time discussing what shouldn't happen; focus instead on what the group can agree to do together. Sometimes certain parts of a project will appeal to some but not others. Define which parts should be left out because they are inappropriate, and which other pieces will remain because, while unappealing to some, they are still important for the project. People sometimes feel they have to block a decision when they really just need to find a different place to plug into the project. Remember that you all agreed to agree on everything, so take time to listen to what everyone feels, wants, and doesn't want to do.

As you work your way through the labyrinth of the group mind, continue to push the process toward the practical ways in which you can manifest your collective goals. If you are using Gobradime, it will lead you directly toward task assessment. This is the essential step in turning theoretical dreaming into focused, tangible action. Work together to develop a list of tasks the group will need to accomplish in order to meet collective goals, and organize those tasks into loose chronological order.

Because consensus groups are based on everyone agreeing to every facet of the project, the ideal is for the whole group to collaborate on a list of tasks. However, it takes far less time and usually works out fine if most tasks are delegated to small working groups and only the most challenging tasks (such as achieving a shared vision or raising a lot of money) are kept within the large group (see the sidebar on page 278). Do what makes sense for the project and collective at hand, but again be receptive to one another and don't go against the large-group decisions by putting tasks on your own list that you know others will strongly oppose.

When Problems Arise

The key to a functional consensus process is the willingness of the participants to trust one another and their ability to conduct mature, responsible relationships. Abusive or otherwise dysfunctional people will find egalitarian group process difficult or impossible.

Sometimes there are minor personality conflicts that can be overcome through some simple problem-solving strategies. Other times it is better

Ideas Into Action

The free-thinking nature of consensus and other egalitarian group processes calls for a decentralized work system in which individuals have a large amount of freedom over their own work. For example, the large group might decide to organize a weeklong "Cities to Gardens" conference; then small groups of two or three will work on developing each day of the conference. The whole group meets once to determine the basic dates and outline of the event, to brainstorm a general list of tasks, and to delegate who will organize which day.

The large group trusts the small groups to come up with relevant, worthy activities for their given day, and pertinent information is posted on a central bulletin board somewhere. If everyone follows through on their personal commitments made at the meeting, the whole group doesn't need to meet again until after the event, to evaluate how it went and to come up with a new project for the group.

When delegating broad responsibilities in the large group or working out logistical details in smaller working groups, I recommend the following process for making sure every detail is covered:

1. **Brainstorm:** Either meet in person or post a list to spell out the tasks that the group agrees to complete. Sort the list into chronological order to create a loose timeline of action.
2. **Volunteer:** Go around the group and take turns volunteering to complete specific tasks. No more than three people need be responsible for any one task. Keep it simple, and encourage people to take on only what they can realistically accomplish.
3. **Assign:** After the volunteer session, go back through and ask everyone to take on a fair share of the tasks that no one volunteered to do.
4. **Redesign:** Now you will be left with a handful of tasks that group members either feel unqualified or refuse to do. Ask the members whether they really want or need these tasks to occur. If possible, redesign your plan of action to eliminate these tasks. If that is not possible, then pool your resources and hire out for someone who can get the job done.
5. **Report:** Create a central bulletin board, website, or whatever to serve as a base of communication for both the large and the small groups. Report progress, unmet needs, changes in the plan, and new opportunities. Use this bulletin board to call a meeting when necessary.

This system works great for getting a large amount of work done with the minimum amount of meeting time. Consensus occurs on every level, in the large group and within the small working groups that have related tasks, and as long as everyone follows through on their commitments the project gets completed quickly and efficiently.

for a person to leave the group or for the group to dismantle. Try to see this not as a failure but as an opportunity to learn and branch off in new directions. Just as in the garden, not every experiment will succeed; the only mistake is refusing to recognize patterns and opportunities.

If you are having trouble finding common ground or getting things accomplished, work through the following steps to look for solutions. These are just a few ideas; experiment with your own collective and individual communication styles to find specific problem-solving techniques that work for you.

Check Your Head

If you find yourself frustrated or disenchanted with your group, the first step is to check your own behavior. As individuals, the best way to contribute to a peaceful society is to be peaceful people. Personal growth is an ongoing process, and if we direct energy at enhancing our own ways of being, we greatly improve our ability to communicate and work with others. It is much easier to change ourselves than to change others, so ask yourself, *What can I learn here?* or *What exactly is the behavior that is causing this emotion?*

Communicating in a nonviolent, egalitarian manner is a learned skill, and unfortunately it's not usually taught in school. So it is up to each individual to learn to interact with others in a way that embraces diversity, promotes sharing, and encourages personal growth. Before you criticize someone else, make sure you are not mirroring her disruptive behavior. Find an alternative to offer her, and find a peaceful way to communicate that alternative.

Few of us are experts at this, but the point is to try. Spend a little time asking yourself questions about your communication skills. What are your strong points? What needs to improve? What baggage are you bringing with you from your past? In what ways were your early examples of interpersonal communication dysfunctional? How are your personal attachments getting in the way of your leadership skills and your ability to fully participate in your community? Identify these issues and resolve them. It is okay to be damaged from your past; most of us are. Nevertheless, it is also okay, and sometimes essential, to change.

Someone once said to me, "Great minds have great flaws." Sometimes people for whom we have a great professional respect

Often the best and fastest way to resolve an interpersonal conflict is by changing your own behavior.

engage in rude or downright abusive behavior, yet they are either unaware or in denial. This not only detracts from their own opportunities but also limits the potential of the whole project.

Many people go their entire lives without learning how to communicate with others in a way that is peaceful, respectful, and mutually rewarding. I went through the first thirty years of my life thinking that to carry on a conversation meant to talk as loud and as fast as I could, and to interrupt as often as possible. I learned the hard way that this is a deeply ineffective way to share ideas with people I trust and respect.

In the decade that I have worked in activist communities, I have been to hundreds of meetings, workshops, and conference panels, and at nearly every one there was at least one person who would continually interrupt, tell long, irrelevant stories, make sexist comments, or otherwise cross the boundaries of the other people in the room. Sometimes that person was me, and I was eventually forced, by my own desire for community, to change.

The point is that if you don't want to work with pushy, obnoxious people who interrupt everyone and disrupt the group, then don't be like them. The old saying "You can catch more flies with honey than you can with vinegar" is true. If you really need to be heard, wait your turn and present your case in a way that is reasonable, realistic, and easy to understand. Often when we wait to speak, others will come up with the same questions and ideas. Allowing room for this empowers the whole group and restores the balance of interaction.

In any situation try to turn problems into solutions, and never be afraid to ask for help from the community. Remember the ecological design principle "Keep your chin up." Be proud of your role in the group and willing to grow in the interests of a healthy community ecology. When we achieve harmony within our relationships with others, we will be that much closer to achieving harmony with all of nature.

Remember, defeat is always temporary.

A basic daily stretching routine like the classic "sun salutation" helps support a healthy body and, in turn, a healthy attitude.

Along with checking your own behavior when things go awry in your group, taking care of yourself before interacting with others promotes healthy relationships all around. If we are not well fed, hydrated, well rested, and free from abuse, we will find it much more difficult to change our lives or our communities for the better. We owe it to ourselves, our collectives, and our planet to take the best possible care of our bodies, hearts, and minds.

One of the best ways to cover all of these bases is to garden. Gardening is great exercise and generates fresh, nutritious food, both of which are important for maintaining a strong, healthy body. In addition, gardening helps us reconnect with nature and is an excellent form of mental therapy: Working with plants has a calming effect and leads to valuable insights about how to deal with internal, emotional conflicts. Beyond gardening, also try stretching, dance, deep breathing, and professional counseling to work through your issues and find the peaceful egalitarian in yourself.

Talk It Out

Once you have gotten to the heart of the issue in yourself, if you still feel angry or uncomfortable about a person or situation, you may need to talk it out. Usually a short conversation is enough to reestablish a basis of unity and get the process flowing again. It helps to go back to notes from previous meetings, backtracking to where the problems began. Then look for alternative ways of working that don't cause conflict within the group.

Work with people you respect, and respect the people you work with.

Sometimes the collective may need to bring in an outside mediator to negotiate issues between people and break up clotted lines of communication. Other times personal issues crop up between individuals in the group. Personal conflicts within a collective can stem from a wide range of issues, from race, religion, and economic status to unintended slips of the tongue that cause a flood of pent-up resentment to spill forth.

If you find yourself in a situation where people have become unable to communicate or work together for any of these reasons, do your best to depersonalize the conversation and return the group to the collective goals. Try the useful clearing technique outlined in the sidebar on page 283, and suggest that everyone take a break to reflect and gain better control of their emotions.

Above all, remember: You can control only your own behavior. Offer suggestions and become a calm place within the storm, but don't try to change, fix, or control your companions. If the group becomes so dysfunctional that you find yourself sucked into unhealthy or abusive behaviors, consider moving on to a group that works better for you.

Set Healthy Boundaries

It is usually worth it to spend time resolving conflict rather than letting a project or relationship fall apart. Sometimes, however, people will cross the line from dysfunction or discomfort to flat-out abuse. As an individual and in groups it is important to set healthy boundaries and to define what constitutes abusive and oppressive behaviors.

As we work together to build a more peaceful, more ecological society, we must develop ways to communicate with one another that encourage honesty, participation, and mutual aid. Never yell at or physically attack another person. This is abuse, and it does not lend well to egalitarian group process.

It is up to you to establish a healthy way of dealing with your group and the problems that arise. If you become overwhelmed, annoyed, disenchanted, or any of the other negative emotions frequently associated with group process, perhaps you aren't setting appropriate boundaries.

Decide what you can and can't do, and what you are and are not willing to deal with. Unless you are called to do social work, dealing with chronic abusers is probably not worth your time. Draw the line and stick to it. If you feel you have tried communicating with someone

Clearing the Air

If two people are having a hard time finding commonality in the group, suggest a clearing session like the ones described in *The Art of Facilitation* by Dale Hunter.[3] Sometimes it is appropriate to engage a neutral third party to mediate, but this is often unnecessary. Find a quiet, neutral space where you can sit comfortably and not be disturbed. Now take turns expressing your commitment to the relationship, your desire to be relaxed and easy to work with, and your love for the person and for the earth. Ground yourselves in your basis of unity.

When you feel ready to communicate, calmly describe your feelings and identify the specific incident(s) that triggered the emotions. Take responsibility for your own feelings but identify what you need to feel safe, respected, and valued. Pay attention to your body language and try to be peaceful and open. Let it all pour out until you feel spent and relieved.

Then it is the other person's turn. Ask her to share her own emotions, to react to your words, and to explain her actions. Do not interrupt; just listen carefully and wait until she too is spent. Sometimes you will need to go back and forth in this fashion until everything is out.

Now you are ready for solutions. Make proposals and come to some agreements about how you will avoid recurring problems in the future.

A similar method can be used to clear a large group: Go around and listen to each individual, writing requests on a large board. Next, ask the group to go through each request and decline, accept, or compromise. This process can defuse even very tense, very dysfunctional situations; often just a few minutes of intentional, open conversation can make a huge difference.

and she continues to cross your boundaries, you are totally justified in asking her to seek counseling, nonviolence training, massage, therapy—whatever it takes. Sometimes an intervention is needed, or a person will be asked to seek professional counseling before returning to the group. If no one else in the group will back you up, check your own behavior again or consider moving on.

Let us go back to the definition of ecological design: Ecological design is a design system for ecological living, with particular emphasis on the relationships among the needs, elements, and participants within that system. The core of ecological living is relationships, whether with ourselves, other humans, or the land or between elements in a system. A successful ecological design depends entirely upon the success of the relationships within. If you want to improve your system, improve the relationships.

Most of us did not learn about egalitarian group process as children and must struggle to define and redefine our roles in each evolving project and the relationships within. However, we can and must learn to get along if we are to build a healthy future, and we can and must teach these values to our children. This is the topic of the next chapter.

12. The Next Generation

The best skill of a good leader is to bring out the leadership qualities in others. For we are all leaders. Every parent is a leader, and every child can become one.

—Graham Bell[1]

Integrating Sector C

Conventional design is predominantly anti-child. Sharp edges, hard surfaces, high windows, toxic environments: These are just a few examples of the exclusion of children from our surroundings. Even if you don't have any children, if you want to build an ecological community you must include the special needs of young people in your observations and planning. Still, many would-be ecological gardens and homesites fail to consider the factors and influences in "Sector C."

The best way to ensure that our projects and designs meet the needs of children is to include them in every level of our work, from goal setting to design and implementation. Even if you are not a parent and have no plans of becoming one, chances are you know someone with children who would appreciate some help, and you might benefit from diversifying the age group of your peers.

All types of projects, in the garden and in the community, benefit greatly from the inclusion of children. Children can contribute fresh ideas and comic relief and add new dimensions to any project. In addition, including children opens up projects to a much wider diversity of participants. Many adults are parents and are much more likely to attend an event to which they can bring their children. Often single parents find it difficult or impossible to attend workshops or community events that exclude children, and by making the extra effort to provide opportunities for children you may double or even triple the attendance.

Not only do projects benefit from having children participate, but the children themselves reap lasting rewards from the inclusion. These rewards include learning about plants, nature, and

Every ecological home and garden should consider the needs and virtues of "sector C."

food, getting more exercise, and developing a stronger work ethic. Children feel empowered through contributing meaningful work and learn to be lifelong learners through witnessing adults sharing skills.

Often children who are included in community projects grow up to initiate projects of their own, and this exponential effect spreads ideas and resources into future generations. Whether you are hosting a community event or just looking for ways to include your own children, here are some effective ways to integrate children into your projects. These range from simply offering child care at community events to organizing projects specifically for younger people.

Schedule with Children in Mind

Schedule meetings and events earlier in the day so that people who have to go to bed early, like children and parents, can attend. Also, plan things for weekends and during school vacations, rather than when children are busy with school. You can also go into the schools to do gardens and other projects; I'll get to that in a minute.

Reach Out to Children and Parents

Go back through your outreach tools and strategies and see how you can make them more welcoming to families. Advertise a child-inclusive policy in flyers, websites, and press releases. Just a few words inviting parents to bring their children can clear up any doubts a wary participant might have about coming.

When you build it, they will come, so follow through and be ready for the explosion of youthful energy, not to mention the potential distractions that come with having children around. Which brings me to the next item.

Provide Child Care

When organizing workshops, seed swaps, and especially multiple-day events, such as a course or conference, be sure to include some sort of plan for child care. Most existing projects assume that the parents will provide their own child care. If you choose to go this route, it's okay, but with a little extra effort you can provide or help organize child care.

The simplest alternative would be to bring a big blanket, a box of toys, books, and art supplies, and pile them up in a soft corner somewhere. The next level would be to hire someone or ask a qualified volunteer to come to staff that space, with the special intention of playing with children at the event. A little more effort can spark a child-care cooperative, where parents take turns providing care during an ongoing series of events.

A simple child-care co-op might work like this: All of the parents have a short meeting in which people choose a safe, central location where the children can hang out and sign up for child-care shifts during an upcoming workshop or event. Sometimes shifts will rotate several times during an event. It is a good idea to keep the children close by, in case something comes up and a parent is needed.

Setting up child care that is a part of, but a bit removed from, the workshop or event is usually the best option when very small children who might not be physically able to participate in the project itself are involved. However, this still creates a situation where the children are kept separate from everyone else, and I think the next strategy makes much more sense.

Designing with Children

Children can participate in all aspects of a project design, whether it is a home system or a community project. I'll use the Gobradime design process from chapter 7 to illustrate this point. Every stage of the design process has a spot for children:

Goals: The needs of children absolutely must be included in this phase. If you have children, or if children will ever visit your home or garden, you will need to consider their needs and potential ways of using the site. It is much easier to design with everyone's needs in mind than to change people's behavior to conform to a design that did not address their concerns.

Observation: Children often see much more than adults do. Their minds are not clouded by the logic and pragmatism of adulthood, and they can see potential that we may dismiss as unrealistic or impossible. Also, children are at a different eye level and see many things that we literally overlook. Let them look, smell, and listen for details, and encourage them to write down or draw what they discover.

Boundaries: Children fit into small places, and their ideas about boundaries, whether physical or otherwise, can help shape a design. A small, seemingly useless corner of the yard could be a fort or secret garden. Children can also help with mapping and measuring a site. In addition, they often help expand the cultural boundaries of a project, because they are less prone to preconceived notions about race, class, gender, or similar issues.

Resources: Just as one person's trash can be another's treasure, resources that you may not see as useful could be a gold mine to your children. Tiny pieces of scrap lumber make great building blocks; discarded books and magazines can be turned into a plethora of fun projects, such as mosaics, beads, origami, or papier-mâché birdhouses. In addition, the children themselves are a wonderful resource of help and ideas, and other parents often make excellent volunteers.

Analysis: Asking children their opinion is key to a holistic design. They will provide you with a range of ideas based on their own needs and perceptions, and these ideas will greatly increase the diversity and resilience of your projects. Their young minds can be surprisingly analytical, and they can help develop

Suggest Meaningful Work for Children[2]

Many communities deny children the opportunity to contribute to the necessary work of their community. They are supposed to be little sponges, soaking up what we choose to teach them and playing sports until they grow up, at which point we expect them to immerse themselves in a useful role and contribute to society. To this end school and work are separated into two distinct activities, and some of the most necessary jobs, such as mothering and gardening, are not considered work at all because they do not generate money.

In my experience children want to participate. If they can talk, they can contribute ideas. If they can think, they can work. Don't assume a seven-year-old can't engage fully in a garden or community project. Indeed, children can hold leadership positions, make executive deci-

new methods and criteria for analyzing your data and resources.

Design: Children can be asked to draw sample designs, and groups of children, if empowered to collaborate on a design project, will learn to work with others toward a common goal. They can also provide fresh insight into patterns and combinations. Children love to do overlay designs with tracing paper and colored pencils, and you may be amazed at the accuracy with which they can create a workable model. It also seems important to note that children often use different paths and engage in different patterns than the adult users of a site; if you have children around, it is prudent and indeed necessary to include these paths and patterns in your design.

Implementation: Children can help implement a project in a multitude of good ways. Work should be age-appropriate, for safety reasons, but give them ample opportunities to challenge themselves. Look at your own list of tasks and ask yourself what you need help with. Ask children what they want to do rather than simply assigning tasks and chores. Tasks that are easily accomplished by children include taking pictures, building compost, sowing and collecting seeds, rooting cuttings, watering, organizing tools, painting signs, feeding chickens, making pottery, and spreading mulch, to name but a few.

Maintenance/monitoring: Send the children around the garden with a checklist to monitor the progress of young plants or document fruit production. Children will often notice if something needs to be changed or adjusted before adults do. Ask them to note and suggest improvements, and listen earnestly to their advice.

Evaluation: Bringing children of all ages into your garden or home and asking them to evaluate it is an excellent way to come up with a diverse set of opinions on how well your system works. Children are usually brutally honest and will often take the path of least resistance. Even just letting a group of children run amok for a few hours is an excellent way to find the natural paths on your site, and their input will undoubtedly inspire your own evaluative process.

sions, and raise most of the money. Ask young people (not the parents) what they want to do, what they are interested in, how they feel they can contribute, and what they need to learn to do so. Then help them in whatever way makes sense for you.

That's not to say we should burden our children with hard physical labor as soon as they're out of the cradle! But we should harvest their abundance of creative energy, respectfully, for the good of the whole. The quickest way to repel children from gardening or anything else is to strap them into a steady regimen of rules, regulations, and drudgery. Find something fun and useful for them to do, and ask whether it interests them.

A great way to empower children is by letting them design and execute their own projects. Provide guidance, but do not supervise. Let them envision and manifest their own ideas, regardless of whether they seem valuable or useful to adults. Give them as much freedom as safety will allow; teach them ways to make decisions and collaborate with other children, but try not to influence their choices. This last concept can be very difficult for many adults to master, but I think you will find that your relationship with children will truly blossom when you invite them to bring their own ideas to fruition. See the sidebar on pages 288–289 for ways to include children in each step of the Gobradime design process.

Allowing children to choose and engage in meaningful tasks teaches them that their contribution is useful and necessary and empowers them to create roles for themselves in the community. Which brings me to my next and most heartfelt suggestion.

Treat Children as Peers

Parents (especially mothers) are usually held responsible for the actions of their children. If a child is rude, violent, or unruly, the parents are blamed. When a parent lives in fear of being judged according to her child's behavior, she is forced into a position of authority and control.

If children grow up around authority and control, they learn to be controlling authoritarians. And while it is parents who choose to make children and care for them—or sadly, sometimes not—it is the respon-sibility of the entire community to create an environment that will encourage children to grow into happy, creative adults. When we see children as peers, not inferior or superior to anyone else because of their age or size but simply occupying their own individual niches in the cycle, then we come closer to an egalitarian, ecological community.

When you interact with a child, pay careful attention to how those interactions are different from those with adults. For example, do you find yourself ignoring the child, changing the tone of your voice, or telling the child what to do—behavior that would be considered very rude if done to an adult? If you do these things, stop. The children I've worked with resent being treated differently just because they are younger. They want to feel comfortable asking questions if they need to and trusted that they can learn and understand anything just as well as you or me.

When children can count on only other children to treat them as equals, they learn to distrust adults and to feel inferior. While it may be necessary to choose vocabulary words that a child can understand, she will respond with more enthusiasm to questions posed in a mature and egalitarian manner. Treat her as a person of less experience, not of less intelligence. Some cultures believe that each new child is wiser than the last, and that children in general are wiser than older people, because they were more recently in contact with the ethereal, cosmic whole.

There will inevitably be times when children exhibit extreme behavior, in the form of a tantrum or by being verbally or physically abusive to others. As discussed in the preceding chapter, adults also sometimes act out in these ways. The natural inclination, in either case, is to shut them down, either by asking them to leave or by forcing the parents to handle the situation. However, if we can see these extreme acts as a call for support rather than a cause for expulsion, and if we can address them as a group rather than isolating the individual, then we will be well on our way to building stronger communities and better lives for everyone, of all ages.

Gardening with Children

One of the best places to connect with children is in the garden. Gardens are full of wonder, and wonder is what leads to knowledge. I remember the first time I gardened with my friend Jasper, who was two at the time. He was sitting next to me, playing in the warm, spongy soil while I weeded a thick patch of overwintered carrots. It was a warm day in early May, and I noticed the edge of a plump young carrot bulging out of the ground. I asked Jasper to watch, and I yanked on the stem. The brilliant orange root burst from the soil, and Jasper's eyes nearly burst out of his

Gardening with children helps instill in them a lifelong ecological ethic.

little face as he exclaimed, "Carrot!" The next ten times I saw him he wanted to eat carrots, and by the time he was four he was working in the garden by my side, planting and weeding carrots of his own.

The first time a child eats vegetables fresh from the garden, her connection with food changes forever. Even a small garden can be a mini adventure park to children, where their imaginations can run wild. In my experience children who visit and participate in farms and gardens are much more willing to eat a wider variety of fruits and vegetables, and of course this improved diet leads to a whole lifetime of better physical and mental health.

When children are included in ongoing garden projects, they blossom right along with the flowers and are soon contributing new ideas and garden designs of their own. Children are often more open to a deep connection with nature than adults are, and you may find that your children are teaching you far more than you are teaching them. Children can help bridge the gap between adults and nature. They can be the ambassadors of the plant world, helping us renew our connection with nature and reminding us of the childlike mind we once enjoyed.

Obviously, while children take great joy in eating directly from the garden, you must educate them about potentially toxic plants. First of all, no garden that may have children in it should ever be sprayed with pesticides, herbicides, or chemical fertilizers. These poisons leave residues for years, and children's small bodies are highly susceptible to such toxins. Second, many edible plants have poisonous parts, such as the leaves of tomatoes and potatoes. These wonderful plants should not be excluded from the garden, but children should be taught always to ask an adult before eating anything new.

Here are some fun and educational ways to share nature with children of all ages. Some of these projects can occur in space of any size; others assume you can find a small plot of land on which to garden.

Make a Discovery Kit

In my favorite children's gardening book, *Roots, Shoots, Buckets & Boots*[3] author Sharon Lovejoy recommends putting together an "explorer's kit" for children that includes an assortment of tools for learning about the garden. What follows is my expanded version, based on my own favorite tools. This simple kit can be made up of mostly recycled mate-

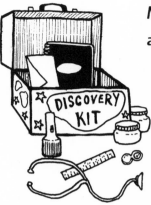

Make a discovery kit for yourself and your children.

rials and will fit into a shoe box or a lunch box. Gardeners of all ages can take their discovery kit anywhere: on a farm visit, to summer camp, or just into the backyard to help them discover and learn about the wonders of the natural world.

Here are some things to include:

- A magnifying glass or hand lens, for looking deep into flowers and getting a close-up view of bugs and other garden finds
- A flashlight, for peeking down gopher holes and for nighttime adventures
- A ruler or measuring tape, for comparing sizes and monitoring the growth of young plants
- Paper bags and small jars with lids, for collecting specimens
- A supply of small envelopes, for collecting seeds
- A pencil, for labeling seed envelopes and other specimens with the date and location
- A handful of garden markers, for labeling new discoveries in the field
- A journal, for recording observations and inspirations
- A stethoscope (if available), for listening to trees (hear them drink!) and underground critters

Make a Garden Coloring Book or Children's 'Zine

If you don't have a space to garden with children, they can still learn about the plants that provide our food by making a food-plants coloring book or informative children's gardening 'zine.

Try this example: Next time you go to the grocery store, have the children make a list of as many different types of food plants as they can find. Read ingredients lists, look in the ethnic food aisle; there are twenty-five thousand edible plants known to humans—how many can *you* think of? Next, get the children to draw pictures of the plants and write captions about where they come from, how to use them, and anything else that seems relevant. Have them draw the pictures in black ink, then photocopy the pictures and assemble them into coloring books, one for each child. Make extra copies to give to friends or send to family members.

Make a Plant Press

Make a simple plant press with two small wooden boards, cardboard, waxed paper, four wing-nut bolts (each five-eighths of an inch), and some ribbon. Cut the boards to make the outside ends of the press. It doesn't matter if they are five by seven inches or eight by ten, but they need to be the same size as each other. Decorate these ends with paint, crayons, or pressed flowers under tape. Drill holes in each corner, and insert the wing-nut bolts. The length of your bolts will determine the maximum thickness of your press. Cut several pieces of cardboard to make dividers, and label one for each new plant family or genus you collect.

Now cut several sheets of waxed paper to double the size of the dividers, and fold them over to make flat envelopes for the leaves, flowers, and sprigs you collect. Attach ribbons to the sides to wrap around and hold everything in, and tighten down the wing nuts as needed to press the plants. Attach a pencil to a string so you can label each new specimen.

Save your favorite specimens
in a plant press.

Start a Bug Farm

An old aquarium tank can be turned into an educational display by filling it with organic compost and adding assorted bugs and worms from the garden and compost. Start by filling a medium-sized tank two-thirds full with moist compost that is about half finished. Cover the compost with a thin layer of regular garden dirt.

This project doesn't work very well with store-bought compost or potting soil, so if you don't have a compost pile or a yard, perhaps you can get a small amount of compost and dirt from a neighbor or community garden nearby. It is a good idea to put a ventilated cover over the bug farm to keep the critters from escaping and keep out cats and birds. Many tanks come with lids, but you can also make a good cover with some cheesecloth and an elastic cord.

Next, cut holes in the lids of several small jars and go out and collect as many different types of worms and bugs as you can find. An old spoon works great as a tool to pick up the little critters if you or the children are squeamish. Put the bugs in the tank and place it in a cool, shady spot. Now the most important thing is to mist it daily with fresh water.

Over the next few days and nights the critters will begin organizing themselves into a living, interactive community. Worms will burrow into the soil, beetles will munch happily away at tiny pieces of debris, and hidden seeds will sprout on the surface of the soil. Watch as the critters decompose the organic matter and interact with one another to build soil and perpetuate life. Unless you drilled drainage holes in the bottom of your tank, your bug farm will last only a short time before it starts to smell bad and become imbalanced. At this point return the soil and critters to the compost pile and start a new bug farm.

Make a Legume Nodule Box

A great way to learn about how legumes fix nitrogen in the soil is to make an observation box. The children's garden at the University of California–Santa Cruz has one of these, and visitors of all ages love to peek at the knobby, nitrogen-fixing bacteria colonies while they grow. Use scrap wood and an old window to build a planter box with one side that you can see through. The box should be at least twelve inches deep and should have plenty of drain holes in the bottom.

A living observation box like this legume nodule display allows us to witness the living soil.

Using plywood and hinges, make a door to cover the window side so that it opens up- or downward, like a bread box. Mount the box a few feet up, at a child's eye level. Fill it with soil and plant fava beans, clover, lupine, and other legumes. As the plants grow you can open the door and peek at the nitrogen-fixing bacteria nodules growing on the roots of the legumes you planted. Notice how different types of legumes produce different sizes or shapes of nodules. Be sure to close the door when you're not observing, because too much light will kill off the roots and beneficial bacteria.

Visit Local Farms

A single field trip to an organic farm or garden will help instill a natural ethic, which will encourage the child to live a more responsible, environmentally aware lifestyle. Children and adults alike will benefit from seeing firsthand where their fruits, vegetables, eggs, meat, and dairy products are grown and processed. A few hours on a farm can generate memories that the child will recall for many years and may provide the inspiration for the child to pursue a career in science, agriculture, land conservation, or ecological living.

To organize a farm visit, go to a local farmer's market or organic food cooperative and ask for contacts at local organic farms. Then call the farmers and ask whether there is a good time to bring a group of children out for a tour. Many farmers are quite open to this sort of thing, and some may already be hosting school or church groups. Tours usu-

A few hours on an organic farm can change a child's life forever.

ally last one to three hours; some farms ask for a nominal per-person donation to help defray the costs of showing you around and letting the children harvest produce to take home.

You may find that you have several farms to choose from. Consider going to all of them, because each place will have something different to offer. One farm may have long rows of vegetables and greenhouses full of salad greens or flowers, while another might host free-range cows and chickens or a few acres of yummy raspberries. Wherever you go, be sure to bring snacks, sunscreen, mud boots, drinking water, and a camera, and be prepared to bring home a plethora of new ideas.

It is also very interesting to visit commercial food production facilities. Giving yourselves an opportunity to compare commercial practices with organic ones will help solidify your goals and may strengthen your resolve to eat and grow organic food. However, industrial farms can be extremely toxic, and many practices, especially those at dairy and meat facilities, can be quite horrible to witness, so please take these things into serious consideration before exposing your children to them.

Plant a Living Playhouse

Just after the last spring frost, mulch or till a small area, from five feet by five feet to six by eight. Scratch in either a square or circular furrow and fill it with the seeds of sunflowers, runner beans, and annual morning glories. Be sure to leave an opening for a door, and scatter white clover seeds all around the rest of the mulched area.

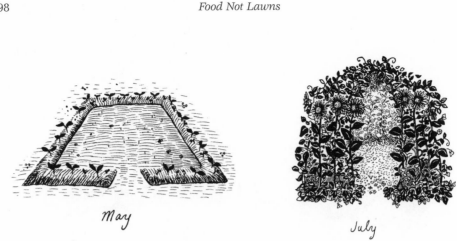

May   *July*

Plant a living playhouse with sunflowers and annual morning glories.

Soon you will see the sunflowers and other plants emerge. Thin the sunflowers to about one every eight inches, and keep a few bean and morning glory plants between. These will climb up the sunnies and eventually will meet at the top, forming a ceiling for the playhouse, which will by then have a carpet of clover and walls made of sunflower stalks. This makes a great shady hideout for children and adults alike, and the multicolored flowers make a brilliant contribution to the land-scape, attract beneficial insects, and produce food.

Get Lost in a Living Maze

You may be able to find a good maze on a local farm, especially during the fall when many small towns boast a haunted corn maze. With a little planning, you can also plant your own corn or flower maze. An age-old tradition, living mazes and garden labyrinths provide a delightful diver-sion from regular garden work and give people of all ages a chance to literally get lost in the plants. You can find hundreds of maze designs in books at your local library, or you can design your own on a sheet of graph paper. A multiple-ring design is relatively easy to create, and it adds an alluring circular focal point to the garden.

Once you have a basic design, stake it out in the garden using small rebar pegs or bamboo poles, with string between them to simulate the walls. Don't forget to make lots of dead ends and leave plenty of open-ings to make the maze extra confusing! Now till or mulch the beds (the walls of the maze). The beds should be eighteen to twenty-four inches wide, with two- to three-foot-wide paths between.

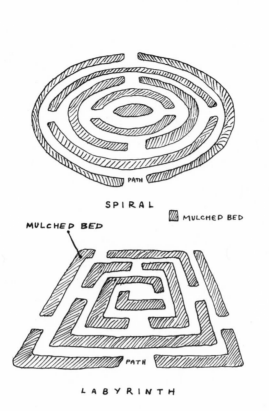

Two ideas for simple maze gardens

SPIRAL

MULCHED BED

MULCHED BED

LABYRINTH

You can grow the "walls" with any combination of plants, but those with straight stalks such as corn, sunflowers, and sorghum usually work best. To grow a permanent maze, try planting boxwood, bamboo, or raspberries. Alternatively, plant Jerusalem artichokes for a seasonal maze that grows all summer and provides tasty tubers through the winter.

Grow a Scratch-and-Sniff Garden

Growing food and sharing surplus with the community are important educational experiences for children. Children love to learn about bugs and plants, to eat fresh food from the garden, and to see beautiful flowers. They also like to touch soft, fuzzy leaves and smell sweet or pungent plants. Many people are kinesthetic learners, and touching things helps stimulate their minds. So why not plant a garden that caters to the senses of touch and smell? Rose campion, lamb's ears, mullein, and comfrey all have wonderful fuzzy leaves, and children will spend hours touching the tiny hairs and comparing textures. Sensitive plant (*Mimosa pudica*) is also a great choice for a kinesthetic garden because the leaves fold up when touched. Be careful of the tiny thorns!

For the sniffing garden, plant lavender, lemon verbena, thyme, rosemary, peppermint, lemon balm, and pennyroyal. Many of these plants release their wonderful pungent aroma in full force when you scratch the surface of the leaf. In fact, most plants in the mint family (Lamiaceae) have either fuzzy leaves or strong fragrances, or both. And be sure to add sweet-smelling classics from other families such as geranium, jasmine, lilies, gardenia, and hyacinth.

Open a Butterfly Buffet

Children love butterflies, and what better way to learn about pollination than to grow a butterfly garden? Even a small container garden can provide shelter and food for a wide range of butterflies and other important pollinators, and a two-thousand-square-foot space can hold enough plants to provide nectar to thousands of butterflies and other beneficial insects.

Plants that butterflies love include lavender, lantana, buddleia, willow trees, thistle, zinnias, daylilies, coreopsis, cinquefoil, dogbane, and black-eyed Susans.[4] And of course no butterfly garden would be complete without milkweed, which provides essential food for endangered monarch butterflies. There are many species of milkweed; most are relatively easy to grow from seed and have exceptionally beautiful flowers.

Plant a Birthday Tree

As a child I received a cherry tree for my birthday, and we planted it in the front yard. We moved away shortly after, but many years later I drove past the house and the tree was still there; it had grown to about thirty feet in height and was loaded with juicy red fruit! Tree planting is a good way to teach children about ecology and about the longevity of the forest. Some people get a live Christmas tree every year, then plant it out.

Whether you choose fruit trees or conifers, you can enhance the landscape while giving gifts that are an excellent alternative to other options such as plastic toys and video games. Trees last much longer than any child's attention span for toys, and they will provide shade, food, and habitat for humans and other animals for many years.

Start a School Garden Project

Many people recognize the benefits of gardening with children, and as a result many elementary and high schools are starting garden projects.

These gardens are usually created by a group of volunteers, often parents, who set up the garden and sometimes train teachers to use gardening to enhance their regular curriculum. Free seeds, plants, and tools can be found by reaching out to parents for donations. In addition, private and federal grant funding for ecological education is often available.

Many schools have a green space that would make an excellent garden, and even very urban schools can usually host a container garden on a section of the blacktop outside. Students gain valuable insight into nature by interacting with the plants and soil; they also learn how to grow food and can provide fresh organic fruits and vegetables to the school cafeteria.

Radishes can be planted in the smallest spaces and provide a fast-growing and nutritious garden experience.

Some schools have large garden programs, while others have just a few planter boxes. Schools in Australia are "learnscaping" school grounds: planting food forests, increasing shade, and developing soft, child-friendly play spaces. Sharing nature with children can be as small or as large a project as you like, depending on the available resources.

In Eugene organic farmer John Sundquist has installed nine gardens for Head Start of Lane County, a low-income public preschool program. He hosts school visits to his farm, River's Turn, in Coburg, Oregon, where he tends thirty-three acres, including ten acres of seed crops, extensive fruit and nut orchards, and more than fifty kinds of bamboo. See the sidebar on page 304 for some of Farmer John's ideas for school gardens.

Favorite Plants for Children's Gardens

No treatise on gardening with children would be complete without a short list of good plants to start with. By no means an exhaustive selection of great plants for children to grow, the following twelve plants can all be direct-sown, grow quickly and easily, and are fun to harvest for food, cut flowers, or seeds.

Corn. Popcorn is always a hit with children, and many varieties grow quite well in a home garden. There is also a vast array of interesting Indian corns available, in a rainbow of beautiful colors. Sweet corn is another option, and nothing compares to a fresh ear right out of the garden as a refreshing snack on a September day.

Gourds. Small gourds grow fast and dry easily to make rattles or small bottles and containers. Large gourds need a longer growing season but make a magnificent addition to the garden; they can be dried and made into birdhouses, bowls, and musical instruments.

Nasturtiums. The leaves, flowers, and immature seeds of nasturtiums are edible and also repel certain insect pests, making them great companion plants. Trailing varieties are a nice addition to a bean tepee or sunflower house, and the bright flowers are a delight to children and adults alike.

Potatoes. Because potatoes can be grown by just throwing them on the ground and tossing some straw on top, they are great fun to raise with children. Also try planting them in a bag or crate: Just fill it one-third of the way with soil, toss in some spuds, and cover with leaves or straw. As the shoots emerge, add more mulch, and in a few months you will have a bagful of fresh sweet spuds to eat.

Pumpkins. Large or small, pumpkins and other squash are a favorite for children of all ages. Giant varieties, such as 'Dill's Atlantic Giant', can grow to up to two hundred pounds and make excellent jack-o'-lanterns. Smaller types are more manageable for small hands and can also be carved or used to make pie, stew, or bread. Some varieties are grown primarily for their seeds, which are a healthy snack and have been known to prevent intestinal worms.[5]

Try making pumpkin tattoos: Use a nail to scratch children's names or little drawings into the skin of immature pumpkin fruits. Be careful not to go too deep—just scratch the surface. When the fruit is mature, the name will appear as a healed scar on the surface, and the finished product will last months longer than a carved pumpkin.

Gourds are easy to grow and can be made into an assortment of useful items like bowls, jars, and musical instruments.

Radishes. Radishes are great for children because they grow very fast and can be planted in just about any space, even a small container. The brightly colored roots are ready to eat in just over a month and can be carved into rosettes or other designs.

Scarlet Runner Beans. Jack and his beanstalk are legendary to many children, and while there are no boy-eating giants at the top of most beanpoles, runner beans are fast growing and produce brilliant red and orange flowers. The seeds are large and speckled purple and can be eaten, replanted, or used for a variety of craft projects, like beads or mosaics.

Strawberries, Raspberries, Blueberries . . . Need I say more? Children love to hunt through the berry patch for a juicy snack, and when they've planted it themselves they feel a sense of pride and accomplishment with every bite.

Sunflowers. They come in many colors, from yellow to orange, white, red, and even tiger-striped. Tall or short, large or small, sunflowers are easy to grow and are a must for any children's garden. The cut flowers last several days, and seeds provide protein and amino acids for young bodies and wild birds alike.

Tulips. Give a child a small shovel and a bagful of tulip bulbs, and when spring comes you will have a yard full of surprises. Tulip flowers are edible and quite delicious, and they help attract beneficial insects into the garden. The general rule for planting bulbs is to bury them twice as deep as they are long, with the pointy end up.

Turnips. Maybe it doesn't seem like turnips would be a hot item in the children's garden, but many varieties grow to be quite large and can be carved and stuffed for a delicious baked meal. John Sundquist grows lots of turnips at his farm, and the children who come out for tours love to see the giant purple, orange, and white roots jutting out of the ground. Fresh turnips smell wonderful, are an excellent source of fiber, and are known to reduce cholesterol.[6]

Zinnias. Last but far from least, zinnias come in every color of the rainbow and are one of my personal favorite plants of all time. They bloom when they reach about three feet in height, just the right height for young eyes and noses to enjoy. One of the many beautiful gifts from Mexico to our gardens, zinnias make excellent cut flowers and can last weeks if you change the water every few days.

Educational Gardens[7]

by John Sundquist

Modern food and fiber production depends on large inputs of oil and natural gas. We must begin now to prepare for the inevitable time when these resources are depleted. We try to design our gardens to be fun and attractive, enduring, and low-maintenance. The rewards of our gardens include food, flowers, exploring our senses, having fun with tools, acquiring life skills, and learning about nature. We learn about the connections among people, plants, wildlife, and microbes. The goal of our efforts is to start children down the path of biological literacy.

The major themes in the garden ideas listed below are biological literacy and landscape design for sustainability. *Sustainability* could be defined as activities that allow people and wildlife to coexist and flourish indefinitely into the future. Children, parents, teachers, and everyone else gain knowledge and skills through hands-on tours, demonstrations, maps and handouts, explanatory signs, and electronic media. Each garden and component would need its own design, but here are some general ideas:

Fun gardens: Landscaped areas allow preschoolers to explore and play on their own terms, observed but not instructed. A variation could be an assessment area where the kids' performance on stepping blocks, balance beams, et cetera could be recorded for evaluation.

Science gardens: How sunlight, climate, soil, and water generate the basic building blocks of life. Understanding the soil food web; photosynthesis; how plants produce our essential oxygen, food, clothing, and shelter; the origins of the proteins, carbohydrates, minerals, and vitamins our bodies need; complementary foods and essential amino acids.

Kinship gardens: Explains the relationships of the plant families, introducing botany and scientific names.

Nature gardens: Interspersed among the other gardens, demonstrating landscaping and construction to support wildlife.

Subsistence gardens: Essential food and fiber production, emphasizing plant guilds and polycultures.

Native gardens: The plants people and wildlife in the area relied on before Europeans arrived.

Ancient food gardens: The crops that nourished previous civilizations around the world.

Unusual gardens: New and different crops, future foods.

Healing gardens: Herbs and flowers grown for health and medicine.

Fiber gardens: Cotton, flax, mulberries (for silkworms), bamboo, and so on.

Aquaculture gardens: Raising water plants and fish.

Fungal gardens: Growing edible and medicinal mushrooms.

Weed gardens: Examples of plants that cause problems through invasiveness, toxicity, et cetera, and keys to identifying these weeds.

Waste treatment gardens: Constructed wetlands that clean human and livestock waste.

Phytoremediation/bioremediation gardens: Plant–fungal–microbial assemblages that detoxify pesticides and industrial waste.

Market gardens: Growing flowers, ornamentals, and food for cash.

We can also organize demonstrations and workshops for necessary skills in topics such as food preparation, preservation, and storage; composting; plant propagation, including seed saving; construction of simple human, animal, bird, and insect shelters; livestock; microbes, worms, chickens; greenhouse and year-round gardening; urban gardening and forestry; and permaculture concepts.

Acknowledgments

Please indulge me while I extend my sincere gratitude toward the extraordinary community of brilliant individuals who brought me to this place. To Taylor Zeigler, my patient and cherished companion, and to Tobias Policha, Nicholas Routledge, Kari Johnson, Sophie Corrigan, and Jane Hayes—soul mates and fellow activists for whom I hold the deepest respect and admiration: Your enduring support and gentle challenges are my life source. This book is as much yours as it is mine.

Thanks to my teachers for believing in me and for treating me as an equal, even when I didn't know what I was talking about: Alan, Linda, and Kusra Kapuler, Carol Deppe, Jude Hobbs, Toby Hemenway, Rick Valley, Tom Ward, Frank Morton, Harald Hoven, Don and Kimberly Tipping, George Stevens, J. J. Happala and John Navazio, who got me started and encouraged me to continue.

Thanks to the artists and activists who inspired me to find creative ways to raise my voice: Ramona Africa, Winona LaDuke, Corbin Harney, Darryl Cherney, Keith McHenry, Terry Compost, Dave Christensen, Peg Millett, Jan Bell, Lil Kreutzer, Spring and Jan Lundberg, Al Decker, Mick and Cindy, Severine Fleming, Lisa SF, Sascha DuBrul, Keja Kramer, Laura Stokes, Phil and Jen Weaver, Randy Shadowalker, Felix, Huck, Woody, Gil, the Superhero Riders, and Jolie Holland—thank you for being my muses.

To Taylor Zeigler, Ralph Lutts, Chris Hables Gray, Muriel Shockley, Kari Johnson, John Zerzan, Ben Watson, and the staff at Chelsea Green, and the others who read and edited the many drafts of this book—thank you for your meticulous editing and priceless insight. To John and Marsha Sundquist, Katie Reinken, Wally Jones, Mike Brunelle, Lazer and Annie Rose, Jake Theisen, Elliot Raesnick, Le Bistro Montage, the crew at Sam Bonds, and the other people who provided me with space, time, refreshments, and understanding while I worked, thank you for putting up with my chaos. Thanks to my first intern, Monica, who dealt well with my fledgling teaching style, taught me how to use my camera, and took the first set of notes that eventually became the outline for this book. And to Jackie Holmstrom, who tirelessly and brilliantly illustrated this text at Mach speed, thank you *so much*—you totally rock.

To my colleagues at Goddard College, the fine faculty who have polished my theories and strengthened my spirit, and especially to the fall

2005 Gamelan tribe—I am forever changed by you. And to countless other friends and relations, including but not limited to Jen Rodenburg, Martita Maderas, Laurena Marrone, Lena Hassof, Stephanie Sanchez, Erin Mirrett, the OCF Recycling Crew, Melissa May, Lisa Anderson, Chris and Karen Keaton, Marjorie and Chicky Reindel, Kris Dicus, Bonnie Behan, Dem-Alisha, Pam Johnson, Rob Bolman, Kathy Ging, Tofu Schwartz, Molly Grant, North Coast Earth First!, the Cascadia Free State, Kirk, Richard, Noah, Virgil, and Emma the dog—from the depths of my fragile heart, thank you.

And finally, thank you in advance to the people who will buy, read, criticize, and use this book—I look forward to hearing what you think. Please feel free to contact me anytime via www.foodnotlawns.com, or through Chelsea Green Publishing Company. I will do my best to read and respond to your questions, concerns, critiques, and suggestions.

For Peace and Organarchy!

H. C. Flores
April 2006

Resources

What follows is an extended list of resources to help you learn more and plug into local projects. Topics are listed alphabetically. Under each topic heading I have listed websites and organizations first, followed by publications, listed alphabetically by author.

I have not read all of these books—though I have read many of them, some are recommendations I pass along from my mentors and peers. To save space, I have annotated only a handful of selections that I most highly recommend; the rest are up to you to discover on your own. Have fun!

Agriculture, Biodynamic

Biodynamic Farming and Gardening Association
25844 Butler Road
Junction City, OR 97448
Phone: 888-516-7797 or 541-998-0105
Fax: 541-998-0106
www.biodynamics.com
The North American hub for the biodynamic farming community. They distribute many of the books below, as well as the *Stella Natura Sowing and Planting Calendar*.

Klocek, Dennis. *A Biodynamic Book of Moons*. Wyoming, RI: Bio-dynamic Literature, 1983.

Philbrick, John and Helen. *Organic Gardening for Health and Nutrition*. Hudson, NY: Anthroposophic Press, 1988.

Schilthuis, Willy. *Biodynamic Agriculture*. Hudson, NY: Anthroposophic Press, 1994.

Steiner, Rudolf. *Agriculture*. Hudson, NY: Anthroposophic Press, 1994.

Storl, Wolf. *Culture and Horticulture: A Philosophy of Gardening*. Wyoming, RI: Bio-dynamic Literature, 1979.

Thun, Maria. *Work with the Land and the Constellations*. Sussex, UK: Lanthorn Press, 1990.

Agriculture, Industrial

Carson, Rachel. *Silent Spring*. New York: Mariner Books, 2002.

Kimbrell, Andrew. *Fatal Harvest: The Tragedy of Industrial Agriculture*. Covelo, CA: Island Press, 2002.

Agriculture and Gardening, Organic

Eco-Farm Association
406 Main Street, Suite 313
Watsonville, CA 95076
Phone: 831-763-2111
Fax: 831-763-2112
info@eco-farm.org
www.eco-farm.org

The Land Institute
2440 East Water Well Road
Salina, KS 67401
Phone: 785-823-5376
Fax: 785-823-8728
www.landinstitute.org

National Sustainable Agriculture
Information Service
PO Box 3657
Fayetteville, AR 72702
Phone: 800-346-9140 (English) or 800-411-3222 (Español)
www.attra.org
An excellent source of information about internships, research projects, funding, and much more.

Northeast Organic Farmers Association
c/o Bill Duesing
PO Box 135
Stevenson, CT 06491
Phone: 203-888-5146
bduesing@cs.com
www.nofa.org
In addition to the renowned annual NOFA Summer Conference, each of the seven state chapters of the Northeast Organic Farming Association provides educational conferences, workshops, farm tours, and printed materials to educate farmers, gardeners, consumers, and land-care professionals. *The Natural Farmer*, the quarterly newspaper of the NOFA Interstate Council, publishes features on organic farming techniques, certification issues, environmental developments as they impact farmers and growers, organic market conditions, and other topics of interest to the Northeast organic community.

Oregon Tilth
470 Lancaster Drive NE
Salem, OR 97301
Phone: 503-378-0690
Fax: 503-378-0809
www.tilth.org
A nonprofit research and education organization certifying organic farmers, processors, retailers, and handlers throughout Oregon, the United States, and internationally. They offer a newspaper with tons of useful news and information about organic food and farming.

Organic Consumers Association
6101 Cliff Estate Road
Little Marais, MN 55614
218-226-4164
www.organicconsumers.org

Organic Trade Association
PO Box 547
Greenfield, MA 01302
www.ota.com

Seattle Tilth
4649 Sunnyside Avenue N. Room 120
Seattle, WA 98103
206-633-0451
tilth@seattletilth.org
www.seattletilth.org
Seattle Tilth inspires and educates people to garden organically, conserve natural resources, and support local food systems in order to cultivate a healthy urban environment and community. Their site has lots of great stuff about children's gardening and organic living.

Acres, U.S.A.
PO Box 91299
Austin, TX 78709
Phone: 800-355-5313
Fax: 512-892-4448
www.acresusa.com
Monthly magazine published since 1970. "The voice of eco-agriculture."

Ausubel, Kenny. *Seeds of Change*. New York: HarperCollins, 1994.

Creasy, Rosalind. *Complete Book of Edible Landscaping*. San Francisco: Sierra Club, 1982.

Fukuoka, Masanobu. *The Natural Way of Farming*. New York: Japan Publications, 1985. In this pivotal book about how to grow food without harming the earth, Masanobu Fukuoka outlines a detailed yet simple system that incorporates rice, barley, fruits, and both annual and perennial vegetables, using seed balls made of clay and compost. It is his personal philosophy of simple, humble living, more than the specific gardening techniques, that puts this book on the list of most valuable references. Fukuoka advises taking responsibility for our lives while still enjoying them. He encourages a focused intentionality toward ecological harmony, coupled with a humble acceptance of the chaotic cycles of nature.

Hart, Robert. *Forest Gardening, Cultivating an Edible Landscape*. White River Junction, VT: Chelsea Green, 1996.

Hemenway, Toby. *Gaia's Garden*. White River Junction, VT: Chelsea Green, 2002. This book presents theories and techniques for home-scale ecological garden design. Much of what I learned about ecological gardening came through Toby Hemenway, either in this book or during one of the many opportunities I have had to study with him directly. *Gaia's Garden* is the premier North American guide to ecological gardening, and an essential addition to any permaculture library. Also check out Toby's website, www.patternliteracy.com.

Jackson, Wes. *Becoming Native to This Place*. Lexington, KY: University Press of Kentucky, 1994.

Jeavons, John. *How to Grow More Vegetables (and Fruits, Nuts, Berries, Grains, and Other Crops) Than You Ever Thought Possible on Less Land Than You Can Imagine*. Berkeley, CA: Ten Speed Press, 2002.

Kourik, Robert. *Designing and Maintaining Your Edible Landscape Naturally*. White River Junction, VT: Chelsea Green, 2005.

Logsdon, Gene. *The Contrary Farmer*. White River Junction, VT: Chelsea Green, 1994.

Rosset, Peter, and Medea Benjamin. *The Greening of the Revolution: Cuba's Experiment with Organic Agriculture*. Melbourne, Australia: Ocean Press, 1994.

Seymour, John. *The Self-Sufficient Gardener*. London: Corgi, 1994.

Shapiro, Howard. *Gardening for the Future of the Earth*. New York: Bantam Books, 2000.

Stout, Ruth. *How to Have a Green Thumb without an Aching Back*. New York: Cornerstone Library, 1973.

———. *The Ruth Stout No-Work Garden Book*. New York: Bantam Books, 1971.

Tilgner, Linda. *Tips for the Lazy Gardener*. Pownal, VT: Storey, 1998.

Weaver, William Woys. *Heirloom Vegetable Gardening: A Master Gardener's Guide to Planting, Growing, Seed Saving, and Cultural History*. New York: Henry Holt, 1997.

Whitefield, Patrick. *How to Make a Forest Garden*. East Meon, Hampshire, England: Permanent Publications, 2000.

Animals and Birds

Feltwell, Ray. *Small-Scale Poultry Keeping: A Guide to Free-Range Poultry Production*. London: Faber and Faber, 1992.

Lee, Andy. *Chicken Tractor: The Permaculture Guide to Happy Hens and Healthy Soil.* Columbus, NC: Good Earth, 1999.

Riotte, Louise. *Raising Animals by the Moon: Practical Advice on Breeding, Birthing, Weaning, and Raising Animals in Harmony with Nature.* Pownal, VT: Storey, 1999.

Biodiversity

Talking Leaves
c/o Lost Valley Educational Center
81868 Lost Valley Lane
Dexter, OR 97431
Phone: 541-937-3351
Since 1989, Talking Leaves has been dedicated to supporting projects that consider the intrinsic value of all inhabitants of the natural world and that work for the survival of intact natural systems both large and small.

Guidetti, Geri Welzel. *From the Ground Up: Build Your Ark! How to Prepare for Uncertain Times.* Oxford, OH: Ark Institute, 1996.

Marinelli, Janet. *Stalking the Wild Amaranth: Gardening in the Age of Extinction.* New York: Henry Holt, 1998.

Shiva, Vandana. *Biopiracy: The Plunder of Nature and Knowledge.* Boston: South End Press, 1997.

Tuxill, John D. *Nature's Cornucopia: Our Stake in Plant Diversity.* Washington, DC: Worldwatch Institute, 1999.

Children

The School Garden Project of Lane County
PO Box 30072
Eugene, OR 97403
Phone: 541-284-9984
www.schoolgardenproject.org

Cornell, Joseph Bharat. *Sharing Nature with Children: The Classic Parents' and Teachers' Nature Awareness Guidebook.* Nevada City, CA: DAWN, 1998.

Fell, Derek. *A Kid's First Book of Gardening: Growing Plants Indoors and Out.* Philadelphia: Running Press, 1989.

Harlow, Rosie, and Gareth Morgan. *175 Amazing Nature Experiments.* New York: Random House, 1991.

Hart, Avery, and Paul Mantell. *Kids Garden.* Charlotte, VT: Williamson, 1996.

Lovejoy, Sharon. *Roots, Shoots, Buckets and Boots.* New York: Workman, 1999.

Sherlock, Marie. *Living Simply with Children: A Voluntary Simplicity Guide for Moms, Dads, and Kids Who Want to Reclaim the Bliss of Childhood and the Joy of Parenting.* New York: Three Rivers Press, 2003.

Stein, Sara. *The Evolution Book.* New York: Workman, 1986.

Wallace, Mary, Lee Mackay, and Dorrie Nagler. *Children and Feminism.* Vancouver, BC: LAFMPAG, 1987. I discovered this revolutionary book several years ago when living with two single mothers. I had no children of my own, and little experience with children, but *Children and Feminism* provided a solid foundation for interacting with young people in a realistic and egalitarian way. It is somewhat obscure, but I encourage anyone who works with children or parents to put in the effort to find a copy. Even if you have no children and don't intend to work with any, the appendix of nonviolent communication alone makes the book worth acquiring.

Community Gardening

Coe, Mary Lee. *Growing with Community Gardening.* Taftsville, VT: Countryman Press, 1978.

Naimark, Susan. *A Handbook of Community Gardening.* New York: Scribner, 1982.

Community Organizing

Bioneers
6 Cerro Circle
Lamy, NM 87540
Phone: 877-246-6337
Fax: 505-986-1644
www.bioneers.org
An educational nonprofit that strengthens and expands networks of practical visionaries working on behalf of the environment and people. They host an annual conference in California.

The Center for Public Integrity
910 17th Street NW, Suite 700
Washington, DC 20006
Phone: 202-466-1300
www.publicintegrity.org

Helios Resource Network
1192 Lawrence Street
Eugene, OR 97401
Phone: 541-284-7020
info@heliosnetwork.org
www.heliosnetwork.org

Our United Villages
www.rebuildingcenter.org/ouv/
With a mission of bringing people together to share ideas that inspire practices that strengthen communities, Our United Villages is dedicated to the idea that communities should make their own decisions about how best to improve their surroundings. They organize interactive opportunities to facilitate this process in localized neighborhoods, then hand full power and credit for the resulting projects back to the people in that neighborhood. Their projects provide an excellent

model for autonomous community action, and are funded entirely by proceeds from their ReBuilding Center (see Recycling). Highly recommended. Check it out.

Prairie Fire Organizing Committee
2502 West Division Street
Chicago, IL 60622-2804
Phone: 773-278-6706
Fax: 773-278-0635
pfoc@prairiefire.org
www.prairiefire.org

Design

Sustainable Education and Ecological Design
(SEED) International
50 Crystal Waters, Kilcoy Lane
Conondale, QLD 4552
Australia
Phone: +61 (0)7 5494 4833
info@seedinternational.com.au
www.seedinternational.com.au
A wonderful website with explanations of permaculture ethics and principles, great photos, and an excellent links page.

Sustainable Living News: A West Coast Journal of Environmental Design
PO Box 45472
Seattle, WA 98145.

Eck, Joe. *Elements of Garden Design.* New York: North Point Press, 2005.

Edey, Anna. *Solviva: How to Grow $500,000 on One Acre, and Peace on Earth.* Vineyard Haven, MA: Trailblazer Press, 1998. A fascinating book about "sustainable solar-dynamic, bio-benign design." Also see the website at www.solviva.com.

Stevens, Peter. *Patterns in Nature.* Boston: Little, Brown, 1974. Out of print and hard to find but excellent and worth the search.

Todd, Nancy Jack. *From Eco-Cities to Living Machines: Principles of Ecological Design.* Berkeley, CA: North Atlantic Books, 1994.

Van Der Ryn, Sim, and Stuart Cowan. *Ecological Design.* Washington, DC: Island Press, 1996.

Zelov, Chris, and Brian Danitz. *Ecological Design: Inventing the Future.* Video, 64 minutes. Knossus, 2000.

Direct Action

Earth First!
www.earthfirst.org
Earth First! is a loosely affiliated network of environmental activists who believe in using all the tools in the tool box, ranging from grassroots organizing and

involvement in the legal process to civil disobedience and more. The links page on their website lists nearly a hundred organizations around the world that support and perform nonviolent direct action.

Food Not Bombs
www.foodnotbombs.net

Greenpeace USA
702 H Street NW, Suite 300
Washington, DC 20001
Phone: 800-326-0959
www.greenpeace.org

Hansen, Ann. *Direct Action: Memoirs of an Urban Guerrilla.* Toronto: Between the Lines, 2001.

Henry, C. T., and Keith McHenry. *Food Not Bombs.* Tucson, AZ: See Sharp Press, 2000. Keith McHenry cofounded the first Food Not Bombs groups in the early 1980s and spawned a food liberation movement that boasts several hundred autonomous chapters worldwide. Food Not Bombs has no formal leaders and strives to include everyone in its decision-making process. Each group recovers food that would otherwise be thrown out and makes fresh, hot, vegetarian meals that are served in city parks, at protests, and at community events to anyone without restriction. This is one of the only books available that contains simple steps to organizing community events, and the format for setting up a local Food Not Bombs chapter can be applied to many different types of projects.

Tracy, James. *Direct Action: Radical Pacifism from the Union Eight to the Chicago Seven.* Chicago: University of Chicago Press, 1996.

Dumpster Diving

Dumpster Diving
www.dumpsterdiving.net
Online discussion forums.

Dumpster World
www.dumpsterworld.com
Online discussion forums.

Ferrell, Jeff. *Empire of Scrounge: Inside the Urban Underground of Dumpster Diving, Trash Picking, and Street Scavenging.* New York: New York University Press, 2006.

Fleming, Leslie. *Dumpster Diving Saved My Life.* Seattle, WA: Peanut Butter, 2004.

Hoffman, John. *The Art and Science of Dumpster Diving.* Port Townsend, WA: Loompanics, 1993.

———. *Dumpster Diving: The Advanced Course, How to Turn Other People's Trash into Money, Publicity, and Power.* Boulder, CO: Paladin Press, 2002.

Ecofeminism

Daly, Mary. *Gynecology: The Metaethics of Radical Feminism*. Boston: Beacon Press, 1978.

Mies, Maria, and Vandana Shiva. *Ecofeminism*. Atlantic Highlands, NJ: Zed Books, 1993.

Ruether, Rosemary Radford. *Women Healing Earth: Third World Women on Ecology, Feminism, and Religion*. Maryknoll, NY: Orbis Books, 1996.

Shiva, Vandana. *Staying Alive: Women, Ecology, and Development*. London: Zed Books, 1989.

Warren, Karen, and Nisvan Erkal. *Ecofeminism: Women, Culture, Nature*. Bloomington, IN: Indiana University Press, 1997.

Ecological Building

Circle Round: The Women's Natural Building Newsletter
PO Box 14194
Portland, OR 97293

Eco-Building Times
PO Box 58530
Seattle, WA 98138

Alexander, Christopher. *A Pattern Language*. New York: Oxford University Press, 1977.

Evans, Ianto, Linda Smiley, and Michael Smith. *The Hand-Sculpted House: A Philosophical and Practical Guide to Building a Cob Cottage*. White River Junction, VT: Chelsea Green, 2002. They also offer internships in cob building. Write to Cob Cottage Internships, PO Box 123, Cottage Grove, OR 97424.

Todd, Nancy Jack, and John Todd. *Bioshelters, Ocean Arks, and City Farming: Ecology as the Basis of Design*. San Francisco: Sierra Club Books, 1984.

Ecology and Science

Berkeley Ecology Center
2530 San Pablo Avenue
Berkeley, CA 94702
Phone: 510-548-2220
Fax: 510-548-2240
info@ecologycenter.org
www.ecologycenter.org

Capon, Brian. *Botany for Gardeners*. Portland, OR: Timber Press, 2005.

Capra, Fritjof. *The Web of Life: A New Scientific Understanding of Living Systems*. New York: Anchor Books, 1996.

Margulis, Lynn. *Five Kingdoms: An Illustrated Guide to the Phyla of Life on Earth*. New York: W. H. Freeman, 1998.

———. *Microcosmos: Four Billion Years of Evolution from Our Microbial Ancestors*. New York: Summit Books, 1986.

———. *Symbiotic Planet: A New Look at Evolution*. New York: Basic Books, 1998.

Moran, Edward. *The Global Ecology*. New York: H. W. Wilson, 1999.

Sessions, George. *Deep Ecology for the 21st Century*. New York: Random House, 1995.

Thomas, Lewis. *The Lives of a Cell: Notes of a Biology Watcher*. New York: Viking Press, 1974.

Education

Goddard College
123 Pitkin Road
Plainfield, VT 05667
Phone: 800-468-4888
www.goddard.edu
My alma mater; offers student-directed, interdisciplinary, distance-learning programs that encourage critical thinking, wide knowledge, personal growth, and thoughtful action.

Freire, Paolo. *Pedagogy of the Oppressed*. New York: Continuum, 1995.

Goldring, Andrew. *Permaculture Teacher's Guide*. London: Permaculture Association, 2000. An anthology of games, outlines, diagrams, and techniques for teaching ecological living to adults. I highly recommend this book for teachers of all disciplines, because it provides such a nice range of ideas for activities to do with nontraditional students. My Gobradime design formula is a mutation of several similar acronyms in this book. Packed with exercises and suggestions for activities to do during a permaculture course, the *Teacher's Guide* yields a diverse array of ways to understand and share the tenets of permaculture in principle and practice.

Nagel, Greta. *The Tao of Teaching*. New York: Primus, 1994.

Postman, Neil, and Charles Weingartner. *Teaching as a Subversive Activity*. New York: Delacorte, 1969. One of my favorite books of all time, this text translates many of John Dewey and Marshall McLuhan's radical education theories into a readable and usable format. The authors provide many witty examples of how subversive and egalitarian teaching techniques empower students and present an argument for teaching students how to teach themselves whatever is relevant to them.

Renner, Peter. *The Art of Teaching Adults*. Vancouver, BC: PFR Training Associates, 1993.

Terry, Mark. *Teaching for Survival: A Handbook for Environmental Education*. New York: Ballantine, 1971.

Elder Care

Oatfield Estates: An Alternative to Assisted Living
4444 SE Oatfield Hill Road
Milwaukie, OR 97267
Phone: 503-653-5656

Oatfield Estates is an innovative residential-care community in Milwaukie, Oregon, focused on healthy living and elder-directed care, with a sustainable connection to nature. Oatfield features a greenhouse that grows thousands of vegetable and flower starts and organic, edible landscapes with perennial fruit and raised beds, some of them wheelchair-accessible. A seed-saving program allows residents to share the bounty with loved ones and contribute back to the community.

Energy and Technology

National Center for Appropriate Technology
815 15th Street NW, Suite 938
Washington, DC 20005
Phone: 202-347-9193
www.ncat.org

Home Power Magazine
PO Box 520
Ashland, OR 97520
Phone: 800-707-6585 (inside the U.S.)
Phone: 541-512-0201 (outside the U.S.)
Fax: 541-512-0343
subscription@homepower.com
www.homepower.com

Anderson, Bruce, and Michael Riordan. *The Solar Home Book: Heating, Cooling, and Designing with the Sun.* Harrisville, NH: Cheshire Books, 1976.

Gipe, Paul. *Wind Energy Basics: A Guide to Small and Micro Wind Systems.* White River Junction, VT: Chelsea Green, 1999.

Kachadorian, James. *The Passive Solar House: The Complete Guide to Heating and Cooling Your Home (Revised and Expanded).* White River Junction, VT: Chelsea Green, 2006.

Pahl, Greg. *Biodiesel: Growing a New Energy Economy.* White River Junction, VT: Chelsea Green, 2004.

Potts, Michael. *The New Independent Home: People and Houses That Harvest the Sun.* White River Junction, VT: Chelsea Green, 1999.

Schaeffer, John, and Doug Pratt. *Gaiam Real Goods Solar Living Sourcebook: Your Complete Guide to Renewable Energy Technologies and Sustainable Living.* Ukiah, CA: Gaiam Real Goods, 2005.

Still, Dean, and Jim Kness. *Capturing Heat: Five Earth-Friendly Cooking Technologies and How to Build Them.* Cottage Grove, OR: Aprovecho Research Center, 1996.

Ethics

Curry, Patrick. "On Ecological Ethics: A Critical Introduction." 1999. Campaign for Political Ecology, www.eco.gn.apc.org/pubs/ethics_curry.html.

The Findhorn Community. *The Findhorn Garden.* New York: Harper and Row, 1975.

Shepard, Paul, and Daniel McKinley. *The Subversive Science: Essays toward an Ecology of Man.* Boston: Houghton Mifflin, 1969.

Westra, Laura. *Living in Integrity: A Global Ethic to Restore a Fragmented Earth.* Lanham, MD: Rowman and Littlefield, 1998.

Festivals

Burning Man
www.burningman.com
An annual technology fest in the desert near Gerlach, Nevada. Very popular with the emerging urban hipster scene, and a useful place to find creative inspiration and meet interesting people, but the festival attitude as a whole is somewhat lacking in ecological integrity.

National Rainbow Family Annual Gathering
www.welcomehome.org
From their website: "Some say we're the largest non-organization of nonmembers in the world. We have no leaders, and no organization. To be honest, the Rainbow Family means different things to different people. I think it's safe to say we're into intentional community building, nonviolence, and alternative lifestyles. We also believe that Peace and Love are a great thing, and there isn't enough of that in this world. Many of our traditions are based on Native American traditions, and we have a strong orientation to take care of the earth. We gather in the national forests yearly to pray for peace on this planet."

Oregon Country Fair
442 Lawrence Street
Eugene, OR 97401
Phone: 541-343-4298
www.oregoncountryfair.org
It is the intention of the Oregon Country Fair to create events and experiences that nourish the spirit, explore living artfully and authentically on Earth, and transform culture in magical, joyous, and healthy ways. They host an annual gathering every July in Oregon and maintain a network of over ten thousand members.

Fibers

Lesch, Alma. *Vegetable Dyeing: 151 Color Recipes for Dyeing Yarns and Fabrics with Natural Materials.* New York: Watson-Guptill, 1970.

Prance, Ghillean, and Mark Nesbitt. *The Cultural History of Plants.* New York: Routledge, 2005.

Food, History, and Politics

Crispo, Dorothy. *The Story of Our Fruits and Vegetables.* Greenwich, CT: Devin-Adair, 1968.

Lappé, Francis Moore, and Joseph Collins. *World Hunger: 12 Myths.* New York: Grove Press, 1986.

Lerza, Katherine, and Michael Jacobson. *Food for People Not for Profit: A Sourcebook on the Food Crisis.* New York: Ballantine, 1975.

Nestle, Marion. *Food Politics: How the Food Industry Influences Nutrition and Health.* Berkeley, CA: University of California Press, 2002.

Root, Waverly. *Food: An Authoritative Visual History and Dictionary of the Foods of the World.* New York: Simon and Schuster, 1980.

Food Not Lawns Chapters

Arcata Food Not Lawns, aka Wild Urban Gardeners, promotes depaving and lawn conversions, operates a tool library, and helps publish *Culture Change* magazine. Excellent site with lots of links.
www.culturechange.org/food_not_lawns.html

Bellingham Food Not Lawns is focused on helping its local community become more sustainable by restoring abused and unused land into organic gardens.
foodnotlawns@gmail.com

Bisbee Food Not Lawns is the newest chapter, hosting workshops and work parties to beautify and unite this small Arizona town.
www.foodnotlawnsbisbee.org

Cascadia Food Not Lawns is focused on promoting peace and sustainability through ecological design, shared resources, and creative community interaction.
www.foodnotlawns.com

Montreal Food Not Lawns publishes a regular 'zine, and its website has tons of great information about food politics, genetic engineering, and much more.
www.tao.ca/~kev

Portland Food Not Lawns. Several autonomous neighborhood groups organize a variety of projects.
www.myspace.com/foodnotlawnsportland

San Diego Food Not Lawns. Organizes a regional conference and maintains a good website.
www.sdfoodnotlawns.com

St. Cloud Food Not Lawns is building local food security through networking with local farmers and growing healthy food. Its website has a nice photo album.
www.localharvest.org

St. Petersburg Food Not Lawns is a loosely affiliated collective of grassroots gardeners promoting urban sustainability by encouraging and assisting in growing food. They apply environmental and anarchist principles including sustainability, reuse, consumption, non-hierarchy, mutual aid, community, consensus decision making, and autonomy.
stpetefnl.cjb.net

Food Storage and Processing

Katz, Sandor Ellix. *Wild Fermentation: A Do-It-Yourself Guide to Cultural Manipulation.* White River Junction, VT: Chelsea Green, 2003.

Keeping Food Fresh: Old-World Techniques and Recipes: By the Gardeners and Farmers of Terre Vivante. White River Junction, VT: Chelsea Green, 1999.

Mollison, Bill. *The Permaculture Book of Ferment and Human Nutrition.* Tyalgum, NSW: Tagari, 1993.

Stoner, Carol Hupping, ed. *Stocking Up: How to Preserve the Foods You Grow, Naturally* (revised and expanded edition). Emmaus, PA: Rodale Press, 1977.

Free Stuff

Try an Internet search for "freecycle" or "barter fair" and your hometown and you'll find a wide variety of excellent resources. Also check out the free stuff section of www.craigslist.org.

Fund-Raising

The Arts and Healing Network (www.artheals.org) is a solid bank of resources for creative people, with many options that allow individuals to find funding for projects without having to go through a corporate nonprofit.

The Fund for Wild Nature
PO Box 42523
Portland, OR 97242
fwn@fundwildnature.org
www.fundwildnature.org
Offers grant funding for a wide variety of environmental activist projects. Deadlines are twice a year, early spring and early fall.

Organic Farming Research Foundation
PO Box 440
Santa Cruz, CA 95061
Phone: 831-426-6606
www.ofrf.org
From the website: "The Organic Farming Research Foundation is a non-profit whose mission is to sponsor research related to organic farming practices, to disseminate research results to organic farmers and to growers interested in adopting organic production systems, and to educate the public and decision-makers about organic farming issues."

Sustainable Agriculture Research and Education Foundation
www.sare.org
From the website: "SARE provides grants and information to improve profitability, stewardship and quality of life. . . . The program is part of USDA's Cooperative State Research, Education, and Extension Service, is managed in partnership with regional land grant hosts, and funds projects and conducts outreach designed to improve agricultural systems."

Hall, Mary S. *Getting Funded: The Complete Guide to Writing Grant Proposals.* Portland, OR: Continuing Education Press, Extended Studies, Portland State University, 2003.
Marchese, Richard C. *Grantwriting: Securing Resources for Non-Profit Organizations.* Espanola, NM: Resource Development Services, 2000.

Genetically Modified Organisms (GMOs) and Biotech

Action Group on Erosion, Technology and Concentration (etc group)
www.etcgroup.org

NW Rage (Northwest Resistance against Genetic Engineering)
www.nwrage.org

Organic Consumers Association
www.organicconsumers.org

Fowler, Cary, and Pat Mooney. *Shattering: Food, Politics, and the Loss of Genetic Diversity.* Tucson, AZ: University of Arizona Press, 1990.
Grace, Eric. *Biotechnology Unzipped: Promises and Realities.* Markham, ON: Fitzhenry and Whiteside, 2005.
Kneen, Brewster. *Farmageddon: Food and the Culture of Biotechnology.* Gabriola Island, BC: New Society, 1999.
Smith, Jeffrey M. *Genetic Roulette: The Documented Health Risks of Genetically Engineered Foods.* White River Junction, VT: Chelsea Green, 2005.
Teitel, Martin. *Changing the Nature of Nature.* Rochester, VT: Park Street Press, 1999.

Greenhouses and Season Extension

Colebrook, Binda. *Winter Gardening in the Maritime Northwest: Cool Season Crops for the Year-Round Gardener.* Seattle, WA: Sasquatch Books, 1989. Though written by and for Northwest gardeners, this book is so packed with valuable information about season extension that I highly recommend it for anyone living in climatic zones 4–9.
Coleman, Eliot. *Four-Season Harvest: Organic Vegetables from Your Home Garden All Year Long.* White River Junction, VT: Chelsea Green, 1999.
Poisson, Leandre, and Gretchen Vogel Poisson. *Solar Gardening: Growing Vegetables Year-Round the American Intensive Way.* White River Junction, VT: Chelsea Green, 1994.
Strickler, Darryl J. *Solarspaces: How and Why to Add Greenhouse, Sunspace, or Solarium to Your Home.* New York: Van Nostrand Reinhold, 1983.
Wahlfeldt, Bette G. *All about Greenhouses: With 15 Build-Your-Own Plans.* Blue Ridge Summit, PA: Tab Books, 1981.

Group Process

Lost Valley Educational Center
81868 Lost Valley Lane
Dexter, OR 97431
Phone: 541-937-3351
www.lostvalley.org
Lost Valley Educational Center is an intentional community and nonprofit educational center dedicated to learning, living, and teaching sustainable, ecologically based culture. They host monthly personal-growth workshops entitled "The Heart of Now," which are said to greatly improve one's ability to solve conflicts between oneself and others.

Butler, C. T., and Amy Rothstein. *On Conflict and Consensus: A Handbook on Formal Consensus Decisionmaking.* The very best guide to classic consensus process. The entire text is available online at www.ic.org/pnp/ocac.
Hunter, Dale. *The Zen of Groups: A Handbook for People Meeting with a Purpose.* Tucson, AZ: Fisher Books, 1995.
Hunter, Dale, Anne Bailey, and Bill Taylor. *The Art of Facilitation: How to Create Group Synergy.* Tucson, AZ: Fisher Books, 1995.

Guerrilla Gardening

www.guerrillagardening.org

Pallenberg, Barbara. *Guerrilla Gardening: How to Create Gorgeous Gardens for Free.* Los Angeles: Renaissance Books, 2001.

Health and Healing

Columbine School of Botanical Studies
PO Box 50532
Eugene, OR 97405
Phone: 541-687-7114
Unique herbal botanical field apprenticeships.

Horizon Herbs
www.horizonherbs.com

The Icarus Project
theicarusproject.net
Mental health for activists and others who don't fit

into mainstream treatment strategies. A nonprofit, community-based website, support network, and underground media project created by and for people struggling with bipolar disorder and other "dangerous gifts" that are commonly labeled as mental illnesses. They believe that when we learn to take care of ourselves, the intertwined threads of madness and creativity can be tools of inspiration and hope in a repressed and damaged world.

Susun Weed
Herbal Medicine and Spirit Healing the Wise
Woman Way
Wise Women's Center
PO Box 64
Woodstock, NY
Phone: 845-246-8081
www.susunweed.com

Burton Goldberg Group. *Alternative Medicine: The Definitive Guide.* Tiburon, CA: Future Medicine, 1999. The essential reference guide for people who want to take control of their own health care.

Cech, Richo. *Making Plant Medicine.* Williams, OR: Horizon Herbs, 2000.

Hausman, Patricia, and Judith Benn Hurley. *The Healing Foods: The Ultimate Authority on the Curative Power of Nutrition.* Emmaus, PA: Rodale Press, 1989.

Heinerman, John. *Heinerman's New Encyclopedia of Fruits and Vegetable* (revised & expanded). Paramus, NJ: Prentice Hall, 1995.

Kloss, Jethro. *Back to Eden: A Human Interest Story of Health and Restoration to Be Found in Herb, Root, and Bark.* New York: Benedict Lust, 1981.

Lust, John B. *The Herb Book.* New York: B. Lust, 1974.

Maggiore, Christine. *What If Everything You Thought You Knew about AIDS Was Wrong?* American Foundation for AIDS Alternatives (11684 Ventura Blvd., Studio City, CA 91604), 1999.

Parvati, Jeannine. *Hygieia: A Woman's Herbal.* Published by the author in 1978. Very difficult to find, but unparalleled as a source of information about herbal birth control and related issues. Highly recommended.

Robbins, John. *The Food Revolution: How Your Diet Can Help Save Your Life and the World.* Berkeley, CA: Conari Press, 2001.

Humanure

Del Porto, David, and Carol Steinfeld. *The Composting Toilet System Book: A Practical Guide to Choosing, Planning and Maintaining Composting Toilet Systems: A Water-Saving, Pollution-Preventing Alternative.* Concord, MA: Center for Ecological Pollution Prevention, 2000.

Jenkins, Joseph C. *The Humanure Handbook: A Guide to Composting Human Manure.* Grove City, PA: Jenkins, 1999.

Van der Ryn, Sim. *The Toilet Papers: Designs to Recycle Human Waste and Water: Dry Toilets, Greywater Systems and Urban Sewage.* Santa Barbara, CA: Capra Press, 1978.

Insects and Pollinators

Buchmann, Stephen L., and Gary Paul Nabhan. *The Forgotten Pollinators.* Washington, DC: Island Press, 1997.

Carr, Anna. *Rodale's Color Handbook of Garden Insects.* Emmaus, PA: Rodale Press, 1979.

Cebenko, Jill, and Deborah Martin, eds. *Insect, Disease, and Weed I.D. Guide: Find-It-Fast Organic Solutions for Your Garden.* Emmaus, PA: Rodale Press, 2001.

Flint, Mary Louise. *Pests of the Garden and Small Farm: A Grower's Guide to Using Less Pesticide* (2nd edition). Los Angeles: University of California Press, 1998.

Inspiration

Berry, Wendell. *Collected Poems, 1957–1982.* San Francisco: North Point Press, 1985. This is just one of Mr. Berry's many amazing books. He is one of the American pioneers in ecological agriculture and well worth discovering if you haven't already.

Bloch, Ernst. *The Principle of Hope.* Cambridge, MA: MIT Press, 1986.

Briggs, John, and F. David Peat. *The Seven Life Lessons of Chaos: Timeless Wisdom from the Science of Change.* New York: Harper Collins, 1999.

Callenbach, Ernest. *Ecotopia* and *Ecotopia Emerging.* See www.ernestcallenbach.com.

Diamond, Jared M. *Guns, Germs, and Steel: The Fates of Human Societies.* New York: W. W. Norton, 1998.

Le Guin, Ursula K. *The Word for World Is Forest.* New York: Ace Books, 1989.

Quinn, Daniel. *Ishmael.* New York: Bantam/Turner Book, 1995.

Starhawk. *The Fifth Sacred Thing.* New York: Bantam Books, 1994; www.starhawk.org.

Intentional Communities

Communities Publications Cooperative
105 Sun Street
Steele, IL 60919

The Farm
www.thefarmcommunity.com
Located in Tennessee, this is one of the USA's pioneers in sustainable living and permaculture education. Their site contains design tips, links and resources, and pages upon pages of useful information.

Directory of Intentional Communities (4th edition). Rutledge, MO: Fellowship for Intentional Community, 2005. Semiannual directory of hundreds of intentional communities around the world, indexed by geographic area, group size and focus, et cetera. Useful for people who are looking for a community to move to, but also makes an excellent travel guide for visiting organic farms and permaculture sites. Also don't miss the Intentional Communities website at www.ic.org.

Roseland, Mark. *Toward Sustainable Communities: Resources for Citizens and Their Governments.* Gabriola Island, BC: New Society, 1998.

Walters, J. Donald. *Intentional Communities: How to Start Them and Why.* Nevada City, CA: Crystal Clarity, 1988.

Internet Hubs and Resources

Craigslist
www.craigslist.org

Global Family
www.globalfamily.net

Green People
www.greenpeople.org

MySpace
www.myspace.com

Mutual Aid
www.mutualaid.org

Sustainable Communities Network
www.sustainable.org

Tribe
www.tribe.net

Zenzibar Alternative Culture Network
www.zenzibar.com

Internships and Volunteer Opportunities

Most of the organizations listed in the resources section, especially those listed under "Permaculture," offer internships, volunteer opportunities, and sometimes jobs. In addition, here are some excellent places to find compiled listings of opportunities from around the world.

ATTRA
www.attra.org

Idealist
www.idealist.org

Organic Volunteers
www.organicvolunteers.org

Short Term Job Adventures
www.backdoorjobs.com

Willing Workers on Organic Farms, aka World-Wide Opportunities on Organic Farms (either way, WWOOF)
www.wwooff.org

Kinship Gardening

Angiosperm Phylogeny Group. *Annals of the Missouri Botanical Garden.* Volume 85, number 4, 1998. A detailed list of plant genera and classifications, based on new genetic data. Alan Kapuler used this data to develop his kinship theories.

Kapuler, Alan. *Peace Seeds Resource Journal.* Published semiannually by Peace Seeds, 2385 SE Thompson, Corvallis, OR 97333; alkapuler@yahoo.com. Alan is my guru and mentor, and I value his work above most everything else. If you have any interest in organics, seed saving, biodiversity, or kinship gardening, get your hands on a set of Kapuler's *Resource Journals.* Also see an extensive review of Alan Kapuler's work at www.organicseed.com.

Lawns

Bormann, F. Herbert, Diana Balmori, and Gordon T. Geballe. *Redesigning the American Lawn: A Search for Environmental Harmony* (2nd edition). New Haven: Yale University Press, 2001.

Jenkins, Virginia Scott. *The Lawn: History of an American Obsession.* Washington, DC: Smithsonian Institution Press, 1994.

Primeau, Liz. *Front Yard Gardens: Growing More Than Grass.* Willowdale, ON: Firefly Books, 2003.

Media and Outreach

International Independent Media Collective
www.indymedia.org

Alexander, David. *Ways You Can Manipulate the Media.* Boulder, CO: Paladin Press, 1993.

Ratner, Ellen, and Kathie Scarrah. *Ready, Set, TALK! A Guide to Getting Your Message Heard by Millions on Talk Radio, Talk Television, and Talk Internet: A Must-Have Resource for Campaigns of All Kinds.* White River Junction, VT: Chelsea Green, 2006.

Ruggiero, Greg, and Stuart Sahulka. *Project Censored: The Progressive Guide to Alternative Media and Activism.* New York: Seven Stories Press, 1999. Highly recommended collection of alternative media resources around the world. Get it, use it.

Permaculture

Alliance for Sustainability
1521 University Avenue SE
Minneapolis, MN 55414
Phone: 612-331-1099
www.allianceforsustainability.net

Aprovecho Research Center
80574 Hazelton Road
Cottage Grove, OR 97424
Phone: 541-942-8198
apro@efn.org
www.aprovecho.net
Aprovecho is a Spanish word meaning "I make best use of." Eight on-site staff study and teach the elements of one approach to a more eco-centered lifestyle: sustainable forestry, organic gardening, and appropriate technology. Up to fourteen interns study with the staff, sharing a life based on voluntary simplicity.

EcoLandTech
www.ibiblio.org/ecolandtech
A meta-link for permaculture-related topics. A great launchboard for further online investigation.

International Permaculture Directory
www.permaculture.net

La'akea Permaculture Hawaii
www.permaculture-hawaii.com
Offers courses and information about permaculture around the globe. Excellent site.

Occidental Arts and Ecology Center
15290 Coleman Valley Road
Occidental, CA 95465
Phone: 707-874-1557
www.oaec.org
OAEC is a nonprofit organizing and education center and organic farm in northern California's Sonoma County. OAEC's programs combine research, demonstration, education, and organizing to develop collaborative, community-based strategies for positive social change and effective environmental stewardship.

Permaculture Portal
www.permacultureportal.com
A must-see website just dripping with practical information. Operated by the Bullocks Brothers on Orcas Island, the site represents many years of combined experience.

Permaculture Activist
PO Box 5516
Bloomington, IN 47408
Phone: 812-335-0383
www.permacultureactivist.net
Permaculture Activist magazine is published quarterly from offices at Earthaven Ecovillage near Black Mountain, North Carolina, where they also offer workshops and internships. Circulated internationally and distributed throughout the US and Canada, the 18-year-old journal covers the development of sustainable culture through ecological design. The extensive website offers international calendars of events; a planetary directory of permaculture links, people, and projects; an extensive catalog of necessary books and videos; lists of permaculture institutes and Listservs; contacts for seeds and plants; and much more.

Bell, Graham. *The Permaculture Garden*. White River Junction, VT: Chelsea Green, 2005.
———. *The Permaculture Way: Practical Steps to Create a Self-Sustaining World*. White River Junction, VT: Chelsea Green, 2005. *The Permaculture Way* shows how to consciously design a lifestyle that is low in environmental impact and highly productive. It demonstrates how to meet our needs, make the most of resources by minimizing waste and maximizing potential, and still leave the earth richer than we found it. Graham Bell discusses human health, community interaction, rural agriculture, urban landscape design, and personal choices. I recommend *The Permaculture Way* as an essential introduction to permaculture, ecological living, and community organizing.
Brown, David, ed. *A Western Permaculture Manual*. Subiaco, Western Australia: Cornucopia Press, 1989.
Holmgren, David. *Permaculture: Principles and Pathways beyond Sustainability*. Hepburn, Victoria, Australia: Holmgren Design Services, 2002.
Jacke, Dave, and Eric Toensmeier. *Edible Forest Gardens*. White River Junction, VT: Chelsea Green, 2005.
Kern, Ken, and Barbara Kern. *The Owner-Built Homestead*. New York: Scribner, 1977. Said to be one of the books that inspired Mollison. I highly recommend this timeless classic on ecological rural living.
Mollison, Bill. *Permaculture: A Designer's Manual; Introduction to Permaculture; Permaculture One;* and *Permaculture Two*. Tyalgum, Australia: Tagari, 1988–1994. These are the premier and, in my opinion, still some of the best permaculture books. The illustrations are excellent and, combined with the witty and informative text, provide a theoretical road map for developing permaculture gardens and communities in almost any setting. Unfortunately, because Mollison is Australian, many of the plant and animal species don't work in other climates. Still, his humor and unique perspective on people, plants, and politics makes these books highly recommendable and a joy to read. Also, look for Bill Mollison's hilarious video documenting four permaculture sites on four different continents, *The Global Gardener with Bill Mollison* (Oley, PA: Bullfrog Films, 1991).

Morrow, Rosemary. *Earth User's Guide to Permaculture.* Kenthurst, NSW: Kangaroo Press, 1993. Still one of the only permaculture books besides *Food Not Lawns* written by a woman, the *Earth User's Guide* is a useful and informative resource for ecological gardeners of all levels.

Whitefield, Patrick. *The Earth Care Manual: A Permaculture Handbook for Britain and Other Temperate Climates.* East Meon, Hampshire, England: Permanent Publications, 2004.

———. *Permaculture in a Nutshell.* East Meon, Hampshire, England: Permanent Publications, 2000.

Plants

Cocannouer, Joseph A. *Weeds, Guardians of the Soil.* Old Greenwich, CT: Devin-Adair, 1980.

Couplan, François. *The Encyclopedia of Edible Plants of North America.* New Canaan, CT: Keats, 1998. Five hundred and eighty-five pages of firsthand information about edible species that grow in North America. Contains nutrition information, parts used, history, etymology, geographical location, medicinal uses, and cooking techniques.

Cunningham, Sally Jean. *Great Garden Companions: A Companion Planting System for a Beautiful, Chemical-Free Vegetable Garden.* Emmaus, PA: Rodale Press, 1998. Illustrated, user-friendly, and highly recommended.

Druse, Kenneth, and Margaret Roach. *The Natural Habitat Garden.* Portland, OR: Timber Press, 2004.

Facciola, Stephen. *Cornucopia II: A Source Book of Edible Plants.* Vista, CA: Kampong, 1998. Includes listings of approximately three thousand species of plants, fungi, algae, and bacteria, with information on edibility, toxicity, nutritional content, geographical regions, uses, and more. Contains detailed descriptions of several hundred cultivars and provides a variety of sources for each species.

Fern, Ken. *Plants for a Future.* East Meon, Hampshire, England: Permanent Publications, 2000. An excellent source of information about multifunctional plants from around the world. Includes cultivation techniques, conservation, and ecology, sorts the plants by application, and provides the most extensive plant-uses appendix I have ever seen. Also don't miss the website, www.pfaf.org, which is a database of over seven thousand useful plants. The sheer richness of options involved means that its search engine can be a little intimidating at first. Some old hands consider it one of the most valuable eco-design resources on the Internet.

Harris, Ben Charles. *Eat the Weeds.* Barre, MA: Barre, 1969.

Hickmott, Simon. *Growing Unusual Vegetables: Weird and Wonderful Vegetables and How to Grow Them.* Bristol, England: Eco-logic Books, 2003.

Hobbs, Jude. *A Guide to Multi-Functional Hedgerows.* Eugene, OR: Agro-Ecology Northwest and Cascadia Landscape Design, 2003–2005. Jude Hobbs is well known as *the* West Coast expert on hedgerow design. She is a permaculture instructor and a teacher and mentor of mine. See her website, www.cascadiapermaculture.com.

Mabberley, D. J. *The Plant Book: A Portable Dictionary of the Higher Plants.* Cambridge, UK: Cambridge University Press, 1996. The most comprehensive book of temperate plants, with easy-to-reference entries containing genus, species, family, description, and origin of tens of thousands of plant species.

National Resource Council. *Lost Crops of Africa.* Washington, DC: National Academy Press, 1996.

———. *Lost Crops of the Incas: Little-known Plants of the Andes with Promise for Worldwide Cultivation.* Washington, DC: National Academy Press, 1989. The same people who brought us potatoes, tomatoes, and peppers also cultivated several other types of edible tubers, grains, and vegetables. I took this book to South America and was surprised to find that even the locals were unfamiliar with many of the foods upon which their culture was founded. Most of these plants will do quite well in temperate climates, and I highly recommend tracking down a copy of the book.

Nugent, Jeff, and Julia Boniface. *Permaculture Plants: A Selection.* East Meon, Hampshire, England: Permanent Publications, 2004.

Pfeiffer, Ehrenfried. *Weeds and What They Tell.* Wyoming, RI: Bio-Dynamic Literature, 1981.

Philbrick, Helen Louise Porter, and Richard B. Gregg. *Companion Plants: Plants That Help Each Other and How to Use Them.* Kenthurst, NSW, Australia: Kangaroo Press, 1991. An alphabetized list of plants and their allies. Highly recommended.

Phillips, Roger. *Vegetables.* New York: Random House, 1993. Part of a highly regarded series of books on plants that includes other titles like *Early Perennials, Late Perennials, Trees,* and many more, *Vegetables* is an excellent place to start finding information about a plethora of edible plants.

Riotte, Louise. *Carrots Love Tomatoes: Secrets of Companion Planting for Successful Gardening.* Charlotte, VT: Garden Way, 1981.

———. *Roses Love Garlic.* Charlotte, VT: Garden Way, 1983.

Schuler, Stanley. *How to Grow Almost Everything.* New York: M. Evans, 1965. An encyclopedia of cultivation instructions for hundreds of plants.

Smith, J. Russell. *Tree Crops: A Permanent Agriculture.* Washington, DC: Island Press, 1987. Considered one of the essential foundation books of permaculture design, and said to have inspired much of Mollison's work, this book is hard to find but well worth the search. Try direct from Island Press: www.islandpress.org or 800-621-2736.

Thomas, Eric. *Hedgerow.* London: Dorling Kindersley, 1982. This beautifully illustrated book tells the story of hedgerows in England: their origins, growth, resources, wildlife, and place in the changing landscape. Very applicable to temperate climates.

Tompkins, Peter, and Christopher Bird. *The Secret Life of Plants.* New York: Harper and Row, 1989.

Recycling

Bring Recycling
Eugene, OR
www.bringrecycling.org

Institute for Local Self-Reliance (ILSR)
927 15th Street NW, 4th Floor
Washington, DC 20005
Phone: 202-898-1610
- or -
1313 5th Street SE
Minneapolis, MN 55414
Phone: 612-379-3815
www.ilsr.org

The ReBuilding Center
www.rebuildingcenter.org
A resale outlet for useful building materials and the primary fundraising body for Our United Villages, a non-profit community enhancement organization (see Community Organizing). Developed by dedicated volunteers, The ReBuilding Center is modeled after successful building material reuse centers throughout North America. Their website boasts a list of over 500 of these centers—go there and find one near you!

ReCycle North
Burlington, VT
www.recyclenorth.org

Food, Fuel, and Fertilizer from Organic Wastes. Report of an ad hoc panel of the advisory committee on technology innovation, National Research Council. Washington, DC: National Academy Press, 1981.

Seed Books

Ashworth, Suzanne. *Seed to Seed: Seed Saving and Growing Techniques for Vegetable Gardeners.* Decorah, IA: Seed Savers Exchange, 2002.

Deppe, Carol. *Breed Your Own Vegetable Varieties.* White River Junction, VT: Chelsea Green, 2000.

Guillet, Dominique. *The Seeds of Kokopelli.* Boston: Kokopelli Seed Foundation, 2000. A wonderful book full of color photos, and available in French or English. Guillet's Kokopelli Seed Foundation (the U.S. branch of the France-based Association Kokopelli) is heavily involved in the protection of biodiversity and in the production and distribution of biodynamic and organic seeds. Also visit www.kokopelli-seeds.com.

Kapuler, Alan. *Peace Seeds Resource Journal.* Published by the author and available through Peace Seeds, 2385 Thompson SE, Corvallis, OR 97333; 541-752-7421; alkapuler@yahoo.com. Alan Kapuler is my mentor and guru and has taught me much of what I know about seed saving, polycultural gardening, kinship gardening, plant propagation, soil building, and interpersonal communication. His life's work has become my own passion, and I highly recommend any and all of his writing.

Klein, Mary Ann, and David O. Percy. *Seed Saving: A Guide for Living Historical Farms.* Accokeek, MD: Accokeek Foundation, 1986.

McDorman, Bill. *Basic Seed Saving.* International Seed Saving Institute, 1994. A forty-eight-page booklet describing useful terms and concepts central to seed saving.

Rogers, Marc. *Saving Seeds: The Gardener's Guide to Growing and Storing Vegetable and Flower Seeds* (revised). Pownal, VT: Storey, 1991.

Stickland, Sue. *Back Garden Seed Saving: Keeping Our Vegetable Heritage Alive.* Bristol, England: Eco-logic Books, 2001.

Turner, Carole B. *Seed Sowing and Saving: Step-by-Step Techniques for Collecting and Growing More Than 100 Vegetables, Flowers, and Herbs.* Pownal, VT: Storey, 1998.

Seed Companies

When you decide to buy seed, it is important to find them as locally grown as possible. Here is a list of bioregional seed sources that support small-scale, organic growers.

Abundant Life Seeds
PO Box 157
Saginaw, OR 97472
Phone: 541-767-9606
Fax: 866-514-7333
als@abundantlifeseeds.com
www.abundantlifeseeds.com

Baker Creek Heirloom Seeds
2278 Baker Creek Road
Mansfield, MO 65704
Phone: 417-924-8917
Fax: 417-924-8887
www.rareseeds.com

Bountiful Gardens
18001 Shafer Ranch Road
Willits, CA 95490
Phone: 707-459-6410
Fax: 707-459-1925
bountiful@sonic.net
www.bountifulgardens.org

Cook's Garden
PO Box C5030
Warminster, PA 18974
800-457-9703
www.cooksgarden.com

Dancing Tree Farm
Bend, OR 97701
Phone: 541-914-4217
dancingtreefarm@mac.com
www.dancingtreefarm.com

Heirloom Seeds
PO Box 245
West Elizabeth, PA 15088
412-384-0852
www.heirloomseeds.com

High Mowing Organic Seeds
76 Quarry Road
Wolcott, VT 05680
Phone: 802-472-6174
Fax: 802-472-3201
www.highmowingseeds.com

JL Hudson, Seedsman
Star Route 2, Box 337
La Honda, CA 94020
www.jlhudsonseeds.net

Johnny's Selected Seeds
955 Benton Avenue
Winslow, ME 04901
Phone: 877-564-6697
www.johnnyseeds.com

Natural Gardening Company
PO Box 750776
Petaluma, CA 94975
Phone: 707-766-9303
Fax: 707-766-9747
info@naturalgardening.com
www.naturalgardening.com

Nichols Garden Nursery
1190 Old Salem Road NE
Albany, OR 97321
Phone: 800-422-3985
Fax: 800-231-5306
www.nicholsgardennursery.com

Peace Seeds
2385 Thompson Street SE
Corvallis, OR 97333
Phone: 541-752-7421
alkapuler@yahoo.com
Peaceful Valley Farm Supply
PO Box 2209
125 Clydesdale Court
Grass Valley, CA 95945
Phone: 888-784-1722
helpdesk@groworganic.com
www.groworganic.com

Salt Spring Seeds
Box 444, Ganges PO
Salt Spring Island, BC V8K 2W1
Canada
Phone: 250-537-5269 (no phone orders)
www.saltspringseeds.com

Seeds of Change
PO Box 15700
Santa Fe, NM 87592
Phone: 888-762-7333
www.seedsofchange.com

Seeds Trust
PO Box 596
Cornville, AZ 86325
Phone: 928-649-3315
Fax: 928-649-8181
www.seedstrust.com

Southern Exposure Seed Exchange
PO Box 460
Mineral, VA 23117
Phone: 540-894-9480
Fax: 540-894-9481
gardens@southernexposure.com
www.southernexposure.com

Sow Organic Seed Company
PO Box 527
Williams, OR 97544
Phone: 888-709-7333
organic@organicseed.com
www.organicseed.com

Territorial Seed Company
PO Box 158
Cottage Grove, OR 97424
Phone: 800-626-0866
Fax: 888-657-3131
www.territorial-seed.com

Underwood Gardens
1414 Zimmerman Road
Woodstock, IL 60098
Phone: 815-338-6279
Fax: 888-382-7041
www.underwoodgardens.com
Victory Seeds
PO Box 192
Molalla, OR 97038
Phone: 503-829-3126
info@victoryseeds.com
www.victoryseeds.com

Seed Organizations

Bay Area Seed Interchange Library (BASIL)
www.ecologycenter.org/basil
The BASIL Project is part of a growing network of concerned farmers and community gardeners dedicated to conserving the remaining genetic diversity of our planet's seed stock. They host annual seed swaps and have a library of healthy vegetable, herb, and flower seeds that are available free to the public.

National Plant Germplasm Service (NPGS)
www.ars-grin.gov/npgs
Focused on preserving the genetic diversity of plants by acquiring, preserving, evaluating, documenting, and distributing crop germplasms to researchers.

Native Seeds/SEARCH
526 N. 4th Avenue
Tucson, AZ 85705
Phone: 866-622-5561
Fax: 520-622-5591
info@nativeseeds.org
www.nativeseeds.org

Organic Seed Alliance
PO Box 772
Port Townsend, WA 98368
Phone: 360-385-7192
www.seedalliance.org

Planting Seeds Project
New City Institute
#26, 721 Millyard
Vancouver, BC V5Z 3Z9
Canada
Phone: 604-255-2326
www.newcity.ca/Pages/planting_seeds.html

Primal Seeds
www.primalseeds.org
From the website: "Primal Seeds exists as a network to actively engage in protecting biodiversity and creating local food security. It is a response to industrial biopiracy, control of the global seed supply and of our food. This evolving tool is designed to empower individuals to participate in the creation of tomorrow."

7Scatterseed Project
PO Box 1167
Farmington, ME 04938
www.gardeningplaces.com/scatterseed.htm

Seed and Plant Sanctuary for Canada
Box 444, Ganges PO
Salt Spring Island, BC V8K 2W1
Canada
Phone: 250-537-5269
www.seedsanctuary.com

Seed Savers Exchange
3094 N. Winn Road
Decorah, IA 52101
Phone: 563-382-5990
Fax: 563-382-5872
www.seedsavers.org
See Chapter 6 for a description.

Seeds of Diversity / Semences du patrimoine
PO Box 36, Stn Q
Toronto, ON M4T 2L7
Canada
Phone: 866-509-SEED
mail@seeds.ca
www.seeds.ca

Sow Organic Seed Co.
PO Box 527
Williams, OR 97544
Phone: 888-709-7333
organic@organicseed.com
www.organicseed.com
Not just another seed company, Sow Organic exists for the purpose of expanding the public domain. Their website contains a ton of useful information. Highly recommended.

Soil

Soil Foodweb, Inc.
www.soilfoodweb.com
An international group of soil biology laboratories analyzing and advising on microbial life in the soil and on plants. I highly recommend this website as a source of information about how to understand and care for your soil community.

Worm Digest
PO Box 2654
Grants Pass, OR 97528
Phone: 541-476-9626
Fax: 541-4764555
mail@wormdigest.org

Appelhof, Mary. *Worms Eat My Garbage.* Kalamazoo, MI: Flower Press, 1997.

Dale, Tom, and Vernon Gill Carter. *Topsoil and Civilization.* Norman, OK: University of Oklahoma Press, 1955. A fascinating treatise on the history of agriculture, from ancient Mesopotamia to the 1950s state of American farms. The authors make clear the fact that our future as a species will utterly depend on our ability to steward the soil that feeds us.

Gershuny, Grace, and Joe Smillie. *The Soul of Soil: A Soil Building Guide for Master Gardeners and Farmers* (4th edition). White River Junction, VT: Chelsea Green, 1999.

Howard, Sir Albert. *Soil and Health: A Study of Organic Agriculture.* New York: Schocken Books, 1972.

Logan, William Bryant. *Dirt: The Ecstatic Skin of the Earth.* New York: Riverhead Books, 1996.

Nancarrow, Loren, and Janet Hogan Taylor. *The Worm Book: The Complete Guide to Worms in Your Garden.* Berkeley, CA: Ten Speed Press, 1998.

Sakura Eigasha. *Life in the Soil.* Video recording. Tawarahon-cho Atami Shizuoka, Japan: International Research Center for Nature Farming / MOA Productions, 1992. Extremely difficult to find but the best video ever made about soil communities. Full-color, microscopic, and time-lapse photography shows soil animals and plants interacting in a variety of natural and agricultural settings. Highly recommended.

Schaller, Friedrich. *Soil Animals.* Ann Arbor, MI: University of Michigan Press, 1968.

Tompkins, Peter, and Christopher Bird. *Secrets of the Soil: New Age Solutions for Restoring Our Planet.* New York: Perennial Library, 1990.

Street Theater

Art and Revolution Convergence
1002-1/2 Dolores Street
San Francisco, CA 94110
Phone: 415-487-5163
www.groundworknews.org/culture/culture
-artrevol.html
A collective of dancers, musicians, puppeteers, and activists, Art and Revolution conducts workshops and organizes street theater around social and environmental justice issues.

Bread and Puppet
753 Heights Road
Glover, VT 05839
Phone: 802-525-3031 or 802-525-1271
Fax: 802-525-3618
breadpup@together.net
www.breadandpuppet.org
One of the originators of giant puppet parades, this collective still hosts internships and annual pageants and tours around the world doing shows about social, political, and ecologically relevant topics.

Bolton, Reg, and Jo Hignett. *Circus in a Suitcase.* Rowayton, CT: New Plays, 1982. Though written specifically for doing children's shows, this contains such a good overview of low-tech performance ideas that I recommend it for performers of all kinds.

Cohen-Cruz, Jan. *Radical Street Performance: An International Anthology.* New York: Routledge, 1998.

Kershaw, Baz. *The Politics of Performance: Radical Theatre as Cultural Intervention.* New York: Routledge, 1992.

Lesnick, Henry. *Guerilla Street Theater.* New York: Avon, 1973.

Simon, Ronald, and Marc Estrin. *Rehearsing with Gods: Photographs and Essays on the Bread and Puppet Theater.* White River Junction, VT: Chelsea Green, 2004.

Van Erven, Eugène. *Radical People's Theatre.* Bloomington, IN: Indiana University Press, 1988.

Transportation, Bicycles

Critical Mass Bicycle Rides
www.critical-mass.info
www.critical-mass.org
From the website: "Critical Mass is a monthly bicycle ride to celebrate cycling and to assert cyclists' right to the road."

Transportation, Biofuels

Biodiesel and SVO Forums
biodiesel.infopop.cc/groupee
Online forums with information on making your own biodiesel and running your diesel engine on SVO/WVO (straight/waste vegetable oil).

Biodiesel Now
www.biodieselnow.com
Online info on biodiesel, but does not talk about making your own fuel.

Frybrid LLC
1218 10th Avenue
Seattle, WA 98122
(by appointment only)
Phone: 206-322-6242
info@frybrid.com
www.frybrid.com
SVO conversion kits.

GoBiodiesel Collective
4684 SE Johnson Creek Boulevard
Portland, OR 97222
www.gobiodiesel.org
A biodiesel consumer co-op.

Golden Fuel Systems (formerly Greasel
Conversions)
HC 73 Box 157D
Drury, MO 65638
Phone: 866-473-2735
charlie@greasel.com
www.greasel.com
SVO conversion kits.

Grease Works
PO Box 432
Corvallis, OR 97339
Phone: 541-754-1897
justin@greaseworks.org
www.greaseworks.org
Biodiesel and SVO services.

Greasecar Vegetable Fuel Systems
221 Pine Street
Florence, MA 01062
Phone: 413-529-0013
info@greasecar.com
www.greasecar.com
SVO conversion kits.

Green Technologies, LLC
150 W. Canal Street, Suite 1
Winooski, VT 05404
Phone: 802-355-3225
sgordon@greentechvt.com
www.greentechvt.com
Manufactures biodiesel from WVO.

Local B100
www.localb100.com
Information on home-brewing biodiesel.

National Biodiesel Board
PO Box 104888
Jefferson City, MO 65110
Phone: 800-841-5849
www.biodiesel.org
Industry group with listings of producers and distributors of certified, "street-legal" biodiesel.

Pahl, Greg. *Biodiesel: Growing a New Energy Economy*. White River Junction, VT: Chelsea Green, 2004.
Ticknell, Joshua. *From the Fryer to the Fuel Tank: The Complete Guide to Using Vegetable Oil as an Alternative Fuel* (3rd edition). Tallahassee, FL: Ticknell Energy Consultants, 2000.

Urban and Inner-City Strategies

The City Repair Project
PO Box 42615
2122 SE Division
Portland, OR 97242
Phone: 503-235-8946
Fax: 503-235-1046
www.cityrepair.org
An excellent example of how a small group of committed citizens can change a large city for the better. From their website: "Born out of a successful grassroots neighborhood initiative that converted a residential street intersection into a neighborhood public square, City Repair began its work with the idea that localization (of culture, of economy, of decision-making) is a necessary foundation of sustainability. By reclaiming urban spaces to create community-oriented places, we plant the seeds for greater neighborhood communication, empower our communities, and nurture our local culture."

Liberated Salad
www.liberatedsalad.com
How to grow a mini oasis in one hour a week.

Path to Freedom
www.pathtofreedom.com
Not waiting on the five-acre rural home to begin realizing their dream, the Dervaes family is living an urban homestead project on a city-sized lot. They document their progress in an urban diary, sharing the successful experiences of a self-sufficient lifestyle and providing informational resources for others interested in simple and sustainable living.

Boland, Jeroen. *Urban Agriculture: Growing Vegetables in Cities*. Wageningen, the Netherlands: Agromisa Foundation and Technical Centre for Agricultural and Rural Cooperation, 2002.
Bryan, John E. *Small World Vegetable Gardening: Growing Your Own in Limited Spaces*. San Francisco: 101 Publications, 1977.

Cheema, G. Shabbir. *Urban Agriculture: Food, Jobs and Sustainable Cities.* New York: United Nations Development Program, 1996.

Corp Rooftop Gardens Task Force of San Francisco Beautiful. *Rooftop Gardens: From Conception to Construction.* San Francisco: San Francisco Beautiful, 1997.

Gardiner, Nancy. *Gardening in Small Spaces: Including Townhouse, Courtyard, Patio, Balcony, Rooftop, Containers.* Welgemoed, South Africa: Metz Press, 2004.

Guerra, Michael. *The Edible Container Garden.* New York: Fireside, 2000.

Olkowski, Helga and Bill. *The Integral Urban House: Self-Reliant Living in the City.* San Francisco: Sierra Club Books, 1979.

Watkins, David. *Urban Permaculture.* East Meon, Hampshire, England: Permanent Publications, 1993.

Wiland, Harry, and Dale Bell with Joseph D'Agnese. *Edens Lost and Found: How Ordinary Citizens Are Restoring Our Great American Cities.* White River Junction, VT: Chelsea Green, 2006.

Wilson, Peter Lamborn, and Bill Weinberg. *Avant Gardening: Ecological Struggle in the City and the World.* Seattle, WA: Autonomedia, 1999. An anthology of essays by ecological gardeners from around the country, this is a little treasure of a book. The last essay in particular, "Paradise Gardening" by Joe Hollis, became a major turning point for my personal philosophy and inspired me to visit Mr. Hollis at his home in North Carolina, where I learned the tenets of paradise gardening and adopted the term for my own work.

Wingate, Marty, and Jacqueline Koch. *Big Ideas for Northwest Small Gardens.* Seattle, WA: Sasquatch Books, 2003.

Wolfe-Erskine, Cleo. *Urban Wilds: Gardeners' Stories of the Struggle for Land and Justice.* Oakland, CA: WaterUnderground, 2001.

Voluntary Simplicity

Culture Change Magazine
PO Box 4347
Arcata, CA 95518
Phone: 215-243-3144
www.culturechange.org

Northwest Earth Institute
317 SW Alder, Suite 1050
Portland, OR 97204
Phone: 503-227-2807
Fax: 503-227-2917
www.nwei.org
They organize community learning opportunities with the goal of "motivating individuals to examine and transform personal values and habits, to accept responsibility for the earth, and to act on that commitment."

Callenbach, Ernest. *Living Poor with Style.* San Francisco: Bantam, 1972.

Elgin, Duane. *Voluntary Simplicity: Toward a Way of Life That Is Outwardly Simple, Inwardly Rich.* New York: Quill, 1993.

Grigsby, Mary. *Buying Time and Getting By: The Voluntary Simplicity Movement.* Albany, NY: State University of New York Press, 2004.

Levine, Karen. *Keeping Life Simple: 7 Guiding Principles, 500 Tips and Ideas.* Pownal, VT: Storey, 1996.

Savage, Scott, ed. *The Plain Reader: Essays on Making a Simple Life.* New York: Ballantine, 1998.

VandenBroeck, Goldian. *Less Is More: The Art of Voluntary Poverty: An Anthology of Ancient and Modern Voices Raised in Praise of Simplicity.* Rochester, VT: Inner Traditions, 1996.

Wigginton, Eliot. *Foxfire 1–7.* Garden City, NY: Anchor Doubleday. This series of books documents the lives of real people practicing simple and rural traditions, with topics such as animal care, homemade banjos and dulcimers, hide tanning, butter churns, water systems, wood carving, hog dressing, log cabin building, mountain crafts and foods, planting by the signs, snake lore, hunting tales, faith healing, moonshining, shoemaking, gourd banjos, and much more. Highly recommended.

Yeoman, John. *Self Reliance: A Recipe for the New Millennium: A Practical "Cookbook" of Tested Ideas to Secure Your Family's Future.* East Meon, Hampshire, England: Permanent Publications, 1999.

Water

Alexandersson, Olof. *Living Water: Viktor Schauberger and the Secrets of Natural Energy.* Wellow, Bath, UK: Gateway Books, 1990.

Christopher, Thomas. *Water-Wise Gardening: America's Backyard Revolution.* New York: Simon and Schuster, 1994.

Emoto, Masaru. *The Hidden Messages in Water.* Hillsboro, OR: Beyond Words, 2004. *The Hidden Messages in Water* introduces the revolutionary work of Dr. Masaru Emoto, who discovered that molecules of water are affected by our thoughts, words, and feelings. Since humans and the earth are composed mostly of water, his message is one of personal health, global environmental renewal, and a practical plan for peace that starts with each one of us. Also see www.hado.net.

———. *The True Power of Water: Healing and Discovering Ourselves.* Hillsboro, OR: Beyond Words, 2005.

Gould, John. *Rainwater Catchment Systems for Domestic Supply: Design, Construction and Implementation.* London: Intermediate Technology, 1999. Design, construction, and implementation of low-tech strategies for collecting and storing rainwater, including how to build various types of rainwater storage vessels.

Kourik, Robert. *Gray Water Use in the Landscape: How to Help Your Landscape Prosper with Recycled Water*. Santa Rosa, CA: Edible Publications, 1988.

Lancaster, Brad. *Rainwater Harvesting for Drylands*. Vol. 1: *Guiding Principles to Welcome Rain into Your Life and Landscape;* vol. 2: *Water-Harvesting Earthworks*. Tucson, AZ: Rainsource Press, 2005.

Leopold, Luna B. *Water: A Primer*. San Francisco: W. H. Freeman, 1974.

Logsdon, Gene. *Getting Food from Water: A Guide to Backyard Aquaculture*. Emmaus, PA: Rodale Press, 1978.

Ludwig, Art. *Create an Oasis with Greywater: Your Complete Guide to Choosing, Building, and Using Greywater Systems*. Santa Barbara, CA: Oasis Design, 2000. Just one of several excellent and essential books by the same author on graywater use in the landscape.

Matson, Tim. *Earth Ponds: The Country Pond Maker's Guide to Building, Maintenance, and Restoration*. Woodstock, VT: Countryman Press, 1991.

Pacey, Arnold, and Adrian Cullis. *Rainwater Harvesting: The Collection of Rainfall and Run-off in Rural Areas*. London: Intermediate Technology, 1986.

Riotte, Louise. *Catfish Ponds and Lily Pads: Creating and Enjoying a Family Pond*. Pownal, VT: Storey, 1997.

Schwenk, Theodor. *Sensitive Chaos: The Creation of Flowing Forms in Water and Air*. London: Rudolf Steiner Press, 1996.

Solomon, Steve. *Water-Wise Vegetables: For the Maritime Northwest Gardener*. Seattle, WA: Sasquatch Books, 1993.

Yeomans, P. A. *Water for Every Farm: Yeomans Keyline Plan*. Southport, Queensland, Australia: Keyline Designs, 2002. Available through Frank Espriella, PO Box 206, Guinda, CA 95637. The premier guide to designing and maintaining farms and garden beds that make best use of land contours to conserve water. Also visit www.keyline.com.au.

Wilderness and Wildcrafting

Columbine School of Botanical Studies
(See under "Health and Healing")

Lomakatsi Restoration Project
www.lomakatsi.org

Walama Restoration Project
www.walamarestoration.org

Gibbons, Euell. *Stalking the Wild Asparagus*. Chambersburg, PA: Alan C. Hood, 1962.

McQuarrie, Jack. *Wildcrafting: Harvesting the Wilds for a Living: Brush-Picking, Fruit-Tramping, Worm-Grunting, and Other Nomadic Livelihoods*. Santa Barbara: Capra Press, 1975.

Pilarski, Michael. *Resource Guide to Sustainable Wildcrafting and Medicinal Herbs in the Pacific Northwest*. Bellingham, WA: Friends of the Trees Society, 2000.

Thie, Krista. *A Plant Lover's Guide to Wildcrafting: How to Protect Wild Places and Harvest Medicinal Herbs*. White Salmon, WA: Longevity Herb Press, 1989.

Tilford, Gregory L. *The Ecoherbalist's Fieldbook: Wildcrafting in the Mountain West*. Conner, MT: Mountain Weed, 1993.

Where to Find These Publications

Many of the titles listed here are obscure, out of print, or otherwise difficult to find in a mainstream outlet.

The first place to check is the library. If your local public or university library doesn't carry a book you want to read, ask them to buy it or order it through interlibrary loan, usually a free service.

If you want to expand your own library, be sure to purchase books directly from the authors or their publishers, usually found easily enough through a keyword search on www.google.com. Most publishers will be happy to send you a catalog. Contact them via their websites or send a SASE by snail mail.

Only as a last resort, buy books through your local bookstores or online stores like www.powellsbooks.com, www.abebooks.com, or www.amazon.com, where you can find used copies of even very rare books, as well as most anything else, but the author receives little or none of the purchase price.

Notes

Chapter One

1. Ernst Bloch, *The Principle of Hope* (Cambridge, MA: MIT Press, 1986). As quoted in Ronald T. Simon and Marc Estrin, *Rehearsing with Gods* (White River Junction, VT: Chelsea Green, 2004).
2. As quoted by Scott London on www.london.com/insight, 25 October 2003.
3. Kenny Ausubel, *Seeds of Change* (New York: HarperCollins, 1994).
4. Among the additives typically banned are hydrogenated fat, aspartame (artificial sweetener), and monosodium glutamate (MSG) (ibid.).
5. Ralph Nader, from the foreword to Martin Teitel, *Changing the Nature of Nature* (Rochester, VT: Park Street Press, 1999).
6. As quoted by Vandana Shiva on www.twnside.org.sg/title/trials-cn.htm, 18 November 2005.
7. Organic Consumers Association, "OCA's Guidelines for Local Grassroots Action," www.organicconsumers.org/cando.htm, 18 November 2005.
8. Grace Gershuny and Joe Smillie, *The Soul of Soil: A Soil Building Guide for Master Gardeners and Farmers*, 4th edition (White River Junction, VT: Chelsea Green, 1999), 50.
9. Tom Dale and Vernon Gill Carter, *Topsoil and Civilization* (Norman: University of Oklahoma Press, 1955).
10. It was through this evolution that a group in Montreal formed around the same time, also calling themselves Food Not Lawns but with a slightly different focus. Though both groups formed without knowing the other existed, we eventually made friends and continue to share resources and information.
11. Sarah Robertson, "History of the Lawn," *Eugene Register-Guard*, 26 April 1995.
12. Richard Burdick, "The Biology of Lawns," *Discover Magazine* 24, no. 7 (July 2003).
13. Joe Hollis, "Paradise Gardening," in Peter Lamborn Wilson and Bill Weinberg, *Avant Gardening: Ecological Struggle in the City & the World* (Seattle, WA: Autonomedia, 1999), 154.
14. Bill Mollison, *Permaculture: A Designer's Manual* (Australia: Tagari Publications, 1988).
15. Maddy Harland, "Creating Permanent Culture," *The Ecologist* 29, no. 3 (1999), 213.

Chapter Two

1. Joe Hollis, "Paradise Gardening," in Peter Lamborn Wilson and Bill Weinberg, *Avant Gardening: Ecological Struggle in the City & the World* (Seattle, WA: Autonomedia, 1999), 162.
2. Bill Mollison, *Permaculture: A Designer's Manual* (Australia: Tagari Publications, 1988), 1.

Chapter Three

1. Tom Robbins, *Even Cowgirls Get the Blues* (New York: Bantam, 1976), 1–2.
2. Graham Bell, *The Permaculture Way* (London: Thorsons, 1992), 202.
3. Rosalyn Creasy, *Complete Book of Edible Landscaping* (San Francisco: Sierra Club, 1982), 17.
4. Ken and Barbara Kern, *The Owner-Built Homestead* (New York: Charles Scribners Sons, 1974), 69.

5. Vandana Shiva, "Now Monsanto Is after Our Water," *The Ecologist* 29, no. 5 (August 1999).

6. Maude Barlow, "The Globalization of Water," *Hope Dance* 5 (November–December 2000).

7. Bill Marsden, "Cholera and the Age of the Water Barons," Center for Public Integrity, www.publicintegrity.org/water/report.aspx?sID=ch&rID=44&aID=44, 18 November 2005.

8. Shiva, "Now Monsanto Is after Our Water."

9. Ibid.

10. Chris Runyan, "Privatizing Water," *World Watch* 16, no. 1 (January 2003), 36–38.

11. Kern, *The Owner-Built Homestead*, 91.

12. Peter Farb, *Ecology* (New York: Time, 1963), 12–13.

13. Roofwater formula from Toby Hemenway, *Gaia's Garden* (White River Junction, VT: Chelsea Green, 2002), 90.

14. Drywell design from Robert Kourik, *Designing and Maintaining Your Edible Landscape, Naturally* (Santa Rosa, CA: Metamorphic Press, 1986), 79.

Chapter Four

1. Chris Roth, "Gardening, Diversity, Peace and Place: An Interview with Alan Kapuler," Talking Leaves (1999).

2. Geri Welzel Guidetti, "From the Ground Up," in Build Your Ark! How to Prepare for Uncertain Times (Oxford, OH: Ark Institute, 1996).

3. Sir Albert Howard, The Soil and Health (New York: Schocken, 1972), 22.

4. Soil Foodweb, Inc., www.soilfoodweb.com, October 2003.

5. Ehrenfried Pfeiffer, Weeds and What They Tell (Springfield, IL: Biodynamic Farming and Gardening Association, 1976), 10.

6. Sources for biodynamic preparation descriptions: Beth Weiting, lecture delivered to Oregon Biodynamic Conference, 2001, and a flyer by the Josephine Porter Institute, Woolwine, VA, 2001.

7. Elaine Myers, "Pee on the Garden," The Permaculture Activist (May 1992).

8. Ken Fern, Plants for a Future, 3rd edition (White River Junction, VT: Chelsea Green, 2000), 21–25.

9. Paul Stamets, www.fungiperfecti.com, October 2003.

Chapter Five

1. Ed Ayres, "The Environment," *Utne Reader Online,* www.utne.com/web_special/web_specials_archives/articles/1826-1.html, 18 November 2005.

2. Joe Hollis, "Eat the Weeds," as found on www.webpages.charter.net/czar207196/eden.htm, October 2003.

3. National Invasive Species Council, www.invasivespecies.gov, November 2003.

4. J. L. Hudson, "Stop the White List," www.jlhudsonseeds.net/WhiteList.htm, 18 November 2005.

5. Sources for edible weeds chart: François Couplan, *The Encyclopedia of Edible Plants of North America* (New Canaan, CT: Keats, 1998); and Ben Harris, *Eat the Weeds* (Barre, MA: Barre, 1968).

Chapter Six

1. Georgie Starbuck Galbraith, *New York Times,* 6 May 1960. As found on www.moore-warner.com/quotes.php, 3 December 2005.
2. Dr. Garrison Wilkes, as quoted in Kent Whealy, "Rescuing Traditional Food Crops," www.primalseeds.org/OTHERSTUFF/new/rescuingcrops.htm, 18 November 2005.
3. Cary Fowler, *Shattering: Food, Politics, and the Loss of Genetic Diversity* (Tucson: University of Arizona Press, 1990).
4. Ibid.
5. Paul Raeburn, *The Last Harvest: The Genetic Gamble That Threatens to Destroy American Agriculture* (New York: Simon and Schuster, 1995).
6. Alan Kapuler, telephone interview, September 2004.
7. Carol Deppe, *Breed Your Own Vegetable Varieties*, 2nd edition (White River Junction, VT: Chelsea Green, 2000).
8. Ibid., 262.
9. Alan Kapuler, telephone interview, September 2004.

Chapter Seven

1. Sim Van Der Ryn and Stuart Cowan, *Ecological Design* (Washington, DC: Island Press, 1995), 9.
2. Patty Ceglia, "The Process of Creativity: A Holistic Approach to Design," *The Permaculture Activist* 12, no. 2 (1991).
3. Van Der Ryn and Cowan, *Ecological Design*.
4. Gobradime is adapted from several similar acronyms found in Andrew Goldring, ed., *Permaculture Teacher's Guide* (London: Permaculture Association, 2000).
5. Ceglia, "The Process of Creativity."
6. Roger von Oech, *A Whack on the Side of the Head: How to Unlock Your Mind for Innovation* (Los Angeles: Warner Books, 1983), 6.
7. John Briggs and F. David Peat, *The Seven Life Lessons of Chaos: Spiritual Wisdom from the Science of Change* (New York: HarperPerennial, 2000).

Chapter Eight

1. Ernest Callenbach, *Living Poor with Style* (San Francisco: Bantam, 1972), 4.
2. Mahatma K. Gandhi, as quoted in *Voluntary Simplicity*, the book that accompanies a discussion course by the same name, given by the Northwest Earth Institute (Portland, OR: Northwest Earth Institute, 1998).
3. Joe Hollis, "Paradise Gardening," in Peter Lamborn Wilson and Bill Weinberg, *Avant Gardening: Ecological Struggle in the City & the World* (Seattle, WA: Autonomedia, 1999), 159.
4. To take the Ecological Footprint Quiz, visit www.earthday.net/footprint/info.asp.
5. Bring Recycling, "Recycling Reaps Rich Rewards," www.bringrecycling.org/newsletters/03fallnews.html, 3 December 2005.
6. *Used News*, newsletter of Bring Recycling (Eugene, OR: Bring Recycling, 2003).
7. See examples of SVO conversion kits at www.greaseworks.org.
8. John Briggs and F. David Peat, *The Seven Life Lessons of Chaos: Spiritual Wisdom from the Science of Change* (New York: HarperPerennial, 2000).

Chapter Nine

1. Peter Farb, *Ecology* (New York: Life Nature Library, 1963), 38–39.
2. Mark Lakeman, City Repair workshop, Eugene Permaculture Guild Annual Gathering at Lost Valley Education Center, Dexter, OR, 2001.
3. Greta Nagel, *The Tao of Teaching* (New York: Primus, 1994).
4. Andrew Goldring, ed., *Permaculture Teacher's Guide* (London: Permaculture Association, 2000).
5. Jude Hobbs, Permaculture Teacher Training, Eugene, OR, August 2001.
6. Neil Postman and Charles Weingartner, *Teaching as a Subversive Activity* (New York: Delacorte, 1969).
7. Keith McHenry and C. T. Butler, *Food Not Bombs* (Tucson: See Sharp Press, 2000).

Chapter Ten

1. Greg Ruggiero and Stuart Sahulka, *Project Censored: The Progressive Guide to Alternative Media and Activism* (New York: Seven Stories Press, 1999), 7–10.
2. Ibid.
3. David Alexander, *Ways You Can Manipulate the Media* (Boulder, CO: Paladin Press, 1993).

Chapter Eleven

1. Bill Cosby, as quoted on www.quotationspage.com/quote/603.htm, 18 November 2005.
2. Nelson Mandela's 1994 inaugural speech, originally written by Marianne Williamson, as found on http://jmm.aaa.net.au/articles/4564.htm, 18 November 2005.
3. Dale Hunter, *The Art of Facilitation* (Tucson: Fisher Books, 1995).

Chapter Twelve

1. Graham Bell, *The Permaculture Way* (London: Thorsons, 1992), 43.
2. Thoughts on meaningful work inspired by Lee Mackay and Mary Wallace, *Children and Feminism* (Vancouver, BC: LAFMPAG, 1987).
3. Sharon Lovejoy, *Roots, Shoots, Buckets & Boots* (New York: Workman, 1999), 137.
4. Louise Riotte, *Sleeping with a Sunflower* (Pownal, VT: Storey Books, 1987), 87–91.
5. John Heinerman, *The New Encylopedia of Fruits and Vegetables* (Paramus, NJ: Prentice Hall, 1995), 390.
6. Ibid., 409.
7. Printed with permission from John Sundquist, River's Turn Farm, Coburg, OR, December 2005.

Index

green
press
INITIATIVE

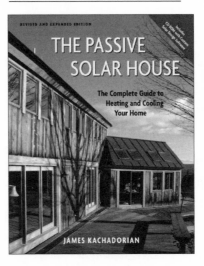

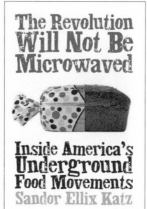
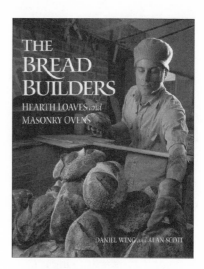

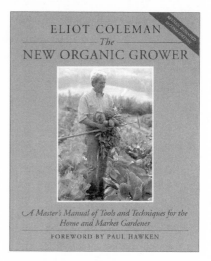